BRAZILIAN PLANNING

BRAZILIAN PLANNING

DEVELOPMENT

POLITICS

AND

ADMINISTRATION

by

Robert T. Daland

THE UNIVERSITY OF NORTH CAROLINA PRESS
CHAPEL HILL

To

Nellie F. Daland

and

John N. Daland

PREFACE

This book really began at the University of California at Berkeley in 1954 when a grant from the Fund for the Advancement of Education of the Ford Foundation enabled the author to spend the academic year with the stimulating faculty of the Department of City and Regional Planning. It advanced a step farther during 1958-59 when, as a postdoctoral fellow in the Metropolitan Region Program at Columbia University, I spent a fruitful year observing the role of planning in the region known as Westchester County, New York. During this time two teachers, the late Hugh Pomeroy and Sy Schulman, conveyed their own excitement about politics and planning.

Research for the present volume was begun in a systematic way in 1961-63 during a tour of duty in Brazil with the School of Public Administration of the University of Southern California, and with the encouragement of Frank Sherwood, chief of party for the school's Brazil faculty. I owe important intellectual debts to the faculty of the host institution, the Brazilian School of Public Administration of the Getúlio Vargas Foundation in Rio de Janeiro. Other support was also provided by that school.

My special thanks go to the Brazilians who allowed themselves to be interviewed for countless hours, helping me to understand the ways of Brazilian planning. Most notably I wish to thank the former Minister of Planning, Celso Furtado, who subjected himself to relentless questioning during much of two days. Mr. A. Theorides of USAID was also most helpful in many ways.

Field work was completed during the summer of 1965 in Brazil, and several persons offered very valuable criticism of a draft of the study. These include especially Professor Cândido Mendes de Almeida, Professor Nelson Mello e Souza, Professor Athyr Guimarães, and my students Paulo Roberto Motta and

Rogerio Feital Soares Pinto. I am also deeply grateful to Professors Ronald Schneider and John Friedman for their constructive comments. I want, additionally, to thank my overworked typist, Mary Barnes, for her loyal service. Stephen Hughes's assistance in preparing the index was most helpful.

I wish also to acknowledge my indebtedness to the Alumni Annual Giving funds of The University of North Carolina at Chapel Hill, administered by the University Research Council, for aid in the publication of this book.

A less tolerant family could not have provided the conditions which made it possible to complete the work.

Finally, the contents and interpretations in the book are my responsibility alone. I have not followed all of the advice which was so generously offered.

Robert T. Daland

Chapel Hill
February, 1967

CONTENTS

BRAZILIAN PLANNING

1

INTRODUCTION

This book is about planning in a developing nation. It begins with a question which is not always regarded as intellectually respectable: Is planning necessary, practicable, desirable, or even possible under the conditions which exist in a "developing" society?

Despite the vast quantities of evidence to the contrary, we continue to assume that planning is the panacea that will rapidly satisfy the "revolution of rising expectations" which is the phenomenon of the post-World War II period.[1] Proceeding on the rational assumptions of planning, national development plans of all sorts are being produced by governmental planners, international agencies, joint commissions, and consulting firms. Many of these plans have been completely disregarded. Others have been "adopted," only to languish in the custody of the government in power. Others have been prosecuted with vigor, but without achieving plan goals.

It continues to be impossible to correlate planning activity with successful development. On the contrary, countries like Brazil seem to have managed a lively economic growth without effective planning as a major cause. Countries like India and Pakistan devote conscientious effort to central planning with modest results.

The view taken here is that the relation between planning and consequent development patterns is yet to be established. It is necessary to take a hard look at the relevance of planning to the development process. Our purpose is to explore this relationship in detail in one country, Brazil, which has a twenty-year history of conscious, institutionalized, central planning.

There are many questions to which answers are needed

1. The phrase was used by Adlai Stevenson, September 16, 1953, *The New York Times*, p. 18 and in *Call to Greatness* (New York: Harper and Row, 1954), p. 44.

about the role and potential of planning in the governmental process. How may the purely rational approaches and techniques of the physical, economic, and social scientist be combined with the norms, values and political impulses of the society? What are the limitations on planning? What procedures and institutions of planning fit differing political environments? What, precisely, are the functions which plans and planning agencies perform in the governmental process? What are the dysfunctions? What are the unanticipated consequences of various planning approaches? What are the differing attitudes toward planning of the chief actors in the governmental arena? The final chapter of this book attempts to deal with these and related questions.

The intervening chapters constitute a case-study of planning in Brazil. Hardly a success story, the Brazilian experience represents the more typical case of a country with a history of planning efforts, each more sophisticated than the last. Despite political and social turmoil, the Brazilians *are* developing planning approaches at national, regional, state, and local levels.

Three general conclusions of this study will be stated here at the beginning so that they may be regarded as hypotheses by the reader. These and their corollaries will be the subject of detailed comment at various points in the book. They may be summarized as follows:

1. The *preparation* of "a national development plan" tends to have positive values for the maintenance and survival needs of the regime.

2. The *implementation* of "a national development plan" tends to have negative values for the maintenance and survival needs of the regime.

3. The negative (dysfunctional) values of plan implementation are related to specific characteristics of the political system.

To the extent that these propositions are valid, the relation between development planning and development is not direct and positive. While no claim can be made that the case of

Brazil is typical of the emerging countries generally, or even of Latin American countries, it is presumed that the Brazilian case will prove highly relevant to that of other countries. In this connection we may note that Albert Waterston's catalogue of administrative obstacles to planning synthesized from his extensive studies, contains very little that is unrecognizable in the Brazilian context.[2] So we are really searching for explanatory propositions of broad validity. Whether we have found any will only become clear when the same questions are raised in studies of other countries.

DEVELOPMENT

To attain an adequate degree of precision in the analysis here presented, it is necessary to devote some attention to the key concepts "development" and "planning."

One may list a host of indicators of "development." These might include gross national product, net product, per capita income, caloric consumption per capita, literacy, automobile ownership, income distribution, land distribution, per cent urban population, civilian control of the government, political stability, cultural output, or political participation. The list may be long or short, and it will reflect the interests and values of the author. In fact, most discussions of development assume Western industrial states to be highly developed, and to exemplify the goals of all the others. This assumption is not to be lightly brushed aside. It is quite apparent that a new aspiration for "development" as quickly as possible has bloomed in many countries of the world. This has occurred both in newly independent nations and in those whose national independence dates back a century or more, as in Latin America. While this is not the place to evaluate the causes of this new aspiration, it is clear that one of its leading elements is the

2. Albert Waterston, "Administrative Obstacles to Planning," 1 *Economia Latinoamericana* (July, 1964), 308-50.

desire to obtain the material standard of living of the wealthy nations of North America and Western Europe.

It is only natural, then, to copy the methods that produced results for the "model" nations. These methods were initially conceptualized in economic terms. When planning was utilized to direct development, economists were the chosen planners, and the plans were economic plans. The efforts to implement these plans, by the nations themselves, by international agencies, or by the United States or other powers offering "foreign aid," soon revealed that development was not a purely economic problem. Massive economic changes affected the political system, social organization, religious institutions, the bureaucracy, and every other element of the society. Development now became "social" and "political" as well as economic. We do not fully understand the relationships between these three major segments of development, but we may safely assume that any major change in any one of them will have immediate effects on the other two.[3] Some kinds of relationships are already quite clear. Education and training are necessary in an industrial society. Education and training have an economic product. They also, however, change the social status of the recipient. They change his political orientation and aspirations. These latter changes may or may not be functional to the economic goals of development. In Brazil it was newly politicized labor organizations that played such a key role in the defeat of the Three-Year Plan.

3. A few of the discussions of these interrelationships are: Gabriel Almond and James Coleman (eds.), *The Politics of the Developing Areas* (Princeton: Princeton University Press, 1960), Conclusion and Appendix I; Dick Simpson, "The Congruence of the Political, Social and Economic Aspects of Development," 6 *International Development Review* (June, 1964), 21-25; Arthur S. Banks and Robert B. Textor, *A Cross-Polity Survey* (Cambridge: The M.I.T. Press, 1963); Phillips Cutright, "National Political Development: Measurement and Analysis," 28 *American Sociological Review* (April, 1963), 264; J. J. Spengler, "Economic Development: Political Pre-Conditions and Political Consequences," 22 *Journal of Politics* (August, 1960), 387-416; Wilfred Malenbaum, "Economic Factors and Political Development," 358 *The Annals* (March, 1965), 41-51; Berthold F. Hoselitz (ed.), *Sociological Aspects of Economic Development* (Glencoe: The Free Press, 1690).

D꞉velopment, then, is major societal change with the object of satisfying the "revolution of rising expectations." Planning for development involves essentially the structuring of changes in the society in such a fashion that changes of a political, social, ideological, or economic order will each reinforce, rather than conflict with, changes in the other realms. Even with complete understanding of these interrelationships, which we are far from having, the planner would not be free to rationalize the society with the object of achieving development. There are cultural limits to change in any society. The planner must therefore determine the limitations within which societal change can be projected, as well as construct a mutually reinforcing system of change. These two tasks present the planner with a problem so complex that we do not presently have well developed tools for him to use. These must include tools of refined political, ideological, psychological, and sociometric analysis in addition to those which the economist has so skillfully provided.[4]

PLANNING

The term "planning" is ambiguous because of its use in two very distinct ways. In its more narrow sense planning refers to the activity of professional "planners" when acting in their professional capacity. In our context the planners tend to be economists. Much of the discussion of development planning employs this usage.

More broadly, however, planning refers to the process by which governments make planning decisions. In this sense planning is both technical and political. It encompasses establishment and support of the planning institution, the conveying of technical solutions into the stream of political decision, and

4. The contributions of the economist are described in Charles E. Lindbloom, "Economics and the Administration of National Planning," 25 *Public Administration Review* (December, 1965), 274-83.

8 BRAZILIAN PLANNING

the creation of attitudes of acceptance for planning decisions, in addition to the purely technical role.[5] These two usages are frequently, though not necessarily, associated with the two general models of planning and decision processes. The more narrow view is most compatible with the "comprehensive-rational" or "synoptic" approach to planning. The broader view tends to match the "disjointed-incremental" strategy of problem-solving and planning.[6] While these two theories have usually been regarded as mutually exclusive, it may be noted that what an individual planning technician actually does as he goes about his work frequently resembles the synoptic model, while decisions of a "policy" nature clearly resemble the disjointed-incremental model.

In this study the term planning will be used in both its broader and narrower senses, as the context will indicate in each case. We will have occasion to argue that the predominance of the purely technical view of the planning process is one of the factors related to the failures of plan implementation.

The usual notions about planning form the basis for the present analysis. Planning, above all, is rational and scientific. Either the synoptic or the incremental approach may be regarded as rational. The real issue concerns the costs of one approach as against the other in any given situation—comprehensivity of information is expensive. However rational planning is, it is employed toward ends which are normatively derived. The planner's first problem is to determine whose

5. This conception of the functions of planning has been developed in Robert T. Daland and John A. Parker, "Roles of the Planner in Urban Development," in F. Stuart Chapin and Shirley F. Weiss (eds.), *Urban Growth Dynamics* (New York: John Wiley, 1962), pp. 182-225. The same kind of thinking is found in Bertram M. Gross, *Activating National Plans*, Occasional Paper, Comparative Administration Group, American Society for Public Administration (Bloomington: International Development Research Center, 1964).
6. These approaches to decision-making, as styles of planning, are discussed in many places. Both are discussed by David Braybrooke and Charles E. Lindbloom in *A Strategy of Decision: Policy Evaluation as a Social Process* (New York: The Free Press of Glencoe, 1963). The synoptic conception is discussed in Chapter 3 and the disjointed-incremental approach in Chapter 5.

ends are to be served. He may, in fact, find it necessary to engage in research as to the goals of the various actors, since goal conflicts represent one of the limitations on plan acceptance. Values and value conflicts are data for the planner.

The planner's second problem, having devised programs leading toward specified goals, is to create a strategy for achieving consideration and implementation of his proposals. This strategy relates to the contents of the plan or proposal and to the institutions available for implementation.[7] It is characteristic of developing nations, even more than of the so called "developed" nations, that the institutions for consideration and implementation of plans do not exist or are not appropriate to the task. Accordingly the planner must participate in the structuring or reform of systems of implementation. This activity involves the planner in a wide variety of activities with which he may or may not be familiar. A good idea of the scope of this activity is conveyed by Saul Katz who has conceptualized a model "system" for development planning.[8] Six action systems provide inputs into the over-all system of action. These include the manpower system, the finance system, the logistics system, the participation system, the legitimate power system, and the information system. Outputs, inputs, components, and constraints are described for the entire system.

Aside from the creation of a concept or system of planning, the planner's third problem concerns who is to oversee, coordinate, and insure the implementation of plans. Is the professional planner to be put in charge of the plans which he

7. Little attention has been given to the strategies and roles of planners within the governmental process except in case studies. The best systematic work has been done by Bertram Gross, most notably in *Activating National Plans*, where he discusses the activation base, obstacles to activation, the activation mix, coping with conflicts, and campaign strategies. Also relevant is his "Managers of National Economic Change," in Roscoe Martin (ed.), *Public Administration and Democracy* (Syracuse: Syracuse University Press, 1966).

8. Saul M. Katz, *A Systems Approach to Development Administration*, Papers in Comparative Public Administration Special Series No. 6 (Washington: Comparative Administration Group, American Society for Public Administration, 1965).

proposed? Does he do this through some super-agency or through some decentralized network of control centers? Whatever the answers to these much-debated questions, it is quite clear that there must be a substantial feedback from the implementers to the planners themselves. In practice the feedback has sometimes been minimal. In other cases, as in the French system of planning, it is the very heart of the planning process and the central planner registers and coordinates plans arising from below. This approach converts implementers into planners. In contrast, the Brazilian case shows how an effort is being made to convert planners into implementers. This contrast poses the implementation question squarely.[9]

Finally, it must be emphasized that we assume that the product of the planning process is a series of decisions. These may be represented by a master plan in a book, or they may be represented in other ways. With or without the book, planning is an unending feeding of rationalizing considerations into the decision process of government—a process whose other major element is politics.

PLANNING AND THE BRAZILIAN BUREAUCRACY

It will be argued in this study that forces internal and external to Brazil have combined to utilize the classical model of bureaucracy as the pattern for structuring developmental planning and administration, and that this model fails to satisfy basic requirements of the Brazilian political culture for identifiable reasons.[10] A considerable literature has developed amending the Weberian theory of bureaucracy in the context

9. The most exhaustive and useful discussion of organization for planning is contained in Albert Waterston, *Development Planning: Lessons of Experience* (Baltimore: Johns Hopkins Press, 1965). This book is based on studies in more than fifty countries and on the extensive records of the World Bank.
10. The classic model of bureaucracy was expressed by Max Weber. See *Essays in Sociology*, translated and edited by H. H. Gerth and C. W. Mills (New York: Oxford University Press, 1946) and *The Theory of Social and Economic Organization*, translated by A. M. Henderson and Talcott Parsons, edited by Talcott Parsons (New York: Oxford University Press, 1947).

of the developed nations.[11] With the recent outburst of work on the developing areas similar consideration has been given to the relevance of classical bureaucratic theory to bureaucracies of the emerging nations. The major work in this field to date is clearly *Administration in Developing Countries: The Theory of Prismatic Society* by Fred Riggs.[12] The present study owes a considerable intellectual debt to Riggs whose book forms a highly relevant framework for the case study at hand. This fact was recently underlined by Lordello de Mello, a well known Brazilian social scientist who, upon completing Rigg's book, observed, "He was writing about Brazil." Riggs's comment about planning in a prismatic society sets the tone for the present investigation: "Tax diversions, moreover, add to the uncertainties of all economic life since they make it difficult, if not impossible, for entrepreneur, government, and bureaucrat to anticipate with any accuracy either future income or future costs. Hence planning rests on a precarious foundation of doubt and insecurity: inability to predict makes it impossible to shape rational courses of action. Prismatic 'planning' is little more than a shadow-play—a mere facsimile of life projected on a chimeric screen."[13]

We will be searching for all the conditions which tend to make of planning a "shadow-play" in Brazil, despite the vigorous efforts to institutionalize it on a bureaucratic basis. This search brings us squarely into the area of administrative ecology.[14] By concentrating on the successive planning experiences of Brazil we will be able to distinguish those transient phenomena related to particular administrations or particular circumstances from the more permanent characteristics and trends in Brazilian planning. With this in view, we proceed to the historical development of Brazilian planning.

11. See most notably Victor Thompson, *Modern Organization* (New York: Alfred A. Knopf, 1962).
12. (Boston: Houghton Mifflin, 1964).
13. *Ibid.*, p. 301.
14. See John Friedman, *The Social Context of National Planning Decisions: A Comparative Approach*, Occasional Paper, Comparative Administration Group, American Society for Public Administration (Bloomington: International Development Research Center, 1964).

2

THE HISTORY AND CONTEXT
OF BRAZILIAN PLANNING

Central governmental planning has come to Brazil, not because of any innate sense of rationality and order such as that
attributed to Germany, or because of a statist ideology as in
the Soviet Union, or yet because of any crisis of survival in a
hostile world as in Israel. In many respects, on the contrary,
the temperament and values of the Brazilian people do not
accept the order, efficiency, and the rationality which planning
implies.

Brazil has backed slowly and haltingly into central planning because it is reputed to be an effective instrument to
shorten the road to achievement of status as a modern, powerful nation with a high standard of living. There is a strong
nationalistic element in this desire. There is the long history
of culture and sophistication in the major urban centers which
breeds an intense pride in the values of Brazilian life. There
is a new awareness that the country's wealth will sustain a
much higher standard of living. The increasing numbers of
Brazilians able to travel abroad using air transportation have
removed Brazil from its previous geographical isolation. The
post-World War II awakening of nations around the world to
the possibilities of progress, and the new interest in underdeveloped countries on the part of the world powers of East
and West, have made new levers available to uncommitted or
partially committed nations.

For reasons such as these there has mounted in Brazil an
urgent desire for the rapid economic development and industrialization which, it is presumed, will automatically produce
the national power and the living standards which Brazilians
crave. Planning is viewed as a major tool of this economic
development.

In this chapter we review the history of planning and its political and economic context.

BRAZIL'S POLITICAL SYSTEM

Brazil's political system during the period of Empire, which ended in 1889, was characterized by an oligarchy with centralized governmental institutions.[1] While many remote parts of this extensive country never really became tied to the unitary state, the thrust of the system was toward nationalism and unity centered around the Court in Rio.

During the Republic, ending in 1930, the monarchy no longer existed to serve this centralizing purpose. Generalizing very broadly, political power resided in the hands of an agrarian, traditional elite whose economic base rested on the export of agricultural products. The main strength of this elite lay in the regions along the coast. Each region, with its characteristic exports—rubber, sugar, cacão or coffee—tended to remain politically autonomous. With poor internal communications, the economic ties of each region were with the port city of the area and beyond to the international markets overseas. Nationalism and unity declined. For the purpose of operating the institutions of the national government, the stronger political chieftains formed coalitions to select a president. Under these circumstances it is not surprising that the large, populous, economically strong states of São Paulo and Minas Gerais managed to dominate the presidency during most of the Republican period from 1889 to 1930 by rotating the presidency be-

1. The key sources on recent Brazilian politics in English are: Charles Daugherty, James Rowe, and Ronald Schneider, *Brazil Election Factbook*, No. 2 (Washington: Institute for the Comparative Study of Political Systems, 1965); Irving Horowitz, *Revolution in Brazil: Politics and Society in a Developing Nation* (New York: E. P. Dutton, 1964); Rollie E. Poppino, "Brazil Since 1954," in José Maria Bello, *A History of Modern Brazil 1889-1964*, trans. James L. Taylor (Stanford: Stanford University Press, 1966); John W. F. Dulles, "Post-Dictatorship Brazil," in Eric N. Baklanoff (ed.), *New Perspectives of Brazil* (Nashville: Vanderbilt University Press, 1966); John J. Johnson, "Brazil in Quandary," 48 *Current History* (January, 1965), 9-15; Andrew Marshall, *Brazil* (New York: Walker and Co., 1966), Chapter 12.

tween themselves. This political alliance is described in Brazil as the politics of *café com leite*—coffee and milk. São Paulo was the chief coffee producer while Minas Gerais had a thriving cattle industry.

The decentralization of power and administration in Republican Brazil was confirmed by the Constitution of 1891, reflecting that of the United States in outward form. The oligarchs, content to retain their political dominance, made little effort to unify the nation or establish a strong national administration. A series of difficulties plagued the Republican governments. Most notably these included disorders requiring military intervention which contributed to increasing chaos in the national finances. It is very relevant to contemporary politics to note the development of the military forces. During the Empire the military was not held in high esteem. During the last half of the nineteenth century, however, a gradual change began to occur. A war with Paraguay greatly boosted the strength of the army. Other uses were found for it as threats arose both from without and from within. At the end of the century, a dramatic rebellion at Canudos in northern Bahia came as a challenge to the new Republic. After a disastrous beginning, the national government finally became serious about the war and achieved a military victory although the threat had been much exaggerated in the country.

After the turn of the century urbanization rapidly increased, spurred by World War I and the first tentative beginnings of local industry. In contrast to Europe and North America, however, urbanization has tended to precede, rather than follow, industrialization. The marginal, but growing middle class of the cities was able to secure some education and represented a potential, though unorganized, political force. The response of the oligarchy to this development was to absorb this incipient middle class into the military and civilian bureaucracy which were allowed to burgeon for this purpose. The bureaucracy, however, was not program oriented, and bred a set of formalistic activities which has been much discussed as the *estado cartorial* or notarial state. Patronage was the basis for recruitment and red tape was a chief product of the system. Red tape not only produced busy-work with which to occupy the new bureaucrats, but through delegating approval powers to various functionaries, permitted the collection of extra-legal revenues for the regime in exchange for rapid processing of the interminable paper work.

The net effect of these changes, however, was not to suppress or co-opt the middle class, which was growing even more rapidly than the bureaucracy. When the São Paulo–Minas Gerais coalition began to crack from internal dissension, just at a time when the political leaders of Rio Grande do Sul had reached a degree of solidarity, Getúlio Vargas became a candidate for the presidency with the support of the other *gaucho* politicians from that state. The victory of his opponent, in an election process controlled by the incumbent administration as usual, was not accepted by Vargas' followers who pushed him reluctantly to the point of military revolution on October 3, 1930. Twenty-one days later the revolution had achieved full success.

These events mark a clear turning point in Brazilian political life. As described by historian José Maria Bello the Republic had shown itself a failure:

After nearly forty years of tormented existence, presidentialism and federalism had proved they could not honestly be applied in Brazil. All their fine concepts had been corrupted in practice. The representative system was a vast hoax, as it had been during the Empire; there were not even national parties, as there had been in the Empire. Government-controlled elections in a patriarchal regime made it possible to select men for their individual worth, but be came dangerous in the Republic when they reflected popular passions whipped up by oppositionist demagoguery. . . . In order to survive, the governments, powerful in many ways and not averse to despotism, were forced constantly to resort to states of siege or to what amounted to the same thing, suspension of constitutional guarantees or civil liberties. Federalism had been converted into intransigent regionalism. Every big state looked up itself as an independent power, with smaller states in its sphere of influence. Alliances between states were formed as in the game of international politics. Through their Congressional blocs, they controlled the president, frequently obliging him to come to terms or negotiate with them. . . .[2]

Vargas immediately moved to change the nature of the regime. He suspended the Constitution of 1891 on November 11 and became unrestricted chief of the provisional government. His career thereafter is unusual. He became constitutional president elected by Congress, a dictator, and later constitutional president elected by the people. Vargas' first years were uneasy, but taking advantage of a partly-manufactured Communist threat, he decreed the *Estado Novo* in 1937 and governed Brazil as a dictator until 1945.

In order to govern effectively a responsible bureaucracy was necessary, and Vargas instituted a series of administrative reforms intended to establish control over the instruments of government. The central focus of these reforms was the establishment of the Administrative Department of the Public Service (DASP).[3] The DASP represented the rational, "scientific," central instrument of administrative control as envisaged in the scientific management movement and as expressed by Willoughby in his *Principles of Public Administration.*[4] As such it was given budgetary, personnel, material, staff services, planning, and control powers. The image of the DASP was that of a technical instrumentality and it became staffed with a new generation of technicians in public administration and planning committed to the new image. In reality, however, the DASP was no more able to separate the exercise of its considerable "technical" powers from the policy-making pro-

2. José Maria Bello, *A History of Modern Brazil 1889-1964*, trans. James L. Taylor (Stanford: Stanford University Press, 1966), p. 255.
3. The leading source on the DASP is Gilbert B. Siegel, "The Vicissitudes of Governmental Reform in Brazil: A Study of the DASP" (Ph.D. dissertation, University of Pittsburgh, 1964).
4. W. F. Willoughby, *Principles of Public Administration* (Baltimore: Johns Hopkins Press, 1927).

cess than does any other agency of real control. The DASP
was a superministry, in fact, exercising controls over the national and state bureaucracies. This new development produced great hostility toward the DASP from within the
bureaucracy and from the political leaders accustomed to derive patronage and income from it. Siegel emphasizes that the
DASP was consciously employed to absorb criticisms against
the new centralization of the regime, allowing Vargas to seem
remote from the details of control. The hostility toward the
DASP of which this is the source, continues to the present day
and explains why subsequent governments have found the
DASP less useful. The decline of the DASP is associated with
the history of the central planning institutions to which we
shall return below.

World War II produced a series of changes in Brazil and in
Vargas' political style. The rigid dictatorship, the political
prisoners, the censorship of the press and the absence of any
system of parties or popular representation in the government
began to seem anachronistic. Twenty-five thousand Brazilian
soldiers were fighting the dictators of Europe in northern Italy
as the war drew to a close. The returning heroes seemed to
have earned a larger voice in politics and the role of the military loomed larger than ever in Brazilian politics.

The new democratic aspirations of the post war world
which affected Brazil were accompanied by economic aspirations as well. The war had cut off imports of consumer goods
and stimulated the substitution of Brazilian goods in their
stead. As industrialization progressed, the new industrialists
identified with economic development goals. The new industrial proletariat held similar developmentalist aspirations and
sought a voice in political decisions. The frustrated middle
class began to find itself a role in the service of the rising
industrial society of the cities.

Vargas was not blind to the new political winds. He announced elections for December of 1945. Parties were legal-
ized. Censorship of the press disappeared and political prison-

ers began to emerge from the jails. The Vargas machine organized the *Partido Social Democratico* (PSD) which chose General Eurico Gaspar Dutra as its candidate. The opposition organized the *União Democrática Nacional* (UDN) and nominated the air force general, Eduardo Gomes. At Vargas' instigation, the labor ministry organized the *Partido Trabalhista Brasileiro* (PTB) as a labor party, which joined in support of Dutra. The elections were calm and, amid a turnout of tremendous numbers of new voters, Dutra was elected. The most bizarre aspect of the situation, however, was that as the election had approached, the Vargas opposition feared he would use his control of the interventors (presidentially appointed governors) in the states to rig the election. Apparently both candidates for president as well as most of the military leaders agreed that Vargas would have to go. The demand for his resignation was delivered October 29, and Vargas quietly acquiesced.

The shrewd dictator, however, had played his cards well. From a radical revolutionary in 1930 he had converted into a proto-fascist between 1937 and 1943 to consolidate power and gain control of the government. With the war, he began to promote economic development, enact social security measures of an advanced type, and convert his image into that of a center-left laborite. Dutra's election is testimony to the success of this strategy, as he received substantial support from both the landed and industrial elites and the laboring class. Gomes received more votes from the middle class of the large cities, but lost elsewhere. Vargas himself continued in politics, winning several posts in Congress—since he could only fill one, he selected a senate seat from his own state of Rio Grande do Sul. When the next presidential election was held Vargas himself became the candidate of the PTB, winning the election from Gomes who was again the candidate of the opposition.

Vargas continued his nationalist-developmentalist policies, but his administration was beset with difficulties. The most severe was the increasing economic crisis. In addition, the military took a dim view of Vargas' Communist supporters and of his new Minister of Labor, João Goulart. The final blow, however, was a series of exposés of the most blatant kinds of corruption in Vargas' official household capped off by the attempted murder of opposition leader Carlos Lacerda at the order of a Vargas henchman. The military again delivered an ultimatum that Vargas should resign, and he committed suicide.

In the next election Juscelino Kubitschek was a coalition candidate for the PSD and PTB parties, winning with the help of the old Vargas machine. His Vice President was João Goulart, the Vargas protégé whose star was still rising. While the naval and air ministers were loath to let the elected ticket take office, decisive action by General Lott saved the day for Kubitschek who was inaugurated on schedule. His role in planning was a decisive one, but remains controversial. While he acted forcefully to carry out his five-year plan, it is alleged that he did so by virtue of an agreement with the agrarian elite to do nothing about land reform. Whether or not this is accurate, the agrarian problem remained to torment his successors.

The 1960 election was the seeming end of the Vargas era. Marshall Lott became the candidate for the PSD. He was opposed by the successful Governor of São Paulo state, Jânio Quadros, who had been succeeded by Professor Carvalho Pinto, Quadros' secretary of finance, now making a reputation for effective planning for the state government. Quadros was not a party man, but was an opponent in São Paulo of Adhemar de Barros, a corrupt party leader of that state. Quadros had earned a reformist, anti-machine image, and received the support of the UDN. His special ability was to appeal successfully to the mass of unorganized voters, railing against the corrupt politicians. Quadros was elected in a landslide vote with a mandate to clean up the government and get on with reforms. The vice president of Brazil can run independently of the president, and in this election João Goulart was again elected as Vice President with the continued support of the labor unions which were his base of political strength. Quadros won some early victories in refinancing Brazil's crushing debts and began to make plans for his reforms. He soon saw that a Brazilian president does not, by virtue of his office, wield sufficient power to achieve basic reforms. The perennially conservative Congress passed none of Quadros' reform proposals. His explorations of means to acquire new powers for the presidency brought down on his head the denunciation of Carlos Lacerda, the perennial critic of incumbents (despite his being a leader of the UDN, Quadros' own party). In addition to this lack of institutional support, as distinct from popularity among the people, Quadros won the enmity of the United States by announcing a new foreign policy. Its keystone was "independence" of the United States and willingness to cooperate with anyone, including especially the Communist countries. Making little progress on his program, the volatile Quadros resigned after seven months in office, presumably anticipating a popular demand for his reinstatement with greater powers. It was his misfortune to have miscalculated.

João Goulart, the Vice President, was travelling in the Far East when the crisis arose. The military forces were basically opposed to the accession of Goulart, despite his obvious constitutional right to the office of president. A few, however, cast their lot with Goulart, including the commander of the Third Army in Rio Grande do Sul, Goulart's home state. Goulart's brother-in-law, Leonel Brizzola, was busy arming a local militia in that state to insure the inauguration. Marshall Lott, now in retirement in Rio, advocated the maintenance of the Constitution. Marshall Odilio Denys, Minister of War, turned to Congress to resolve the impasse. It seems likely that had Congress still been meeting in Rio under the watchful eyes of the generals, it would have yielded to the military pressures. Secure in Brasilia, however, it took an independent line and worked out a compromise which the military accepted. Goulart would remain as a figurehead president and the country would be governed by a Council of Ministers responsible to the Congress in a parliamentary form of government. The military ministers resigned to make way for the new appointees. Parliamentarism was a failure, however, and Goulart spent his first year preparing for a plebiscite to return to presidentialism which was successful in early 1963. The planning effort of the Goulart administration and its consequences are detailed below. He found no way to co-opt the military, however, and ultimately sought to control it by divisive tactics while at the same time threatening to prosecute thorough agrarian reform. Either of these would have been a rash act and the combination was fatal. As Goulart fell more and more under the influence of his radical left advisers, the military forces executed a coup d'état, removing Goulart from office in April, 1964.

Military tolerance of civilian rule was now exhausted. Castelo Branco was appointed President, and ruled in the name of a military junta. The Constitution was frequently amended by decree, though the Congress was permitted to continue subject to the decrees emanating from the military command. For the first time in Brazilian history, the military ruled directly for a time sufficient to reconstitute the political system in the form it deemed desirable. The old political parties were abolished to limit the number of legal parties to two or three. Two new "parties" arose of which one, the Aliança Renovadora Nacional (ARENA) was the "government" party to which the majority of politicians gravitated. The opposition party, the Movimento Democrático Brasileiro (MDB) was composed of a variety of dissidents unwilling to associate with the party of the Revolution. Election of the president and of the governors was made indirect. The new chief executives would be elected by the legislative bodies of states and nation. Castelo Branco was scheduled to serve until March, 1967, by which time the new constitution would presumably have taken shape. Electoral "reforms" virtually guaranteed the election of ARENA's candidate, the Minister of War, General Costa e Silva, by

October of 1966; he was to take office at the end of Castelo
Branco's term. Broad authority was exercised to remove the
political rights of opponents of the regime for a period of ten
years. This power was exercised with enthusiasm, not only
against adherents of the Goulart regime, but increasingly
against supporters of the 1964 Revolution who won the enmity
of the new regime. The best known politicians who were removed from the political arena were former President Kubitschek and Adhemar de Barros, perennial candidate and Governor of São Paulo at the time of his removal. The threat of
similar action silenced many another opponent of the regime.

Under these conditions overt opposition to the regime appeared fruitless, and as the indirect election approached, the
MDB was debating whether or not it would be of any value
even to contest the election. A no-contest might be the most
damaging strategy to dramatize the shift toward dictatorship.
This strategy was pursued, and no opponent was designated
by the MDB. Long before the election public discussion shifted
from *who* the new president would be to what policies he would
be likely to adopt and whom he would appoint to the cabinet.
These developments created a new situation in terms of potential for plan execution. If the old political battle impaired
plan implementation, what might be achieved through a military monopoly of governmental power?

THE BRAZILIAN ECONOMY

Prior to World War II the Brazilian government did not
intervene in the economy and by no stretch of the imagination could it be said to have had an "economic development"
policy. Automatic "protection" of such industry as began to
form derived from World Wars I and II and from the depres-
sion. It became cheaper to manufacture some products at
home.

During the *Estado Novo*, however, developmentalist and
nationalist economic policies began to assert themselves. Bra-

zilians expected a rising standard of living as a result of improved communications and awareness of the world abroad. Special urgency was given to this expectation as a result of a postwar population boom in Brazil as elsewhere. A population of 30 million in 1920 had grown to 40 million in 1940. By 1960 the growth curve produced a population of 71 million. Without rapid economic growth the standard of living could not hold its own, to say nothing of increasing.

The need for a change in the structure of the economy seemed even more apparent as a result of the decreasing strength of the prices received for the traditional agricultural exports following the favorable prices of World War II. Brazil's terms of trade have steadily declined since 1954. As balance of payments problems steadily became worse, the government adopted controls on foreign exchange—initially to adjust the balance of payments, but later to encourage the development of an industrial base. The substitution of local manufactures for former imports became firm policy. As Brazilian manufacturers produced a product similar to one that was imported, it was automatically awarded tariff protection.

The beginnings of state intervention in the economy came with Vargas and increased during his time in office. The famous Instruction 70 nationalized exports of agricultural commodities and alienated the agrarian elite. Vargas presided over the establishment of a major government steel plant and its later expansion. Major hydroelectric dams were built. A national gasoline monopoly, Petrobrás, was established. The Rio Doce Valley Company was established to enlarge mining operations. A national electric company, Eletrobrás, was being urged by Vargas, but this became unfinished business at his suicide, to be taken up later by Jânio Quadros.

Policies such as these did in fact produce a great change in the economy. The share of agriculture in the gross domestic product dropped from 27 per cent in 1947 to 22 per cent in 1961. During the same period the share of industry increased from 21 per cent to 34 per cent. The post war years brought an extremely high annual growth rate. After 1948 the real growth of the domestic product averaged just under 7 per cent up to 1961. In that year it was 7.7 per cent. In 1962 the growth rate suddenly dropped and in 1963 it was only 1.6 per cent. At this point *annual* population increase had reached an amazing 3.1 per cent. These figures dramatically illustrate the deterioration of the Brazilian economy in terms of social potential during the Goulart regime. Even assuming equal distribution of the fruits of development—which was far from the actual case—the standard of living had to go down.

While economists have not developed figures to show the impact of these economic changes by economic class, they have achieved something of the same effect by noting the differential economic growth by regions. Regional disparity is even more politically dangerous than class disparity. In terms of balance of trade as between the states of the poor Northeast and the rich Center-South, the Northeast had a negative balance in every year between 1948 and 1959 except for a very slight plus balance in 1956. The Northeast contains 25 per cent of Brazil's population but earns about 10 per cent of the national income. The states of the Northeast all earn far less than the national average per capita income. Similar disparities, but less pronounced, may be observed as between the West and Northern regions on the one hand and the prosperous South on the other.

These economic factors are complicated by violent changes in the rate of inflation in Brazil. The long term trend has been inflationary for many decades. The most reliable figures on inflation are calculated by the Economic Research Institute of the Getúlio Vargas Foundation—a politically independent semi-governmental research and education entity. According to this source, inflation was about 6 per cent in 1947. Ten years later it had grown to 13 per cent. By 1963 and 1964 it had reached the neighborhood of 80 per cent. During the period of planning from 1961 to the present, the effect of inflation on economic development was a matter of political con-

troversy, as will be noted below. As a result, and due to a
highly unreliable data collection system, the rate of inflation
became a topic of controversy among economists committed
to one or another political position. The relation between economic growth and inflation is generally suggested by the following table:

RELATION BETWEEN ECONOMIC GROWTH AND INFLATION

Year	Real Growth Rate of Domestic Product	Per Cent Rate of Inflation
1947	1.8	6
1948	9.5	4
1949	5.6	6
1950	5.0	11
1951	5.1	11
1952	5.6	21
1953	3.2	17
1954	7.7	26
1955	6.8	19
1956	1.9	22
1957	6.9	13
1958	6.6	17
1959	7.3	52
1960	6.3	24
1961	7.7	43
1962	3.7	52
1963	2.1	80
1964	3.4	79-92
1965	3.7	30-63
1966	(first 6 months)	25

Source: 1947-1963 Conjuntura Econômica and Revista Brasileira de Economia,
March, 1962; 1964-1966 estimates covering the range of controversy
among a variety of Brazilian sources as reported in the Brazilian press.

The above table, assuming it is accurate, gives some basis
for either of the prevalent theories about the relation of inflation to development: that it helps and that it hinders. In the
banner production year of 1961, inflation was a high 43 per
cent. In the almost as good year 1957 it was only 13 per cent.
On the other hand, the very poor year 1947 had only 6 per cent
inflation, while the almost as poor year 1963 had a shattering
80 per cent inflation. Since 1963 production has increased

slightly while inflation had gradually decreased though the exact amounts are in doubt.

These "facts" about the economy suggest that the answer to the key economic questions still remain unclear, and thus are fair game for the politician. Does inflation help or hinder development? For the rich, for the poor, or for everyone? How much governmental intervention in the economy, and what kind, will produce maximum economic growth? How much reliance on the foreign investor is desirable in terms of sound growth patterns? Since the economists do not have conclusive answers, development planning includes not only technical inputs, but also ideological conflicts among technicians. The ideological differences among technicians are but one short step removed from the ideological and partisan differences among politicians. These relationships will become much clearer as the roles of politician and technician in Brazilian planning are developed in later chapters. We now turn to a brief history of planning efforts as such.

PLANNING UNDER THE ESTADO NOVO

During World War II, the dislocation of trade stimulated a desire to develop Brazilian sources for materials which could no longer be secured on the wartime market. From the point of view of the United States, which helped in the early stages of Brazilian planning, hemisphere sources for war materials in short supply were needed. This motivation was consistent with the internal forces in Brazilian life. From the point of view of the growing Brazilian nationalist movement, economic self-sufficiency was an element of nationhood. From the point of view of the rapidly increasing population of destitute and very poor people, economic development seemed the only road to a higher standard of living. From the point of view of private business, development meant an enlarged local market and greater profits. From the point of view of government, hard pressed for increased sources of tax income, development rep-

resented a broadening of the tax base on which the government rested. From the point of view of the international
community, the development of all of the underdeveloped
areas meant progress toward the elimination of the tensions
which perpetuate wars and instability in the world at large.

Economic planning as such began in 1942 when the Brazilian government obtained the services of a group of ten engineers and other specialists led by Edward S. Taub, a civil
engineer, all from the United States. This group produced a
plan of investment for a ten-year period to cost a total of four
billion dollars. The interest of the United States in this activity
was to use Brazil as a pilot area to test modern methods of
industrial development. The report was kept secret for many
years, and with the end of war, as well as of the Estado Novo,
the matter was dropped.

In the meantime, however, the DASP had prepared the
first of a series of five-year plans known as the *Plano Quin-
quenal de Obras e Reaparelhamento da Defesa Nacional*.
Hardly a plan in reality, this project was merely a list of capital
expenditures. Its contribution to the concept of planning, however, lay in its five-year duration and its characteristic as a
supra-agency budget. No special arrangements were made for
the execution of this plan, and the degree to which it was
"implemented" is still unknown. Certainly it never reached its
life expectancy of five years.

The following year, 1943, another U.S. mission was dispatched to Brazil with roughly the same objectives as the Taub
Mission. This group, the American Technical Mission to Brazil, was known as the Cooke Mission after its chief, Morris L.
Cooke. Its status was more official than that of the Taub Mission. The group was sponsored by the *Centro de Estudos de
Problemas Brasileiros* of the Getúlio Vargas Foundation, and
it worked as a counterpart to a similar group of Brazilian technicians. Research was done on various subjects such as production transport, fuel, petroleum, energy, textiles, minerals,
chemicals, education, and the improvement of the San Fran-

cisco Valley. Various proposals were made, but the price tags
were not indicated. The research report did not constitute a
plan, but is significant for two reasons. First, it was a basis for
work of later economists involved in planning. Secondly, it
expressed the rationale later adopted for the Alliance for Progress. On the other hand, its utility was limited because it was
kept secret until released by the U.S. government in 1948.

At the end of 1943 a decree-law of Vargas established a
second five-year plan, called the *Plano de Obras e Equipa-
mentos e dá Outras Providências*. This was another public
works budget intended to extend through the years 1944-1948
inclusive. While still hardly a "plan," this project did provide
the elements of a system of implementation. A billion cruzeiros
were to be provided each year of the five years from specified
sources. These funds were to be administered by the Minister
of Finance on the orders of the President. This plan, or
budget, like its predecessor was prepared by the technicians of
the DASP. Little is known about the degree of achievement
of the plan, or its actual longevity.[5]

In 1945 the situation of Brazil changed precipitously. Vargas left the presidency, World War II and its stimulus to planning ended, and a new constitution was written, being adopted
in 1946. The new constitution did not establish any agency
for national planning, though the two most depressed areas of
the country found the opportunity to establish regional planning and development agencies. Three per cent of national tax
income was set aside for economic improvement in Amazonia,
to be supplemented by state and local funds, and a similar
provision was included for the benefit of the Northeast. These
provisions led to the creation of major federal agencies to administer the plans for these areas, requiring the subsequent
coordination of nationally prepared regional plans with nationally prepared national plans.

5. Extensive efforts have been made by Brazilian scholars, notably Professor Benedicto Silva to secure information on implementation of these early
plans. These were foredoomed to failure due to a total lack of relevant records.

THE SALTE PLAN

During the Dutra administration (1946-1950) the DASP technicians again set to work making plans, with the assistance of technicians from the São Paulo state government, showing a considerable continuity in the plan-making function during the decade of the forties. As a result of the several previous planning efforts of the national government, the creation of regional agencies, and the legacy of uncompleted plans and unused reports, the SALTE Plan was prepared to coordinate existing plans.[6] This was the first of a number of efforts to "coordinate" a complex of planning activities. This plan, however, was confined to the four key fields of health, supply, transport, and energy. It was written during 1946 and 1947 and was submitted to Congress by President Dutra in May of 1948, to cover the five years 1949-1953.

The difficult career of this plan proved instructive. Shortly after its proposal by the President, the Economic Council of the National Federation of Industry, the major Brazilian trade association, said the plan would not work since it called for a greater expenditure than could be met with available funds. During 1949, however, Congress appropriated 1,900,000,000 cruzeiros to initiate implementation of the plan, but failed to authorize the plan itself. The funds were to be disbursed by the Ministry of Finance after approval of the President. Most of the funds were in fact disbursed, but no record remains as to the objects of the expenditure. In 1950 only thirty-seven-and-a-half million cruzeiros remained to be carried over to the new fiscal year.

It was not until 1950 that the SALTE Plan was officially sanctioned by Congress, despite the fact that funds had been spent on it during the previous year. The plan was now to cover the years 1950-1954, and was to be administered by an Administrator General with a staff of six assistants and a sup-

6. The initials refer to the four areas of the plan, *Saude* (health), *Alimentação* (food supplies), *transportes* (transportation) and *energia* (electric power).

porting staff. An immediate confusion was built into the law, since an old decree-law of 1943 was made applicable to the new planning effort. By that law, the Minister of Finance was given power to budget and spend the funds of the plan, subject to approval of the President. By 1950 the DASP had acquired the budget function. As a result, there appeared two claimants for the control of SALTE expenditures: the Minister of Finance and the Director General of DASP who was also Administrator General of the SALTE Plan. The President solved the problem by lending his ear to one or another of the two as his fancy might lead. In 1950 little of the money appropriated was given to the SALTE administrator for disposition. In addition, no regular provision was made for administrative expenses of the planning office, and its position was extremely weak. While the idea of planning as a regular governmental function had gained much ground, the political and administrative will to insure implementation of planning was totally lacking. Up to 1950, institutionalized central planning could not have had any impact whatever on the course of Brazilian development. The stage was set, however, for more successful attempts.

With the return of Vargas, central planning gained more support. In 1951 he asked for a change in the law governing the SALTE Plan. He noted that the funds for the plan either were not available or had been spent on other things. He asked that the plan be scaled down to fit actual resources for the purpose, thus making it realistic. In addition, a sum equal to 2 per cent of SALTE funds was authorized for administrative expenses of the SALTE office. The President now delegated to the Administrator General of the plan the authority to distribute the funds, though he retained the authority to approve or disapprove of these decisions. Since the funds were to be spent by the regular governmental agencies, a procedure had to be developed to decide which agencies would receive available funds. The process involved application to the administrator of the plan, and ultimate approval by the President. A minor, but enlightening, footnote on this period of planning administration is the fact that the new Administrator General of the SALTE Plan appointed by Vargas in 1951, Arízio de Viana, was able to fire 23 of the 31 members of the SALTE staff as unnecessary for the conduct of the work of the office. At the same time, Viana recognized that while field inspection of projects undertaken under the plan would be desirable, competent staff for the purpose was not available.

The essential function of the SALTE Plan office was now to assign available SALTE funds to specific agencies eligible under the plan—that is, to decide on the priority of implementation of plans. Thus, a primitive mechanism for implementation was beginning to develop. Meanwhile the techniques of economic research, another ingredient of sound planning, were more or less independently being created in Brazil.

A third mission of U.S. experts was requested by the Dutra government and it arrived in Brazil in 1948, led by John Abbink. This group, together with a Brazilian counterpart staff, composed the Joint Brazil-United States Technical Commission. The leader of the Brazilian staff was Otávio Gouveia de Bulhões. Bulhões was a young lawyer–economist who was to spend much of his career in the Ministry of Finance associated with planning in various capacities. He was interim Minister during the transition between Quadros and Goulart in 1961. Twice he served as Executive Director of the Superintendency of Money and Credit, the credit control agency. He also became known outside Brazil at the United Nations and as Vice Governor of the International Monetary Fund. Ultimately he was appointed Minister of Finance in the Castelo Branco cabinet.

The new Commission prepared another report, this time emphasizing the broader problems of the Brazilian economy, without reference to matters of wartime supply. Such questions as the balance of payments and measures needed for economic stability in the face of inflation now received attention. While no plan was produced, some specific recommendations were made. Of these some were carried out, such as the reorganization and re-equipment of the railroad system. Others, like tariff reform, were not acted on. This report added to the economic studies available to later planners, but it was in no sense a plan itself.

In the meantime, significant developments had occurred outside Brazil whose impact soon was destined to be felt within the country. The United Nations had been created, with its interest in economic development of the less developed countries. The International Bank for Reconstruction and Development now stood ready to give loans for development projects. The Economic Commission for Latin America, a branch of the U.N., located an office in Rio de Janeiro and was receiving aid for economic studies from the Brazilian government. In the United States the Act of International Development was passed in 1949. As soon as the United States indicated it was ready to cooperate in furthering the economic development of Brazil, the Brazilian government replied that it would be desirable to establish a Joint Brazil-United States Economic Development Commission. This was done, and the Commission operated during 1951, 1952, and 1953.

The purpose of the new Commission was to render the necessary technical assistance so as to speed the preparation of applications for loans for development projects, which would be submitted to the United States and international lending agencies. The theory was that certain key types of investments could have a stimulating effect on the further investment of purely private funds. That is, loans from public funds would be made for the purpose of eliminating bottlenecks in basic economic sectors such as transportation and power, without which increased private investment would be very unlikely. Thus it was the job of the Commission not only to make technical studies, but to make planning decisions with regard to what projects needed subsidy in order to achieve a balanced development of the Brazilian economy, and then to prepare the projects so as to meet the technical standards required by foreign financing institutions.

The integration of this planning activity with the Brazilian policy-making hierarchy was achieved through the device of a special Brazilian commission which supervised the work of the Brazilian Section of the Joint Commission. This special commission was composed of the ministers of finance, foreign affairs, agriculture, and transportation and public works. A key member of the Brazilian staff of the Commission was Roberto de Oliveira Campos, another economist to leave a deep imprint on the course of Brazilian economic planning.

Robert Campos was born in Mato Grosso in 1917, and was educated as an economist, among other places at George Washington University and Columbia University. At the age of 32 he entered the foreign service of Brazil by examination. He served as secretary to the Brazilian delegation at the Bretton Woods Conference, thus being familiar with the international Monetary Fund and the World Bank from their inception. He served as Brazil's economic counselor at the United Nations under Dutra, and returned to Brazil to join the Joint Commission staff. When the National Development Bank was created in 1952, Campos became a director. Later he became superintendent of the Bank, and ultimately, under Kubitschek, its president.[7] He was associated with Quadros as an adviser during his brief term of office. Despite earning a reputation in radical nationalist circles as an *entreguista*—signifying one who sells out to foreign interests—he was appointed Ambassador to the United States by João Goulart. In 1963, however, he resigned this post, feeling he could not represent the increasingly extreme policies of the Goulart administration. He was brought back as Minister of Planning by the regime of the 1964 Revolution. Brazil has had no more influential a planner than Campos.

7. Campos, however, was dropped from this office in mid-1959 when Kubitschek decided to take a more independent line on financial policies rather than to accede to pressures of the IMF. Campos has been generally sympathetic to IMF policies.

Planning by the Commission was done on a relatively short term basis, not waiting for the impact of expected tax reforms. Total sums estimated as available were those presently within sight from Brazilian and international sources. The International Bank indicated what it regarded as a realistic expectation from that source. Criteria for decisions on projects included projects which would be: (1) conducive to the elimination of bottlenecks or to the creation of basic conditions for economic growth, (2) complementary to, rather than substituting for, private investments, (3) susceptible to reasonably quick realization, and (4) financed by non-inflationary means. Based on these criteria, transportation and energy projects seemed to be the most potentially productive. Ultimately, the Commission recommended forty-one individual projects as deserving of subsidy from public funds.[8]

No effort was made to correct regional imbalances in development. Rather, productivity was regarded as more important. The total cost of the projects in funds from all sources was estimated at about 22 billion cruzeiros. By the time the report was completed, the SALTE Plan was in full swing, though far from fully implemented. According to the Report of the Commission, the administrator of the SALTE Plan was most cooperative in accommodating to the newly forming program of the Commission. When the next administration appeared on the scene many months later, its planning agency, the Council for Development, took up the program of the Commission and incorporated it into its broader Program of Goals. Thus the work of the Commission represents the first phase of a planning effort which has been substantially continuous for the past fifteen years, beginning on the basis of partial planning only in two economic sectors, with a short run perspective and the prospects of a quick payoff. Before turning to the next chapter in the planning story, under the

8. Institute of Inter-American Affairs, Foreign Operations Administration, *Report of the Joint Brazil-United States Economic Development Commission* (Washington: Institute of Inter-American Affairs, 1954), p. 79.

Kubitschek administration, let us turn back to characterize the role of the National Bank for Economic Development, created to finance development projects.

THE NATIONAL DEVELOPMENT BANK

On June 20, 1952, the National Bank for Economic Development (BNDE) was created at the instigation of the Commission. This action was a recognition that planning requires special machinery for implementation. Heretofore the administrator of the SALTE Plan had merely controlled the distribution of funds to regular governmental agencies. The function of the new bank went far beyond this. Its purpose was to obtain funds from international sources as well as domestic sources, a function requiring great finesse. Projects had to be developed and their details negotiated as between the Brazilian agency or company which would receive the money and the international agency providing the money. Priorities had to be established to guide application of the funds.

The BNDE was created as a direct result of the work of the Joint Commission during its period of research, and was originally intended to carry out the program of the Commission, known in the regulations of BNDE as the *Plano de Reaparelhamento e Fomento da Economia Nacional.* This program initially included primarily transportation and electric power projects, but later was expanded to include the entire basic industrial complex of Brazil.

The administrative device chosen to implement economic planning was the *autarquia*, a type of independent agency with the characteristics of a government corporation. This assured the freedom of action and flexibility needed in its banking-type operations. The Bank was created as an agency subordinate to the Ministry of Finance but with considerable independence. Like most Brazilian independent agencies, it has two directing bodies which in theory include a policy-making board and an administrative board. The policy organ consists of a board of four members. These are a president appointed by the President of Brazil and subject to summary dismissal, a superintendent with a five-year term, and two additional directors for four-year terms. All are appointed by the President of Brazil. The administrative council consists of seven men also appointed by the President, of whom one is the president of the Bank. The remaining six have three-year terms. This council meets weekly and handles the on-going administration of the Bank.

The Bank is engaged in six basic types of operations, both in national and foreign currency. From funds provided by the government of Brazil, the Bank makes repayable loans (accounting for 79 per cent of total financing as of May 15, 1962), participates as a partner in certain enterprises for which it provides part of the funds (accounting for 18.3 per cent of total financing), participates through direct investment in certain enterprises where insurance and capitalization companies controlled by the bank actually provide the funds (accounting for 2.7 per cent of financing), and financing the manufacture and sale of goods produced in the country (a new activity in 1962). Operations in foreign currency include chiefly the guaranteeing of supplier credits obtained by the Brazilian enterprises from foreign suppliers of equipment or for operations undertaken in its own name or that of the national treasury, and obtaining credits in foreign currency for transfer to Brazilian organizations empowered to carry out development projects. By May of 1962 these operations had amounted to a cumulative contribution to the economy of 85.7 billion cruzeiros and 632.6 million dollars. Funds from national sources have been obtained from appropriations of Congress, from a surtax on income, from compulsory deposits by savings banks and insurance companies, and from the sale of surplus wheat from the United States. Some of these funds are specifically earmarked for the Federal Electrification Fund, the National Highway Paving Fund, the Railroad Rehabilitation Fund, the Merchant Marine Fund, and the National Port Fund. International

HISTORY AND CONTEXT   37

sources include the World Bank, the United States Export-Import Bank, the Alliance for Progress of the United States Agency for International Development (and its predecessors) and several countries of Western Europe.

In making its decisions, the Bank receives applications for assistance from governmental and private institutions. It serves as a clearinghouse for such applications. Within its system of goals, directives, and plans, the Bank determines the source of funds most appropriate to satisfy the application, or it rejects the project entirely. Up to 1962, the Bank was able to satisfy only 40 per cent of total requests. The Bank operates through seven divisions including economics, international operations, projects, control of applications, finance, juridical and administration. The total staff of the Bank is well over 500, including more than 300 technical and professional personnel.

In view of the scope of operations of the Bank, it is clear that a continuous process of decision-making had been created to make decisions on major economic investments for Brazil. The program of the Joint Commission was only a starting point. Accordingly, what in essence was a planning organ was established within the Bank, and is known as the Department of Economics. Here are centered the research functions. Studies are made of monetary and fiscal policy, the balance of payments, and national income. Annual modifications of the investment program are both for Brazil as a whole and for the regions of the country.

That this planning role of the Bank is a conscious one is indicated in its official reports: "the relationships of the Bank with the government require, obviously, a direct participation in planning and in the execution of the governmental policy in the area of economic development."[9] It is apparent, then, that the Bank has developed not only as a continuing mechanism for the execution of plans, but also as a planning agency prop-

9. BNDE, *Exposição Sôbre O Programa de Reaparelhamento Econômico* (Rio de Janeiro: Banco Nacional de Desenvolvimento, 1958), p. 39. Unless otherwise indicated, all translations from Portuguese sources are by the author.

er. It has never claimed to be a comprehensive planning agency, however, since its efforts are confined to the capital investments portion of the economy.

The creation of BNDE came at a time when the United Nations also had an interest in the economic development of Brazil. One of the subsidiary agencies of the U.N. is the Economic Commission for Latin America with an economic research staff located in Rio de Janeiro. Recognizing that continued study of the Brazilian economy was necessary, the BNDE magnified its own efforts by signing an agreement with the secretariat of ECLA in April, 1953, which provided that a joint team of economists from the Bank and from ECLA would make a complete study of the Brazilian economy. This study had been recommended by the General Assembly of the United Nations.

THE PROGRAM OF GOALS

Together with the previous work of the Joint Commission, this new study laid the basis for the first real "economic plan" for Brazil. Despite the considerable amount of "planning" that had been done, one key element was still missing. This was the element of comprehensiveness. Previous planning had been done for the most part with special objectives in view or on an emergency basis. The new concept was that specific goals should be developed for every major sector in the economy, so that economic progress could proceed on a coordinated and mutually supportive basis. This concept was implemented early in the administration of President Juscelino Kubitschek with his Program of Goals. The resulting five-year plan, covering the years 1956-1960 inclusive, was not literally comprehensive, since it did not cover all the economic sectors. It was a great advance, however, in that it did cover most of them. Previous effort had been devoted primarily to planning for transportation and electric power investments.

As has become customary in Brazil, the new administration

desired to conduct planning through its own instrumentality. The BNDE continued its project financing, but a new Council of Development was created by decree on February 1, 1956 and provided with a technical staff. At the same time, the Program of Goals was announced. This was being drawn up hurriedly within the BNDE, and was based on the studies of the CEPAL-BNDE group and of the Joint Commission.

The plan itself consisted of thirty specific goals in the fields of energy, transportation, food supply, basic industries, and education of technical personnel. The projects necessary to implement these were listed, together with the estimated cost. In the report to the President at the end of the five-year period covered by the plan, the results are added up.[10]

The function of the Council was to monitor the degree to which the goals were being carried out by BNDE and other agencies, and to recommend to the President any needed changes in the goals and the ways of implementing them. It was a purely advisory and planning staff for the President. The Conselho itself consisted of a total of 17 persons under the chairmanship of the President. These included virtually all the ministers of state and in addition the Director General of the DASP, the President of BNDE, the President of the Bank of Brazil, and the chiefs of the military and civil cabinets. The planning staff, therefore, reported directly to the top policy-making group of the administration.

THE PLANO TRIENAL

Brazil had two new presidents during the year following the end of the Program of Goals, and a major political crisis. Jânio Quadros came to power, announced his plan for government in July, created a National Planning Commission (COPLAN) in early August, and at the end of that month resigned from office. The decree establishing the Commission

10. Conselho do Desenvolvimento, *Relatório do Período 1956-1960* (Rio de Janeiro: Presidência da República, Conselho do Desenvolvimento, 1960).

directed that the staff of the Council, the planning agency of
the Kubitschek administration, be turned over to COPLAN.
In view of the political crisis, this particular directive was not
carried out. There now existed two national planning agencies
charged roughly with the same responsibilities. The Council,
however, was an advisory body. COPLAN, while it did not
yet have authority to insure execution of plans, had at least
paper authority to enforce "coordination" of the planning done
by various governmental entities.

The unreality of the situation is underlined by the fact that
while two planning agencies now existed in competition, their
collegial directorates consisted of virtually the same group of
people. The new Commission consisted of the President of
Brazil, the ministers of state, the civil and military cabinet
chiefs, the Coordinator General of the Technical Staff of the
President of Brazil, the Director General of DASP, the Executive Director of the Superintendency of Money and Credit
(SUMOC), and the Technical Director of the COPLAN staff.

Neither agency had a substantial staff, and the political
crisis was not conducive to deliberation and planning. When
the new parliamentary cabinet, the Council of Ministers, came
to power in September, 1961, it immediately published its
basic program of government. This program listed seven general objectives including increase of the gross national product
at a rate of 7.5 per cent annually, promoting full employment,
elimination of tensions due to inequality of income, price
stabilization, reduction of regional inequalities, improvement
of the balance of payments situation, and correction of structural deformities in the economy. These were to be achieved
through tax reforms, improving the employment of investments, development programs, and mobilization of foreign resources. To achieve these goals, it was announced, COPLAN
would be re-created to work on three levels: an immediate
emergency plan consisting in part of existing projects for some
of which foreign financing was already available, a five-year
plan, and a long-range plan with a twenty-year perspective.

Both the Council and the Commission were quiescent during most of 1962. Their common governing board was deeply occupied with political developments, and a succession of prime ministers presided over the cabinet. The climax came in January of 1963 when the plebiscite restoring presidentialism took place. This solution to the political crisis was anticipated by several months by President Goulart and Prime Minister Hermes Lima. On September 27, 1962, the Prime Minister signed a decree creating the post of Minister Extraordinary for Planning, and Celso Furtado was designated as the minister.

Furtado had already left a deep mark on Brazilian planning. He was born in Brazil's Northeast in the state of Paraiba. In 1944 he received a degree in juridical and social sciences at the University of Brazil. He continued his formal education at the University of Paris and later at Cambridge University, pursuing his interest in economics. At Cambridge he spent a year in research. Since 1949 he had pursued a career as economist and planner in Brazil, first serving with the United Nations on the Economic Commission for Latin America (ECLA). He was chief of the economic development group of ECLA, and later chief of the ECLA-BNDE mixed group. His studies were not by any means confined to Brazil, but covered other Latin American countries as well. In 1958 Furtado was appointed a director of BNDE. In the Bank, Furtado was the intellectual leader of a group of economists who believed economic development in Brazil required basic "structural" changes in the economy, and that these could best be achieved through planning and implementation of plans by the state. In 1958, President Kubitschek sought the aid of the Bank in recommending solutions for the serious drought problem which was just recurring in the Northeast. Furtado produced a brilliant and imaginative report on the subject which was presented to the President. On the basis of this report the Superintendency for the Development of the Northeast was created in 1959.[11] While the law creating the agency, known

11. Law No. 3692, December 15, 1959.

as SUDENE, was awaiting approval of Congress, Kubitschek lost no time in putting Furtado to work by creating the Council for the Development of the Northeast (CODENO).[12] When the law was finally passed, Kubitschek appointed Furtado as the first superintendent, and he became not only a theoretician and planner, but now an administrator of the program he himself had developed. Jânio Quadros retained Furtado at his post in 1960, as did Goulart in 1961.

Prior to his appointment as Minister, Furtado had canvassed the staffs of both COPLAN and the Council to determine which would serve best as the staff for his work. He determined that COPLAN offered the greater potential, and immediately began to strengthen its staff through requisitions of economists from various other agencies.

While the technical staff of COPLAN was acquired by the new minister, the collegial directorate was not. Furtado reported directly to the Prime Minister, and after the plebiscite to the President of Brazil. The Commission itself withered away from disuse.

When Furtado was appointed in September, he was directed to prepare a national development plan. Two years of the five-year term of the President of Brazil had now elapsed, and accordingly the decision was made to produce a three-year plan of economic and *social* development. The new Minister was to "coordinate" the plans and activities of the regional planning agencies, as well as plans for foreign aid to Brazil. Within two-and-a-half months of intensive effort, Furtado's staff had produced a sophisticated three-year plan which immediately became known as the *Plano Trienal*, to cover the period 1963-1965.

The story of what happened to the Furtado plan and to the planning machinery which made it is told in the case study which constitutes Chapter 5 of this study. In brief, the policies of the plan had been accepted by the administration and put into effect. For various reasons, these policies could not be

12. Decree No. 45.445, February 20, 1959.

maintained, however, and Furtado and San Tiago Dantas, the Minister of Finance, were removed from the cabinet, as part of a general renovation in which every member was replaced.

In mid-1963 a new "planning" agency, an Office of Coordination of National Planning, was created in the President's office. It was to be concerned primarily with securing funds for various projects. This agency was a stop-gap measure, and a new system of national planning was being proposed as a part of the general administrative reform recommendation of Amaral Peixoto, Minister Extraordinary for Reform. This recommendation involved a "national planning system" composed of a planning council at the top, a secretary-general and staff, and a similar council and planning staff in each of the ministries.

These plans came to nothing, since the Goulart administration survived for only a few more months. During these months the actual decisions on economic policy were formulated in the Ministry of Finance to which Carvalho Pinto, the respected former governor of São Paulo, had succeeded. The leadership in such decisions had already shifted in considerable degree from the Ministry of Planning to that of Finance during the days of Furtado and Finance Minister San Tiago Dantas. Under Carvalho Pinto this trend was strengthened. In short, the pattern of "planning" had now reverted to decision-making by a single strong individual, relying on whatever advisers and technicians throughout the government he might choose to use. In view of the way in which the Furtado and Kubitschek staffs had been recruited, this was not actually so much different from previous practice. It was a highly personalistic style of "planning," devoid of the trappings of institutionalization.

Carvalho Pinto, however, was strongly committed to the idea of planning, and was in fact famous for development planning in his own state of São Paulo. He determined that the Goulart administration was not congenial to the methods and objectives which he sought for Brazil, and in a few months resigned from the cabinet. During the last weeks of the Goulart regime there was no semblance of planning whatever, despite the continued existence of COPLAN and the Council as nonfunctioning shadow-like agencies, now completely insulated from the centers of decision.

On March 31, 1964, the opposition to Goulart launched the "revolution" which was completely successful within three days. A completely new government was soon formed under the presidency of General Castelo Branco. The revolution was based on a variety of complaints, especially the financial and economic chaos into which the country had been thrown. It seems clear that the total and even dramatic failure of planning by the Goulart regime was an element in his downfall. This fact was quite clear to the new administration which set out to rebuild a planning program for the country.

THE PROGRAM OF ACTION

The revolution of March 31, 1964, represented the most extreme shift in governmental power in Brazil since the beginning of the Vargas era in 1930. It would not have been surprising, then, if it had taken considerable time to initiate the processes of deliberate planning. What is surprising is that this was done so soon after the revolution. In a matter of weeks Castelo Branco had called in Roberto Campos and appointed him Minister Extraordinary for Planning and Economic Coordination.

There can be no doubt that Castelo Branco wanted effective planning and, above all, control over the economy. He appointed the most effective team he could possibly get to implement these aims. The new Ministry of Planning again gathered together a staff of economists and others from various agencies and set to work on a new three-year plan. Again, it was deemed important to have a plan immediately. During May, June, and July of 1964 the plan was created. In important respects it was similar to the Plano Trienal. The plan went to Congress on August 13, 1964. It was intended to cover three years, but the first of these was 1964, already more than half over. As usual, the plan was to cover the period of the incumbent administration. Initially Castelo Branco was expected to continue in office until the end of Goulart's term, which would have been January 31, 1966. This would have required elections in October of 1965—much too soon for the Revolution to consolidate its position. On July 22, 1964 a joint session of the Congress extended Castelo Branco's term to March 15, 1967.

Immediate measures were taken to implement the Program of Action (PAEG) as will be explained below. An advisory Council (CONSPLAN) was created in 1965 representing various economic groups in the population. This was the first experiment in formal structuring of the consultation function in Brazilian planning. In 1965 steps were initiated to give final and official form to the organization of the Ministry of Planning and to define its powers of implementation. At the same time, the long awaited task of creating a ten-year "perspective" plan was initiated with the use of outside consultants and work groups within the Ministry.

During 1966 the question was not whether the new planning system would survive, but whether the new president, presumed to be General Costa e Silva, would maintain the same policies. He asserted that he would while conveying the definite impression that certain controls would be softened and that planning would be "humanized."

The twenty-five year history of Brazilian planning has shown considerable impetuosity in the use of planning, a tool not well understood by the chief executives of the nation. No really effective central planning institution had developed, with the exception of the relatively stable National Development Bank concerned with micro-planning. The development of a planning staff had been hit-and-miss. The administrative and political complexities of planning had received little if any attention. But the gains in planning had been notable as well. Planning had become well recognized as an essential function of the national government. Having a plan had become important. Groups in the body politic had become accustomed to discussing and studying the successive plans. Through the Advisory Council they could now participate to some degree in planning. Most of all, a highly competent corps of Brazilian planners—economists—had been trained over a fifteen-year period. Despite the appearance of chaos in planning organization, the same key names had appeared among those making economic development decisions over the years. They may have been used inefficiently, but they represented a substantial resource which can be exploited in future planning.

The issues of plan-making, organization for planning, and techniques of implementation are treated in the fourth and fifth chapters of this study. In the next chapter, however, we turn to a description of the nature and content of the plans themselves.

3

THE SUBSTANCE AND PROCESS
OF PLANNING

Any discussion of planning rests on a somewhat superficial basis until the actual content of the plans is specified. This is not to assume that plans, once devised, will necessarily be carried out. Planning documents serve a variety of functions. These functions may or may not be rationally related to the explicit goals of planning. Certain purposes are achieved through plan-making even if plans are not implemented. We take the position, then, that the planning document is always important, even if the goal achievement which follows is minimal. The intriguing subject of the functions of plans and of planning is discussed chiefly in the last chapter. This chapter compares the four most recent Brazilian plans: the SALTE Plan, the Program of Goals, the Plano Trienal, and the Program of Action.

Three kinds of plan content are important in this discussion: (1) type of analysis in the plan, (2) stated goals, and (3) the arrangements recommended for goal achievement. Because of the variety of content in plan documents, we refer to the last of these three as the "plan proper." This category is the action agenda. In this discussion the Plano Trienal is treated at greater length than the others since it is the subject of the political case study in Chapter 5. Special emphasis is given in this chapter to the Plano Trienal as a political statement to serve as a backdrop for the case study. Each plan will be characterized separately, followed by a comparative analysis. Since plan content is intimately related to the *process* of plan-making, this will be the concluding subject in the chapter.

CHARACTERISTICS OF THE SALTE PLAN

Four broad sectors were chosen as objects of national planning under the SALTE Plan: public health, food supply, transportation, and electric power. These were considered the crucial points in the economy at which to stimulate economic growth. Each of the four was an obvious major factor in economic growth. Transportation and energy are both essential elements of the infra-structure for any industrialized nation. Agriculture (food supply) provided the manpower pool from which an urban industrial labor supply would have to come; and it required production methods of such efficiency that foreign exchange would not be exhausted by food imports when industrial investment was needed. Public health figures dramatically proved the erosion of the labor supply produced by morbidity rates which in some diseases approached a hundred per cent in some regions.

The choice of these four sectors demonstrates a development from the previous two plans which concentrated almost exclusively on the infrastructural elements of transportation and energy. A somewhat broader view of economic planning had arrived with the SALTE Plan. It is instructive to compare the sectors of the SALTE Plan, however, with those included in later plans. The major sectors which were absent were education, industry, fiscal and monetary policy, foreign trade, housing, and public administration. Only later did the inclusion of these areas appear essential.

In three of its four sectors, the SALTE Plan was strictly a governmental program. This was true of health, food supply, and transportation. In the energy sector, however, it appeared essential to consider the total picture. The governmental program in energy turned out to be only 9 per cent of the country's total. Thus the SALTE Plan was comprehensive neither in the economic sectors which it covered, nor in encompassing all economic activity both private and public. In general, the program covered only the national government, with state and local programs coming in for little attention. It was probably a good thing that the plan did not attempt to be more comprehensive than it was, since it was never carried out in its entirety in any event. The manner in which it was conceived and assembled suggests one reason why this was so.

The SALTE Plan contains no over-all framework within which its parts fit, other than the general goal of increased economic development to produce more societal income and thus a higher standard of living. In one sense, its function was not so much to produce economic changes in the society as to serve a closer range, pragmatic function. According to Mário Bittencourt Sampaio, Director General of the DASP at the time the plan was made, a major purpose was to strengthen the DASP as an institution and save it from falling prey to its enemies.[1] The particular competitor of Sampaio was the Minister of Finance, Pedro Luís Correa e Castro. One of the main issues between them was the division of responsibility in the area of programming and budgeting. The SALTE Plan provided a rather dramatic justification for assigning more of this activity to the DASP, at a time when the work of two U.S. economic missions had already popularized the idea of economic planning, and a third mission was arriving in Brazil to constitute part of the Joint Brazil–United States Technical Commission. This last group arrived just as President Dutra was presenting the SALTE Plan to the Congress in May, 1948. Sampaio assigns much of the credit for the survival of the DASP during this period to the formulation and publication of the SALTE Plan, which gave the DASP an "economic planning" image.[2]

1. Interview with Sampaio, May 28, 1963.
2. A related incident is worth preserving. At the time the SALTE Plan went to Congress, Sampaio was in France attempting to purchase a refinery for Brazil. Due to the insistence of the French that Brazil buy a large number of war surplus locomotives (originally from the U.S. invasion forces), this negotiation had broken down, and Sampaio was about to return to Brazil. At this point the Brazilian Minister of Finance, incensed over the publication of the SALTE Plan by the DASP, resigned. Word spread that Sampaio would be the new Minister of Finance. This prospect was even worse from the point of view of the Minister who quickly rescinded his resignation and re-

Since there was an element of political urgency in the completion of the plan, the work procedure followed in its preparation is not surprising. In the absence of any permanent planning staff, the work was assigned to groups of technicians, each group working on its own particular area, drawing on the sources of information and aid available in the ministries, and in the case of the food supply studies, using the expert staff of planners of the São Paulo state government. With no professional planner coordinating this operation, what happened was perhaps inevitable. Each sector, and often each portion of each sector, produced its own "plan" unrelated to that of any other sector. Much good work was done, data were analyzed, problems were spotted, and various goals were established. These goals were used as a setting for a specific list or "plan" of specific initiatives. In addition, the cost of accomplishing each unit of the "plan" was simply the sum total of amounts which each work group decided was necessary for its own particular area of interest. In effect, the result was a collection of project budgets such as might be turned in by a group of ministry planning offices. Critics later said that the plan was chiefly defective in that it bore no relation to available resources. A rationale for financing the "plan" had been developed, but this bore little relation to the actual prospect of providing the funds needed. This is not to say that Brazil could not have provided the funds in question given certain political and administrative conditions. Since these conditions did not exist, however, it is fruitless to argue that the plan was realistic as a budget guide. It did, however, serve an institution-building function for the DASP, as well as fulfilling an educational function. The failure of the plan in terms of implementation, and its association with the increasingly unpopular DASP, were factors contributing to the change of tactics under Kubitschek, who established a permanent planning

---

turned to work. In the interim, the French, feeling that they were dealing with a potential minister of finance, reconsidered their decision, and sold the refinery before it was learned that the old Minister of Finance would be retained.

agency with a permanent technical staff independent of both the DASP and the ministries.

The SALTE Plan was constructed by technicians of various sorts, including engineers, public health experts, agricultural experts, and economists. It was by no means purely an economic analysis. It was a project and problem-oriented approach, and the criterion of need in each case was basically what had developed within each professional group itself. The economic effects and other unanticipated consequences of actually carrying out the plan were not systematically studied. All of these characteristics of the SALTE Plan and the process of creating it were deliberately rejected during the next planning phase under the Kubitschek administration, which pioneered a new approach to national planning in Brazil.

CHARACTERISTICS OF THE PROGRAM OF GOALS

The "plan" of the Kubitschek administration is technically a tremendous advance over that of the SALTE document. It began to incorporate the notion of continuous planning. It is true that a single planning document was produced. In a broader sense, however, this represented only a stage, and not the final stage, of the plan. The first element of the broader plan was the political testament and campaign platform of presidential candidate Kubitschek, a book published during the campaign of 1955.[3]

Here, among other things, he developed the notion that if Brazil's resources were properly applied, that is, to those objects which would most promote economic growth, then rapid progress could be made in all areas of national life. What was the role of the state in this process? Kubitschek described this as a guiding and motivating role, but definitely not a directive and compelling one. He said:

3. Juscelino Kubitschek de Oliveira, *Diretrizes Gerais do Plano Nacional de Desenvolvimento* (Belo Horizonte: Privately printed, 1955).

I believe that the guided development of our economy must not
have as a consequence only the increase in the degree of intervention of the State, but must envisage, above all, the substitution for
sporadic and uncoordinated intervention of the State, the formulation of an organic program within which private initiative recog-
nizes the general goals that economic development requires and
the incentives that the State establishes. Toward this end, the program of the Government that I propose to lead foresees, initially,
the adoption of a "National Plan of Development," in which are
determined the objectives and the necessary conditions in order
that private initiative, with the aid of foreign capital and the effective assistance of the State, can accomplish the great task of our
progress and anticipation.[4]

On assuming office, Kubitschek immediately followed
through on the program foreseen. The second element of the
broader plan was the statement of thirty key goals to be
reached by January of 1961. These were announced in February of 1956, immediately after Kubitschek had taken office.
They were not hastily devised, however. Both the goals and
his book had been based largely on the projections and other
work of the CEPAL-BNDE mixed study group which had been
initiated in 1953 under the leadership of Celso Furtado.

The thirty goals had a dramatic impact in addition to establishing specific targets to be achieved. They were published
in a space of two printed pages, and were widely distributed.
In this plan, the sectors presumed critical to economic development were more broadly conceived than in the SALTE Plan.
They included energy, transportation, agriculture, as did the
SALTE Plan, but in addition, eleven specific goals in the area
of basic industry. These were concerned with steel, aluminum,
non-ferrous metals, cement, alkalis, cellulose and paper, rubber,
mineral exports, automobile industry, naval construction, and
heavy machinery. The final sector was education of technical
personnel. The majority of the goals were specific quantitative
goals to be reached by the end of the quinquennium such as:

4. *Ibid.*, p. 26.

oil production of 100,000 barrels daily, paving of 5,000 kilometers of roads, increase in the number of agricultural tractors in use to 72,000, production of 170,000 automotive vehicles in the year 1960.

The real "planning" began after the goals had been established. In 1956 the Development Council, to be described in detail in the next chapter, was created to engage in continuous planning. This was Brazil's first permanent central planning agency.

During 1956 the Council's staff broke down the thirty goals into the specific "projects" intended to achieve them. These were to be carried out by the government, by mixed enterprises, and by the private economy. Some of the studies made at this point bore fruit. They led to the establishment of USIMINAS, a state-federal mixed enterprise in the state of Minais Gerais, obtaining of a 125 million dollar loan from the Export-Import Bank of the United States for re-equipment of ports and railroads, and to the establishment of the nationalized auto industry in Brazil. During 1957, all this work was combined into a single program and published in a three-volume, 150-page work in 1958.[5] It is this program, worked out during the presidential term, that is now thought of as the "Program of Goals." During the study period the year 1956 rapidly passed out of the plan, so the quinquennium was shifted forward and the 1958 version of the plan deals with the years 1957-1961.

The Program of Goals comes to grips with the knotty question of how to finance the plan. The economic projections tended to show that Brazil had the capacity to finance the projects planned. When the bill was totalled up, however, the funds were not all in sight. Of a total of estimated needs from Brazilian sources of 338 billion dollars, only 285 billion was estimated as actually available. Of 2 billion, 318 million U.S.

5. Conselho do Desenvolvimento, *Programa de Metas* (Rio de Janeiro: Presidência da República, Conselho do Desenvolvimento, 1958). Vol. I, *Introdução*; Vol. II, *Energia e Transportes*; and Vol. III, *Alimentação, Indústrias de Base, Educação*.

dollar needs to be provided from foreign sources, 669 million
were apparently not available from any known source. While
in a sense these facts prejudiced the plan from the start, at
least there was a clear distinction made between money on
hand and money wished for.

The source of the goals varied according to the subject
matter. In the case of the basic industries, the goals were
developed by the Council itself. In other cases the interested
department established the goals. In still others, work groups
had to be established to integrate the thinking of the several
departments and of whatever private industry was involved.

The 1958 report indicates that the Council intended to follow up on effectuation of the plan through obtaining periodic
reports from all concerned. To a considerable extent this was
in fact done, though the reporting did not insure that the goals
were reached. The report also emphasizes the important role
of the president in supporting the program, and the key role
of the Congress in appropriating funds for the annual budgets.
The relation of the plan to budgeting is recognized: "In truth,
this program, involving the forecasting of budgetary sums distributed over several years, represents an effort at systematization of the budgetary task. . . ."[6]

Finally, the Program of Goals was reported on during its
life in annual and other reports of the Council. The final report, covering the entire five-year period (1956-1960) of the
Kubitschek administration, was published at the end of 1960
in four volumes.[7] At the end of the period, some goals had
not been attained fully, as in the case of agriculture. In some
cases ground had actually been lost in terms of the indices
cited in the plan, as in the case of transport. In the case of
the automobile industry, the goals had been exceeded.

6. *Ibid.*, Vol. I, p. 60.
7. Conselho do Desenvolvimento, *Relatório do Período 1956-1960* (Rio de
Janeiro: Presidência da República, Conselho do Desenvolvimento, 1960). Vol.
I, *Setor de Energia*; Vol. II, *Setor de Transportes, Setor de Alimentação*;
Vol. III, *Serviços Portuários e de Dragagem*; and Vol. IV, *Setor de Indústrias
de Base. Setor de Educação.*

The Program of Goals was a great advance over previous plans. Nevertheless, it was still basically an economic plan, and covered a major part, but not all, of the economic sectors. It dealt only to a limited extent with fiscal and monetary policy. It dealt with foreign trade only in a fragmented fashion. The one noneconomic sector included in the goals was education, and this from a special point of view. The governmental sector was not dealt with except in terms of specific major investments as in transportation and energy. At the end of Kubitschek's term there was still a long road to travel in planning despite significant advances.

CHARACTERISTICS OF THE PLANO TRIENAL

The document entitled "Three-Year Plan for Economic and Social Development, 1963-1965" is not a complete blueprint for solving the problems of Brazil. In all honesty, it could not be, since the knowledge and means for a complete solution are not at hand or are not apparent. In fact, "the plan" consists of a weaving together of a diverse set of elements, all relevant to the planning problem of Brazil. These elements may be grouped into our three categories: the analytical basis of the plan, the goals of the plan, and the instrumental means by which the goals will be carried out. We will describe the first two of these elements briefly, and then evaluate the plan proper in great detail. After thus describing the contents of the document, we will consider the plan's characteristics as a political statement.

The great bulk of the 150-page plan, in its published version, is devoted to analysis. Data is presented showing the performance of the economy over recent years, the indicators of the present state of the economic system, and projections for the period of the plan—1963, 1964, and 1965. In a few cases longer time periods are the basis of analysis. For example, the discussion of nuclear energy covers development up to 18 years in the future. Much of the analysis of the agricultural sector extends eight years ahead. Unlike many plans, however, the data does not dominate the analysis. An even more important component is the intellectual rationale which interprets the significance of the data, indicating road-blocks to economic progress and areas of possible flexibility and manipulation. In a very real sense, the validity of the "plan" depends on the competence of the economic analysis and its interpretive rationale. The present study is in no sense an evaluation of this competence.[8] Its intention is rather to describe the planning *process* and relate it to the broader governmental process of which it is a part.

The second element of the plan consists of statements of goals. These are presented at several levels of generality. At the broadest level the plan was intended to provide for growth in the national income in order to raise the standard of living. This growth was stated in operational terms as seven per cent per year growth in the national income (i.e., economic development) which corresponds to 3.9 per cent per year increase in per capita income. In order that increase in income be real, a second goal was to control inflation. In operational terms, inflation was to be limited to 25 per cent in 1963 (half the rate of 1962), 15 per cent in 1964, and 10 per cent in 1965. The document recognized that the measures which promote one of these goals tend to conflict with the other one. At the next lower level of generalization, the goals to be achieved (in order to attain the higher goals of planning) are institutional in nature, and are referred to as "basic reforms" in the structure of the Brazilian system. These include administrative, banking, tax and agrarian reform. These reforms were deemed necessary in order to create conditions under which the measures recommended by the plan could be taken.

The specific measures that constitute "the plan" in its literal and immediate sense, are scattered throughout the published

8. For an economic evaluation, see 16 *Revista Brasileira de Economia* (December, 1962). The entire issue is devoted to a series of articles evaluating various aspects of the Plano Trienal.

document. This "action agenda" is so intermixed with the
rest of the document that it is often difficult to separate it from
the matrix within which it appears. It takes many forms. For
example, the action items of the plan contain such matters as
the following: (a) "raising the tax burden" (p. 43);[9] (b) "cur-
tailment of scheduled public expenditures" (p. 43); (c) "it is
essential to reduce progressively the current consumption subsidies" (p. 45); (d) "government action . . . should be concentrated on incentives to the export activities" (p. 52); and (e)
"intensify pre-investments relating to the survey and evaluation
of natural resources including agricultural resources so as to
benefit regions having poor financial resources of their own
. . ." (p. 65). All of these items appear in the first three of
four major sections of the plan. It will be noted that they are
not expressed in quantitative terms, and they are not related
to particular money expenditures. They are, in fact, simply
policy *directions*. This is not to criticize them. Many plans are
expressed in money amounts, while policy directions are disregarded, a practice which represents blind planning. The
policy directions contained in the Plano Trienal are *guides* to
planning rather than blueprints.

The major portion of the "plan" covers "sectorial programming." The sectors are education, health, natural resources,
transport, communications, electrical energy, nuclear energy,
oil, coal, fishing, agriculture, mining, and manufacturing. An
analysis is made of trends and conditions in each sector, but
the "plans" for the sectors are highly variable in their nature.
The educational plan consists of two items which are really
goals: (a) "six years of elementary education to all Brazilian
residents of the urban districts and four years to all Brazilian
residents of the rural areas," and (b) "junior high school
[*ginásio*] educational opportunities to 40 per cent of the population ranging from 12 to 15 years, senior high school [*colégio*]

9. All page numbers in the plan are from Presidência da República, Estados
Unidos do Brasil, *Three-Year Plan for Economic and Social Development*,
1963-1965 (Rio de Janeiro: Serviço Grafico do IBGE, December, 1962).

education opportunities to 20 per cent of the population with ages ranging from 16 to 18" (p. 69). Following this, the plan is expressed in money terms broken down by each of the three years of the plan and for major categories of educational expense. There is no evidence presented that the goals can actually be achieved with the funds indicated. Moreover, the sums of money apparently (but not explicitly) include resources of unspecified origin from "abroad."

Again, the resources required to carry out the Cartographic Plan (for natural resources) are three billion cruzeiros for 1963, five billion for 1964, and six billion for 1965. Of these sums, the 1963 budget assigns 1.5 billion for 1963. If funds from foreign sources cannot be obtained, the plan goes on, the sum from the 1963 budget will be spread over the entire three years so that "part of the projects contemplated for 1963" can be carried out during the life of the plan (p. 75). This, at least, is an honest plan.

In other sectors, the "plan" consists of stating the program to govern expenditures of funds actually budgeted from existing sources. In still other cases, the expenditures are directly tied to the program, but it is not quite clear that the listed funds are actually expected to be available. In some cases the funds to carry out the plans are projections based on various assumptions.

In some categories, the contribution to "planning" consists of establishment of priorities for spending funds. Thus the nuclear energy program states, "First, such funds will go almost only to preinvestments, that is personnel training and project design. Only after a more advanced stage is attained the actual projects will be carried into effect" (p. 89). "Funds budgeted for 1963 . . . are considered to be insufficient to cover the costs of the program" (p. 89).

The sector covered in the plan most intensively is agriculture. After a thorough analysis of agricultural problems, and the projected need and potential for expansion of production for various crops and products, generalized policies are stated for improving the situation such as: (a) "It is the responsibility of both the Federal and State Governments to stimulate the establishment and expansion of rubber tree plantations, especially in economically underdeveloped regions with good ecological conditions" (p. 120); (b) "take the necessary steps for placing fertilizers within the reach of the greatest possible number of farmers with the necessary adjustments to the price and credit policies to this end" (p. 128); and (c) "concentrate, on a priority basis, all new investments (for warehouses and silos) on projects capable of bringing about a wider utilization of regional networks" (p. 129).

In the plan, the industrial sector is given relatively brief treatment. The dominant fact that industrial growth over the past five years had never been under 11 per cent annually is the evidence of the vitality of Brazil's new industrial complex. No real plan of governmental action for industry is presented, though some relevant considerations are pointed out: (a) "the exchange policy and the foreign trade policy must consider the special concessions for the exportation of manufactured and semi-manufactured goods" (p. 135); (b) "it is desirable that larger investments [in aluminum and lead] be made in order to expedite the rate of substitution of imports, for which requirement the country is exceptionally endowed" (p. 138); (c) "the subject industrial group [chemicals] should be given the special attention of the government since it includes the production of petrochemicals, alkalis, fertilizers, pulp and paper, all of great value in the economic development process" (p. 139).

All of these kinds of variations in the nature of "plans" presented reflect the realistic problems of planning. In many cases data on past experience is incomplete or is unavailable entirely. In such a case there is no basis for projections. Some economic factors can be predicted over a period of several years ahead, thus allowing specific plans to be made with regard to them. Other factors and indices are variable and unpredictable beyond a few months. Moreover, the plans of

government cannot constitute a complete and detailed blueprint unless all factors in the economy are under the control
of the government. Brazil's institutions provide for a wide area
of activity for private enterprise, which the government, in
fact, has often attempted to broaden in various ways. Thus a
consideration of sectors dominated by private activity cannot
produce governmental plans with immediate and complete
solutions to economic ills. In such a situation only peripheral
governmental policies, stimulants, or other aids can come to
bear. All of these factors must be borne in mind as we comment on the extent to which the Plano Trienal forms a basis
for guiding governmental policy.

THE PLANO TRIENAL AS A POLITICAL STATEMENT

Perhaps more than any of the other Brazilian national plans,
the Plano Trienal performed a political function. In a culture
in which personality and shifting coalitions are dominant factors and policy is obscure, the plan outlines a clear set of
policy directions to which the Goulart government became
committed. This policy statement provided a different kind
of basis for support or opposition to the government than is
customary in Brazil. The consequences of this fact are traced
in a later part of this study. The present purpose is merely to
characterize the political nature of the document.

Ever since the second administration of Vargas (1950-
1954) the pressures for substantial reform in the Brazilian society have been growing. Specifically the demands express the
desires of the great mass of the population for a larger participation in the benefits of the Brazilian economy. Vargas himself did much to precipitate the expression of these demands,
and his protégé, João Goulart, became firmly committed to
them during the course of his rapid rise to power. They are
expressed in the over-all objectives of the Plano Trienal as
three of eight major points:

To assure a rate of growth of the national income commensurate with the expectations of better living conditions which at present motivate the Brazilian people. . . .

To create conditions for a larger share of the fruits of development to the population, the real salaries of which must grow at least as much as the increase in productivity of the economy as a whole, in addition to the adjustments for the increase in the cost of living.

To intensify substantially the Government action in the fields of education, scientific and technological research and public health, in order to assure a rapid improvement of the human element as a factor in development and permit the access of an increasing number of the population to the fruits of cultural progress (p. 7).

While these points are expressed in very general terms, the means to achieve them are made more specific in the other five of the eight objectives. These five cover such measures as directing investment in the economy, the containment of the national budget, restrictions on credit, the limitation of imports vis-à-vis exports, and an increase in the rate of capital inflow. The rationale for use of these five major measures is convincingly presented in the plan itself.

The great political fact about the Plano Trienal is that it faces up to the inevitable imperative of any rational approach to planning, namely, the conflict between lesser short run benefits as against greater long run benefits. In brief, to change the structure of the Brazilian economy to the future advantage of the mass of people requires present sacrifices of various kinds. The very people who demand reforms often object to the essential means by which they must be brought about. Every one of the five categories of measures listed above adversely affected the self-perceived interests of one or more groups. The way in which these groups responded is related at a later point. By way of illustration, however, two early reactions to the plan will be mentioned here. The plan proposed a strategy of containing the size of the federal budget. A ceiling of 40 per cent on salary increases for civil servants and the military forces was established. An immediate campaign to break through this aspect of the plan was undertaken within the labor movement and the armed forces. This campaign served to aggravate a crisis within the military leadership of the country which had highly political ramifications.

Another of the goals of the plan was to increase the level of capital inflow into Brazil from foreign countries. This goal ran directly counter to the prime plank in the platform of various leftist and nationalist groups in the country which opposed foreign influences of any kind from the United States or Western Europe, and specifically the "exploitation of capitalist imperialists." The two main sources of funds from abroad were the United States government and the International Monetary Fund. The Fund was viewed as a tool of the United States. Accordingly, both these sources were viewed as "Yankee imperialism," a slogan which brings a tremendous political response in Brazil as in most of Latin America. These and other issues set against the plan many of the avowed spokesmen for the very beneficiaries of the plan themselves—the mass of poor people. Under the plan it was no longer intended to follow the ancient demagogic rationale of voting against all taxes and for all expenditures.

Beyond this major function of the plan as a rationalizer of political action, there were several other facts of political significance. In Brazil, as in much of the world, political and economic events are commonly interpreted in terms of a left-right dichotomy, however inept this oversimplified notion may be. Goulart came to power with a basically leftist image. To draft his plan of government he appointed Celso Furtado, Superintendent of SUDENE, who also had a leftist image. The reaction of many people to the plan depended more than any other one thing on whether the plan seemed to be socialist or not. Ready-made groups of both supporters and opponents were prepared for a leftist document. While the plan has been condemned as perpetrating every sin from the extreme left to the extreme right, the fact is that it is not by any means a socialist document. While seeking strong government intervention in certain economic areas, these are in every case justified as instrumental to the goal of stimulating development within the existing norms of Brazilian society. Moreover, the plan itself is specifically committed to the preservation of the free enterprise economy. The flavor of this commitment is conveyed in such passages as the following:

The decisions relating to capital formation in a free enterprise economy are not made in isolation. They result from the interaction of complex forces. On the other hand, there is the supply of resources in the capital market, which depends mainly on the level of overall economic activity; on the other hand, there are the short-run prospects for business profits, the degree of confidence in institutional stability, the long-range outlook for the economy. The progress in the understanding of these processes, achieved to a large extent in the last two decades, has made possible the planning techniques adapted to free-enterprise economies . . . (p. 11).

It had long been generally assumed that planning would be possible only where economic decisions were wholly centralized. This would be true if the conduct of businessmen failed to conform to a pattern as far as investments are concerned. Once these patterns and the major factors underlying the behavior of investing businessmen are identified, it would not be difficult to conceive policies designed to guide the capital formation process in free enterprise economies . . . (p. 11).

Planning is not intended to determine in detail what should take place in the economic system. It is designed to anticipate the major structural changes required to sustain a certain pace of development . . . (p. 12).

Action from the public sector is designed to enable certain objectives to be successfully achieved and decisions to be made at the appropriate time in order to ease internal tensions as much as possible. These investments, because of the important part they play in the capital formation process, could be classified as strategic. With respect to all other investments the responsibility for which pertains almost solely to private business, planning action should be carried on in a far more indirect manner . . . (p. 12).

Brazil overcame, during this period, [the past ten years] its most difficult stage in the process of industrialization. It has transcended the light industry stage of finished products and entered boldly the heavy industry stage. It conquered disbelief and indifference as regards the country's industrial possibilities, and won over the traditional sector more concerned with the import and the export trade, which always looked upon industrialization with doubt. Furthermore, an entrepreneurial class has developed, aggressive and dynamic, whose interests at stake make the process irreversible . . . (p. 131).

In short, the Plano Trienal did not represent a new political philosophy breaking violently with the past. The reforms advocated in the agrarian, tax, banking, and administrative system sprang not from an ideological base, but from the needs for institutional changes which would remove barriers to the major plan goal of increased economic development. However rational the basis for the plan, however, its reception was influenced strongly by the ideological positions of the various political actors, as will be shown in Chapter 5. At this point suffice it to say that the plan was based on the ideological *status quo* and had the effect of committing the Goulart administration firmly to this position, providing a new fixed point in the political structure.

Just as the plan gave no comfort to the socialists, neither did it gratify the radical nationalists. As noted above, far from advocating elimination of foreign capital from Brazil, it pointed to the need for increased investments from abroad. Moreover, it contained no recommendations for expropriation or otherwise acquiring the major foreign-owned enterprises in the country. Evidently foreign ownership was not regarded by the planners as an exploitative roadblock to development.

A recurrent political theme in Brazil has long been the correction of regional disparities. These disparities—the result of many factors of physical geography, historical development, and cultural behavior—can be measured in economic, social, or political terms. The Plano Trienal documents this disparity in economic terms, tracing its historical causes. It shows that the exchange policy of Brazil during the postwar years until the middle of the decade of the fifties produced income transfers from regions with an export balance, like the Northeast, to areas with an import balance like the Center-South. With a change in exchange policies in 1956 the situation began to improve. Other policies also contributed to this end as represented by the creation of regional development agencies in the Constitution of 1946, investments of Petrobrás in the Northeast, and others. These kinds of regional policies are described as "differential favors." The plan merely expresses support for continued differential favors, recommending three general policies to this effect. It is virtually a continuation of the regional policies of the Kubitschek administration.

Potentially, a policy of special aid for any region is an added political lever for the administration. Grants may be withheld pending fulfillment of conditions, and these could conceivably be of a political nature. Recognizing the high incidence of political unrest in the Northeast of Brazil and the development of peasant leagues with ideological leadership of a strongly radical type, the policy of regional favors achieves special significance.

Perhaps the most important political aspect of the Plano Trienal is the movement toward centralization of economic decisions. In the public debates about the plan, this aspect has received little attention, though it is clearly outlined in the document itself: "What is immediately envisaged by planning in Brazil is this ranking of problems in order to create conditions to permit the introduction of more effective decision-coordination techniques within a few years . . ." (p. 13).

What this implies in political terms is suggested as follows:

Economic planning is not an objective which can be achieved at once. It is ultimately a government and management technique and should as such be gradually introduced as the political, institutional, and administrative set-up admits of it. There cannot be any planning, for instance, if the Legislative and Executive branches of government fail to work in tune with fairly harmonious views, if within the Executive Branch top officials fail to make decisions in concert, if monetary authorities fail to obey a single command, and if such a command is not tuned with fiscal authorities, if the Administration is not adequately integrated to perform regularly the tasks which are assigned to it . . . (p. 13).

Where is the "single command" with which all legislative and executive authorities must remain in concert? The answer to this question seems to lie in the section of the plan on administrative reform. Here there appears a blueprint for a national planning system to coordinate the planning, and control the execution of the work of all the administrative agencies of the government, including the regional development agencies. Moreover, in order to effectuate this national planning structure, specific administrative reforms are recommended, including, among others: (1) the removal of some agencies reporting directly to the president from direct access in order to make his job manageable, (2) the reorganization of finance agencies to insure that more of the taxes levied are actually collected, (3) the reorganization of the entire accounting and control system, and (4) the control of budget execution by the central planning agency.

Enough has been said to underline the number of interests that would be vitally affected by this centralization in the decision mechanism of the government. The key existing control points would be subordinated to another control center, to some undefined degree. Existing bureaucratic machines would be disrupted through reorganization. Freedom of action would be restricted in many ways. Even the legislative body would have to conform in some degree. As soon as the Plano Trienal was published, these realizations gave rise to the epithet "superministry" as applied to the projected new ministry of planning. Nothing less than a new allocation of political power within the bureaucracy was in prospect. Shifts in power allocation are always obtained only against violent struggle on the part of those who expect to lose influence, status, and prestige. The evaluation of the degree to which the

execution of the plan was impaired by the lack of this centralization of decision-making is considered in another portion
of this study. At this point it is possible to conclude that tremendous political opposition could arise from any attempt to
implement the administrative reorganization of the planning
structure of the government on anything other than a slow,
piecemeal basis. The plan itself, in fact, foresees this development only in a time perspective expressed as "within a few
years."

THE PROGRAM OF ACTION

The Brazilian revolution successfully initiated in early April,
1964 produced a completely new government. The effect of
the revolution on planning in Brazil is of considerable interest
both in terms of planning and of the process of "revolution."
One might expect any genuine "revolution" to produce a plan
radically different from its predecessor. The Brazilian revolution was more than a mere coup, despite the negligible amount
of blood spilled—considerably less than in the Los Angeles in-
surrection of 1965. The Brazilian government has increasingly
identified the "revolution" with the program of the regime in
a usage familiar in such places as Nasser's Egypt, Mexico, or
for that matter in various Communist countries. Thus "the
revolution" is a continuing and uncompleted project.

This type of "revolution" demands a program which would
presumably be reflected in any national plan. We must therefore inquire what were the goals of the "revolution" in Brazil?
Remarkably, we can turn to no revolutionary manifesto, document, or program to find an answer. The truth is, the Brazilian
revolution has no new ideology to offer. The closest we can
come to an official justification of the revolution is the statement in the *Ato Institucional*, the original constitutional act of
the new government. In the preamble are listed two objectives
of the revolution: (1) to restore economic and financial order,

and (2) to drain the Communist abscess which had infected all levels of the Brazilian government.[10]

The first of these two objectives is directly relevant to the planning program of the new government of Castelo Branco. What program was to guide the restoration of economic order? Some supporters of the revolution believed that a mere ousting of Communists and a return to free enterprise would do the trick. The new President, however, well realized that changes in the structure of the economy were indeed necessary, and he appointed planners who agreed. Moreover, he appointed planning leaders who had for years been involved in economic research and administration in Brazil. The plain fact is that the real goals of the revolutionary government were substantially the same as those of President Goulart's planners. It is hardly a surprise, then, that the new plan which emerged was, in its crucial aspects, similar to the Plano Trienal. The program which had been embraced but never implemented by the Goulart administration was now revived by Roberto Campos and Castelo Branco. True, there were changes in emphasis. The new planners had learned some things from the failures of the previous plan. Let us consider the differences and similarities more specifically.

The Program of Action covers three years—1964, 1965, and 1966. Actually it was not completed until the midpoint of 1964. It was created in three months as was the Plano Trienal. The same subjects are dealt with in the Program of Action as in the Plano Trienal for the most part. However, a few new or greatly expanded areas of interest appear in the Program, such as housing, social welfare, salary policy, and tax policy. Moreover, the published version of the Program is considerably longer than that of the Plano Trienal.[11]

In general, the Program contains a more comprehensive and complete analysis of problems of the economy than in

10. *Ato Institucional*, published in the *Diário Oficial*, April 9, 1964.

11. *Programa de Ação Econômica do Govêrno 1964-1966* (Síntese), (Rio de Janeiro: Ministério do Planejamento e Coordenação Econômica, November, 1964).

any previous plan. The great bulk of the document is of this nature. In essence, the economic analysis runs as follows. Inflation has reached proportions which have produced a balance of payment disequilibrium, and have endangered continued economic growth. This must be checked if growth is to continue. Controlling inflation could tend to retard growth, however, and this is to be avoided during the transition period. In particular, unemployment must be fought. Basic reforms are needed in taxation, land tenure, education, and governmental personnel administration. Increased "socialization" is to be fought. This could result from gradual increases in government investment in the presence of lack of investment stimuli in the private sector. Minimum levels of public and private investment must be maintained, especially in transportation, power, education, and housing. Much of this investment must be governmental, and the containment of public expenditures must stop short of this type of investment.

The goals of the Program of Action, similarly, are the goals of the Plano Trienal, with some shift in emphasis. The first and foremost goal is to restore the rate of economic growth to previous levels, meaning seven per cent per year. From 7.3 per cent in 1961, this rate had dropped to 1.4 per cent in 1963 during the last months of the Goulart administration. The seven per cent growth rate would, in view of projected population increases, produce an increase in per capita income of 3.3 per cent annually. Secondly, the Program intends to curb inflation, so as to achieve reasonable price equilibrium by the beginning of 1966. Third, the plan proposes to absorb the continuously expanding labor force and to adopt policies which will not reduce labor's share of the national wealth. Fourth, a general goal is announced of ameliorating regional, sectoral, and social imbalances by means of improvement of social conditions. Finally, it is proposed to correct the balance of payments deficit. The Program did not emphasize the refunding of foreign debts as had the Plano Trienal, since considerable success in this area had already been achieved. It managed to focus on protecting the status of labor without conveying the impression of distributing the rewards of economic development more evenly through the population. The Program's stated goals do not mention changes in the structures and institutions of society or in the means of governmental control though they may be inferred. These differences are much more matters of strategy than of goals. In all essential respects, the goals of Brazilian planning have remained constant.

The "plan proper" of the Program of Action is the point at which it differs the most from the Plano Trienal. Again, the difference may be essentially a matter of strategy. In any event, the Program is less specific. Policy objectives, policy measures, and policy directions are clearly indicated in general form, but the Program by no means contains a budget covering projects to be undertaken during the three years of the plan. Rather, it is much like a perspective plan in its content. The following are typical elements of "the plan," which is divided into "general instruments," "sectoral policies," and "social and regional improvement." "The Policy of controlling the lending capacity of commercial banks and of selective control of bank credit will be exercised by the utilization of two principal instruments: Variation of minimum reserves that the commerical banks must maintain by order of SUMOC [Superintendency of Money and Credit] and variation of limits and conditions under which commercial banks have access to the credit facilities that the Monetary Authorities award them through rediscount permits of the Bank of Brazil" (p. 70).[12] "Extension of the area of incidence [of the income tax] toward the end of avoiding concentration of collections from a small group of contributors. Within this principle, the Congress already revoked, according to a message of the Executive, constitutional exemptions from the income tax for professors, authors, journalists, and judges" (p. 80). ". . . an objective for intensive training of labor . . . must embrace somewhat more

12. All page numbers in this section refer to the published version of the Program of Action, *ibid.*

than 200 thousand individuals, between 1964 and 1970" (p. 118). "The Plan of Action aims . . . to create conditions that stimulate the entry of external resources, with a view of accelerating the rate of increase of the internal product" (p. 142). "To proceed with measures aimed at reducing expenditures in foreign exchange for the importation of petroleum and its derivatives . . ." (p. 166). "For the improvement of Social Welfare emergency arrangements are not sufficient . . . what is imperative . . . is to submit legislation consisting of a complete revision in order to correct distortions in the field of welfare administration . . ." (nine guidelines for this revision are then listed, p. 222).

It is extremely difficult to extract action elements of "the plan" from the general discussion of trends, projections, analytical, and explanatory comments, and other commentary, because of the very general nature of the policies recommended. This demonstrates the perspective nature of the plan document. What should be emphasized very strongly, however, is the planning activity which was actually concurrent with the preparation of the *Program of Action* document. Very specific measures were being taken which were not parts of the plan document which went to Congress in August. By the time the plan was published in December, it contained comments explaining the measures already taken, and a summary of these actions between April and November of 1964. During this period, at least, the Program of Action was as much an explanation and justification of the government's reform program as it was a guide to that program.

The major reforms undertaken during the eight-month period included a law to stimulate personal savings and corporate reinvestment; compulsory capitalization of public utilities by users of the services; revision of gas taxes in order to make the road construction program self-financing; change in the law on profit remittance in order to stimulate the use of foreign capital; and establishment of a series of industrial credit institutions. These measures were all directed at stimulating growth.

Measures aimed at curbing inflation included elimination of import subsidies for wheat, petroleum, and newsprint (thus reducing the governmental budget), reduction of the deficits of various government corporations through adjustment of rates, elimination of uneconomical services, improvements in efficiency, and other measures; reduction of expenditures in government departments; increases in income, sales, and stamp taxes; creation of a new type of government bond with an escalation clause; introduction of an escalation clause on fiscal debts; an escalation clause, in effect, on credit to the private sector; and wage readjustments for the previous two years rather than at the previous peak.

Employment and housing objectives have been approached through a new law creating a financial system for financing of new housing on a mass basis for low income families, and through revision of the rent control law. The balance of payments situation was attacked through modifying the exchange rates in favor of exporters; the profit remittance law mentioned above; a law for financing exports; simplification of the bureaucratic procedures necessary for exports; and concession to exporters of foreign exchange for imports. Improvement of the agricultural sector was sought through the establishment of a system of agricultural credit; importation of fertilizer financed through AID counterpart funds; revision of the minimum price laws; and enactment of an agrarian reform bill. In addition, a banking reform law was enacted; a law for the financing of primary and secondary education was passed; and the Advisory Planning Council was established. Other measures were enacted in 1965 including a law to reward businesses that had held the price line and penalize those that had not; a wage reduction law, especially for government employees; a compulsory loan for persons receiving more than a specified salary; and an agreement with the United States guaranteeing investments in Brazil. Finally, toward year's end a tax reform law was enacted and a National Transportation Council was created. The BNDE established a variety of funds for stimulating various sectors of business and manufacturing (FINAME, FIPEME, FUNDECE, FUNDEPRO, and FINEP), and the newly created Central Bank established FUNAGRI, a fund to administer the use of resources for agricultural development.[13] At the end of 1965 loans from USAID, IMF, the World Bank, and the Inter-American Bank totalled more than a billion dollars since the advent of the Castelo Branco regime.

Lower priority reforms received attention in 1966, including a reorganization of the merchant marine, creation of a new unemployment compensation fund, reorganization of the social security system, and the establishment of several new entities including the Advisory Commission on Industrial and Commercial Policy, a Fund for Research on Industrial Technology, the Brazilian Tourist Institute, the National Council on Foreign Commerce, and others. In May of 1966 it became possible to loosen credit restrictions somewhat. This final year of the Program of Action also saw continued support from abroad. U.S. aid had increased from 350 million dollars in 1964 to 560 million dollars in 1965 and appeared destined to increase still further. The IMF provided a 125 million dollar standby loan for stabilization purposes, the Inter-American Bank gave loans for more projects in industry, agriculture, roads, and ports, and in July Minister Campos traveled to Paris to a meeting of the World Bank. There he presented a report on the success of the Program of Action and an agenda of thirty-four projects needing financing by the Bank.

All of these initiatives and achievements were viewed in the Ministry of Planning and Economic Coordination as part of a continuing process of planning consistent with the Pro-

13. An excellent survey of economic developments for the year 1965 is found in an extensive supplement to the *Jornal do Brasil* called "Revista Económica," Volumes I, II, and III, February 10, 1966. FUNDEPRO (established in 1966) finances basic and general consumer-goods industries. FINAME finances the manufacture and sale of capital goods produced in Brazil. FIPEME provides credit for the investments of small and medium-sized companies. FUNDECE provides working capital. FINEP provides credit for the preparation of technical products. FUNDEPRO is described in Brazilian Government Trade Bureau, *Brazilian Bulletin* (May, 1966), p. 5.

gram of Action, but not as a final fulfillment of it. By August
of 1965 the top staff of the Ministry was asserting the notion
that the Program of Action was merely the first of a series of
planning statements which would be produced over the years.
Steps had already been taken both to prepare a plan covering
the period 1967-1977 and to coordinate the planning process
with annual budgeting and administrative processes, thus moving in the direction of detail and specificity in planning implementation. The President himself, in a knowledgeable dis-
course on planning, had listed the key steps which Brazil must
take to include: (1) permanent institutionalization of the
planning machinery in a Ministry of Planning; (2) the collection of accurate statistical information needed for planning;
(3) preparation of detailed regional and sectorial plans; (4)
the integration of these into a long-range plan of development;
and (5) institutionalization in permanent character of the relationships between planning and execution.[14]

THE PLANS COMPARED

In order to visualize the developing trends in Brazilian
planning it is useful to compare the plans. Any number of
bases of comparison might be chosen. We concentrate here on
goals, scope of plans, programming arrangements, relation to
the private economy, political role, and the plan-making process.

All the plans have come perilously close to the thinking
that regards economic development of Brazil as the panacea
that will attain all social objectives. This type of thinking sets
up economic development as an ultimate goal, beyond which
there is no point in looking. Fortunately, there is a perceptible
trend away from this line of thought. In the SALTE Plan,
judging by the document itself, the basic motivations were

14. Castelo Branco, "Os Estágios Do Planejamento Econômico Brasileiro,"
Address at the opening of the course on economic programming for the
Ministry of Planning, May 11, 1965.

exclusively economic. True, one of the major sectors covered was health. But the purpose in improving the nation's health was clearly stated as improving the human being as an efficient piece of the economic machinery. This is the engineer's approach. With the Program of Goals, a few lines are devoted to the ultimate goal—man himself—but with two important qualifications: "In its widest sense, the investment projects are composed in such a way, above all, so as to elevate the standard of living of the Brazilian people, to the maximum degree compatible with the conditions of economic equilibrium and social stability."[15] One might think that economics and social stability were *components* of standard of living rather than limits, but in any case, the human being now becomes the object of the plan. This in itself was a triumph. The Plano Trienal carries the same basic goal, but develops it to add the democratic factor. In that plan the benefits of a rising living standard are to be systematically controlled so as to distribute them more evenly than heretofore throughout all groups in the population. To speak approvingly of the democratization of planning goals, however, must not blind us to the fact that equal distribution of benefits probably conflicts with a maximum rate of economic development. Certainly this is true in the short run. The Program of Action is not specific on this point, speaking only of "social disequilibrium," whatever that may mean.

The shift in emphasis as to goals has been accompanied by a broadening of the scope of the plans. The SALTE Plan contained the three economic sectors of agriculture, transport, and energy, plus health. The Program of Goals dropped health, but continued the three basic sectors of the previous plan. The big addition of the Kubitschek era was to include a heavy emphasis on basic industry. This is in no criticism of the SALTE Plan, since the infrastructural elements of energy and transportation systems are in a real sense basic to any development of industry. The Program of Goals began after five more years of development than did the SALTE Plan. The

15. *Programa de Metas*, Vol. I, p. 18.

goals included, in addition, that of training technical personnel. This is an increasing problem as the extent of industrialization increases. The Plano Trienal dealt with various embellishments representing the now even more advanced degree of industrial development.

The great advance of the Plano Trienal lay not in sector analysis, substantial as this was, but in other elements of content. This plan moved from the collection of micro-plans, which is substantially what the Program of Goals represented, to a macro-plan for the economy. In order to do this, the plan document necessarily had to include both an analysis of how the economy as a whole performed and what policies would need to be applied to make it perform in the fashion desired. In addition to specific policies, such as exchange controls, for example, it was necessary to deal with the basic institutional reforms required by economic development. These were administrative, banking, fiscal, and agrarian reforms. This represents a tremendous broadening of the scope of planning and changes it from the almost simple exercise of listing capital investments to the fantastically complex task of restructuring the processes of the society. More than this, this new broad approach strikes at the fixation on the panacea of economic development itself. Here, as if almost unconsciously, there is recognition that treatment of the economy is inseparable from treatment of social and political institutions. No one can doubt that agrarian reform and administrative reform strike at entrenched socio-political institutions. The very name of the Plano Trienal became "Three-Year Plan for Economic and *Social* Development." It is true that the plan itself does not include the studies and recommendations for the four areas of institutional reform. It merely rationalizes the need for them. But the door was opened.

The Program of Action receded, if anything, from the broad scope encompassed in the Plano Trienal, though the difference is more a matter of phrasing and attitude than of plan content as such. The Program contains sections on education, public health, social welfare, and housing. In each case, however, these subjects are discussed *because of their effect on the economy* in much the style of the SALTE Plan. Housing programs are needed to provide employment in the construction industry. Low education levels are slowing development of the economy. Governmental welfare funds are not on a sound basis. Only in discussing regional disparities does the concept of social justice creep in (p. 225). In general, however, the Program is an economic program without physical, social, political, or administrative dimensions. Benjamin Higgins, the Brazilian government's top economic planning consultant, even suggested that in the perspective plan the rather ambiguous reference in goal number three to social welfare policies ". . . perhaps should not be included as part of the aims of economic development policies as such."[16] This avoidance of the noneconomic goals, so common in development plans, may be based on a variety of assumptions such as: (a) if the economy is treated, other problems will take care of themselves automatically, (b) economic problems are more basic than social problems, and must be treated first—after the crisis is resolved other types of planning may be done, or (c) sociopolitical planning is dangerous and all plans must be couched in purely economic terms.

As the discussion to come will show, Brazil's present planners have not proven reluctant to struggle with socio-political planning, and we presume the exclusively economic mien of the Program of Action is a matter of strategy. It is relevant to note that the Ministry of Planning has recently employed various "comprehensive planners" with the mission of developing a "national system of regional and local integrated planning," which would comprehend physical, administrative, and social as well as economic planning.[17]

16. Benjamin Higgins, "The Economic Development of Brazil," a draft outline of a Perspective Plan Document, mimeographed, no date, p. 20.

17. This is documented in a mimeographed report of the regional and municipal planning division of the Ministry of Planning, presented to the Seminar on State Planning of the Center for Economic Development of ECLA

How do the plans provide for programming the necessary implementing actions? This is a constant dilemma in a mixed economy, part governmental, part private. The usual answer is to say that governmental programs may be programmed centrally, while private activity is subject to indirect controls, stimuli, guidance, and incentives. Let us consider primarily governmental programming.

Ideally, a development plan, to be implemented by any government might look about as follows. There would be a clear statement of goals. The means would be programmed. By this is meant that the plan proper would include in every section a statement of the units of work necessary to reach the goal, and the priorities to guide performance of the various units. In terms of the specific planning document, these units would then be assigned to a particular year for implementation, and to a specific governmental entity or combination of entities. This plan of work would then be expressed in terms of the total cost, which in turn would be broken down into costs of the work to be performed in each year of the plan. These sums would constitute part of the regular governmental budget.

There have been cases when this "ideal" plan was actually put on paper, but such a plan has always departed far from reality. The difficulty is that no plan of economic development for a nation as complex as Brazil could possibly be this complete. If there were no limits to available financial resources of the country, the plan could be complete, and sums assigned to achieve any possible goal. In real life, however, resources are too limited to achieve all the legitimate goals of a population. This is no reason to abandon the goals. Through planning, it may be possible to achieve the closest possible approach to the goal with available resources. Thus it is more important to have the proper *direction* set forth to reach the

and the National Economic Development Bank, entitled "Anotações Referentes a Implantação de um Sistema Nacional de Planejamento Integrado, em Nivel Regional e Local" (July, 1965), p. 4.

goal than to imagine *all* the steps necessary to achieve it. For this reason we cannot expect any realistic plan to be complete in the sense described above.

Certain expectations, however, can be sought in planning. The *first* of these is that the portion of the work that can be accomplished with available resources during the term of the plan must be clearly stated. The *second* is that the work to be performed be related to the specific sums of money needed to perform it. The *third* is that these sums of money be directly and clearly related to the governmental budget. The SALTE Plan does not deal with any of these matters in any meaningful way. The Program of Goals contains some of these elements of programming, but none was effectively carried out. Since so much of the planning was done during the period to which it applied, no real system of relating planning to the annual budget and extending the five-year period by one year each year was developed. Brazil has never overcome through administrative means the hiatus represented by a change in presidential administrations. The Plano Trienal was deficient in all three areas as well. Like its predecessor, this plan was being programmed during the triennium. The plan contains the policy *directions* but in most cases these are not broken down into the amount that can be accomplished during the three-year term of the plan. Secondly, most of the plans are not costed. It is not clear how much will be available and allocated to the plan. General expectations and needs are set forth in money terms, as well as statements of sums available. Usually these sums are clearly stated to be less than needed. Finally, sums available for execution of the plan are not related to the budget. This relationship was left to be worked out later as the budget process proceeds.

The Program of Action contains even less programming than the Plano Trienal. In this case, however, no attempt was made to produce a detailed plan. The real substance of programming has been in progress, or is planned, as a next stage in a longer planning process. No doubt the same could have been said of the Plano Trienal had it attained a longer life. In any event, the planners of the Campos ministry have a lively appreciation for the very intimate relation between planning, programming plans, and the budget and administrative process generally. For this reason a considerable amount of effort has been devoted to budgetary reform by the Branco government. As early as 1964 budget ceilings were employed for the first time in Brazil's history at the beginning of the budget process.

The degree of control has increased during the history of Brazil's plans. The SALTE Plan was concerned chiefly with the governmental portion of the economy. The Program of Goals extended to the private sectors as well, but solely on a sectorial basis. The two more recent plans, approaching the matter from the standpoint of macro-economics, necessarily dealt with the entire economy. The Plano Trienal, however, seems to have been designed with a view to greater centralized governmental control. Despite the many control measures enacted pursuant to the Program of Action, the planning approach being designed seems to be aimed at something more closely approaching the "indicative planning" of the French variety. Certainly this would be true if in fact sectorial and regional planning precedes integration of these elements into a national plan as the Branco speech implies. This impression is reinforced when we consider the interest in a regional and local planning "system," and the implementation arrangements being planned, as will be described in the next chapter.

The four plans have had quite different political significance. The SALTE Plan emanated from the sub-presidential level to serve a survival function for the DASP. The Program of Goals was a campaign document, and proved of enough political value that Kubitschek, when he announced his new bid for office, stressed that he would provide a new program of goals. For him the plan was a political success. The Plano Trienal was produced to fill a needed program gap for the Goulart administration. With the benefit of hindsight it is clear that Goulart reaped nothing but trouble from the plan—as from most of his other political ventures. It is too soon to evaluate the political impact of the Program of Action. If the government is successful in combatting the critics of the Program, it is conceivable that it will prove to have been the first Brazilian plan to achieve substantial movement toward its goals. This could only produce political benefits. In any event, the Branco government is more solidly committed to the process of rational planning than any previous Brazilian government.

A final point of comparison will help to introduce the subject matter of the next chapter. There has been a perceptible tendency in the plan-making *process* employed by the Brazilian plans. The SALTE Plan was constructed on an *ad hoc* basis. The Program of Goals converted to a system of more or less continuous planning through use of a presumably permanent planning agency. The same tendency was continued in the Plano Trienal process, though important elements of discontinuity crept in as a result of political and personnel changes. Despite these negative developments, however, there was still a perceptible movement toward a new type of continuous process, particularly as represented in the Furtado proposal. The new element is the concept of central planning as integration of regular and continuous planning done at the agency level. This development, and its intellectual sources in the administrative reform movement, is traced in the next chapter. In terms of process, the Program of Action is an extension of the trend expressed during the previous administration. The organization of the system of planning has been worked out in greater detail by the present administration. There is perhaps a greater sense that in the long-run planning cues will come from below rather than from above. Accordingly, there is apparently a greater emphasis on regional, state, and local planning—in the plans for planning. In part, however, this may be a function of the greater length of time available to the planners of the Castelo Branco government.

To sum up, the trend is clearly in the direction of creating a continuous planning process throughout the agencies and levels of Brazilian government which will operate within the context of a long-range set of policies, perspectives, or goals. Annual and short-range plans, programs, and projects would be produced and directly related to the annual budget process, which would be transformed into a sophisticated program budget. There is a long way to go before this kind of an ideal will be reached, but the essential concept has already been embraced. Should this trend continue, "the plan" document may become insignificant or even disappear altogether except as a public relations instrument. As the process of planning changes, the nature of "the plan" must inevitably change as well. This relationship will be explored further as we consider the administration of planning in the next chapter.

4

THE ADMINISTRATION

OF PLANNING

When planning agencies are created, their organizational relationships almost always depend on very temporary conditions, often of a political nature. The original arrangements for planning may be very inappropriate at a later turn of the political wheel. One might argue from this fact either that planning administration *should* be subject to change as political conditions evolve, or that there is a need for more stability and continuity in the planning establishment. We are not prepared to take either position as a general proposition, since a good case can be made for either side. We can, however, come to certain conclusions with reference to Brazil.

Six chief issues sum up the dilemmas of planning administration. First, given any specified planning goals, should initiative in planning come from a central agency or from decentralized planning units in the departments, regions, states, and municipalities? Realistically, some initiatives will originate in all these places. The question is, what are the consequences of one mix as against another? Very closely related to this question is the second: Where does final decision lie on the substantive matters of planning as between central and decentralized entities? One could conceive of central decision in key matters after initiatives arise from the agencies and units of government. In a sense, the French system approximates this. One can equally well conceive of initiatives from the center, with final decision resting in the decentralized entities. State planning in the United States often displays this pattern. Both of these questions are very clearly related to such variables as the constitutional division of powers within the governmental system, the location in government of planning talent, the configuration of political decision centers, the homogeneity and size of the nation in question, and perhaps others.

A third and difficult dilemma is whether or not the professional planners should also be the implementers of plans. On the one side is the general line of argument which has been referred to by Frederick Mosher and others as Gresham's law of planning—responsibility of an agency for implementation with its attendant crises and deadlines tends to drive out the contemplative, postponable activity of long-range research and study on which good plans presumably ought to be based. In addition to this, the political involvements which inevitably attend implementation tend to feed back into the plan making process to produce negative effects when judged by the explicit goals of planning. The other line of argument holds that planning cannot be "realistic," especially in terms of political limitations, unless the planners constantly are forced to test their decisions against the hostile pressures at play in the political arena. This process provides the feedback which will permit maximum adjustment of "rational" plans to the "irrational" forces which cannot be disregarded in the short run. Some of the more relevant variables which affect this decision include the confidence which the political elite has in the professional planners, the public image of the planners, and the administrative skills of the planners (reflecting the composition of the planning profession and recruitment patterns for planners).

A fourth dilemma concerns the degree of coercion—especially from the central government—to be used in implementation of planning. It is generally recognized by every authority on planning that participation of those who must implement, and of those to be affected by plans, is desirable in the planning process. Arrangements for such participation may even be observed in the highly centralized Soviet system of planning. The most common expression in the documents and discussions relating to the planning function, however, describes the role to be played as one of "coordination," a hopelessly ambiguous, and therefore convenient, term. This is not the place to list, in increasing order according to the amount of coercion to be used, the very many devices used in "coordination." These range from a simple information clearing house to the dictation of plans and of implementational measures. Some of the variables most relevant to this problem of planning are the degree of pressure for change to which political authorities are subjected, the types of noncoercive levers available to implementers, traditional levels of tolerance for coercion by central authority, and degree of certainty that plans will produce the effects predicted.

The fifth matter, less a dilemma than a choice among many possibilities, is the nature of the technical staff for planning. Some mix as among economists, project engineers, administrators, physical planners, social scientists, statisticians, and a wide variety of research specialists, must be determined. The relevant variables here are the past traditions in the country, the national image of what "planning" is, the availability of these various technicians, the relative status in the country of the professions listed, and of course the planning goals which the country is seeking to achieve.

A final dilemma, and one to which little systematic thought has been given, is the nature of the mix between technical and political factors in planning. By "technical" factors is meant rationality solely in terms of the explicit and accepted national goals of planning. By "political" factors is meant the rationality of any constituent groups in the nation which are able to press for their goals at the centers of political decision when these goals are in conflict with the explicit national goals. The conceptual distinction is a useful one, despite the difficulty in making it operational. The position taken here is that if the planning process is essentially a technical one in its earlier stages, the final result will be much different (both in terms of the nature of the plan and the degree to which it is implemented) from the case where the earlier stages are subject to "political" guidance with the later stages devoted to technical preparation of programs based on those guidelines. The vari-

ables relevant to this question seem to be the attitude of the
planners themselves as to this question (often stemming from
professional doctrine), the level of understanding of planning
on the part of political decision-makers, and the political insight of the planners.

It is readily apparent that these six problems of planning
administration are highly interrelated, as are the variables
listed above. In addition to these variables, there are some
general ones which appear to affect most or all of the questions
listed above. These include factors which affect the bureaucracy in general such as the degree of achievement orientation
among administrators and employees, bureaucratic traditions
with reference to whether functionaries are actually expected
to perform work or not, morale in the public service, and the
degree to which the red tape syndrome is present.

In this chapter we shall explore the manner in which variables such as those listed above have produced a resolution of
the six dilemmas in the case of Brazil.

ORGANIZATION FOR PLANNING

In Brazil the evolution of organization for planning, in general, has followed a typical pattern. First, plans have been
created with no governmental agency established for the purpose whatever. Second, plan-making agencies of a temporary
character have been created to administer particular plans with
no clear definition of the role or powers of the agency. Finally,
efforts have been made to establish a permanent system of
planning with defined powers of plan-making and execution.
Only the most preliminary steps have been taken into the third
stage at the national level. One or two states and regional
authorities, like SUDENE, have progressed farther in this direction. This discussion will focus on the nature of the organ
of direction of the planning apparatus, the internal organization of the planning agency, its external relationships, and the
nature of the technical planning staff.

The directing organ for planning. When the SALTE Plan was drafted there was no planning agency. The plan was drafted by DASP technicians plus some others recruited from the state government of São Paulo. Finally, in 1950, a General Administrator (*Administrador Geral do Plano SALTE*) was appointed by the President.[1] The administrator was virtually without authority. While he was directed to "coordinate" the plan, he was given almost no means of doing so, in a clear case of broad responsibility and no authority. In fact, his formal authority was confined to receiving whatever of the SALTE funds were released to him by the President, and depositing them in the appropriate account of the Bank of Brazil for the designated spending agency. His discretion was limited to setting priorities as between implementing agencies in the distribution of these funds—a discretion exercised by President Dutra in practice. Beyond this, the function was clerical, being performed by one accountant.

What made the position tenable at all was the fact that the administrator of the plan was also the Secretary General of the DASP, and whatever influence he exerted probably stemmed from the latter role. It perhaps underscores the point more effectively to indicate what the administrator could *not* do. While he had few funds to distribute, as it turned out, he had no way whatever of checking on how they were used, once allotted. This is why no one knows to this day how much of the SALTE Plan was accomplished. There was no mechanism of feedback to report on progress toward plan goals in any particular sector of the plan. Finally, the administrator had no staff of planners to do advance planning. It is difficult to escape the conclusion that the incipient planning mechanism under the SALTE Plan was significant chiefly for what it showed of how *not* to plan. The assigned job of "coordinating" the plan was impossible with the means provided.

Since the DASP did not prove an effective home for planning, and probably for other reasons, the Kubitschek admin-

1. Decree No. 28.225, June 12, 1950.

istration turned to the device of a council, and created the Council for Development (Conselho do Desenvolvimento) in 1956.[2] The Council, in fact, consisted of the cabinet plus the other key officials of the administration.[3] This arrangement is intended to insure that the planning agency is intimately geared to the current political realities gaining direction at the very top level and reporting there. In theory this system would gain top level political commitment at an early stage in the planning process. There is a danger, however, in this form of planning leadership. The span of attention which planning can gain from the men who run the country at the top power center is often relatively brief. The validity of this arrangement relies heavily on the attitude toward planning held by the chairman of the Council—who is the President of the Republic. He calls for meetings of the Council. Kubitschek, founder of the Council and deeply interested in its work, insured for it a key place in the pattern of top level decision-making. Continuing to exist under Quadros and Goulart, however, the Council became completely inactive in terms of planning leadership.

The Council's powers were all advisory. In essence, it was expected to direct economic research, formulate plans, and be informed about the results. The assumption on which this approach is based is that the function of planning is essentially to formulate sound decisions and feed these into the regular decision-centers of the government to be implemented by the various ministries and other organs. Given the make-up of the Council, this has a certain logic. The line of communication is open.

2. Decree No. 38.744, February 1, 1956. Slight changes were made by Decree No. 38.906, March 15, 1956, and Decree No. 43.395, March 13, 1958.

3. Specifically the members were the President, Minister of Justice and Interior, Minister of the Navy, Minister of War, Minister of Aeronautics, Minister of Foreign Affairs, Minister of Fazenda, Minister of Transportation and Public Works, Minister of Agriculture, Chief of the Military Cabinet, Chief of the Civil Cabinet, President of the Bank of Brazil, President of the Economic Development Bank, and Minister of Health. In 1959 the Minister of Education and Culture, Minister of Labor and Social Welfare, Minister of Industry and Commerce, and the Director General of DASP were added.

The direction of the work of the Council on a continuing basis was the responsibility of a member of the Council, designated by the President of the Republic, called the Secretary General. This position was a political rather than a technical one. It is a position of prestige, and as is typical in Brazil, could be held by a person with various other responsibilities at the same time. As a result it was a part-time activity. The last Secretary General, for example, was Leocádio de Almeida Antunes who was also the President of the National Economic Development Bank. Full-time, technical direction of the staff was centered in no one place.

The role of the Council changed over time. Under Kubitschek it formulated the Program of Goals for the five years of the administration, and in so doing was at the center of the national policy-making process. After Kubitschek, the Council was not used in this way. Various special studies and projects were assigned to it, in some cases feeding into the national plan produced elsewhere. As a central planning agency it suffered from the lack of any philosophy of continuity in planning, monitoring planning, and continuously feeding back recommendations for updating the plan in force. Its fortunes rose and fell with the single five-year plan which it originally created.

When Jânio Quadros took office a new planning agency was created in August, 1961.[4] The question immediately arises, why was a new planning agency created when one already existed with a substantial and presumably successful record? Was it a new type of organization that was desired? Was a new function to be performed? Was the old planning agency associated with failure? The best evidence available suggests that fundamentally it was none of these. Rather, the reason may be spoken of as "political." Jânio Quadros came to office with no conception as to the requirements for governmental planning, though he was strongly motivated to produce change in the existing administrative system in order to give it a

4. Decree No. 51.152, August 5, 1965.

thorough cleansing. His campaign organization did not carry over to any considerable degree into his administration. Upon his election he did not immediately turn to the task of mapping out the policies of his administration. As the day for inauguration approached, and in anticipation of the need to give an inaugural address, Quadros hastily gathered together a staff of advisers. A number of these were technicians and planners drawn from the campaign staff of General Lott, one of the candidates Quadros had defeated! Some of these men, including Roberto Campos, had previously served Kubitschek in planning roles of one kind or another.

Like Kubitschek, Quadros was reluctant to delegate authority in the area of planning and his intention was to keep it within the technical staff of the President—the Assessoria Técnica da Presidência da República. As director of this staff, Quadros appointed Cândido Mendes de Almeida who was the director of the national railroad system during the Kubitschek administration. Mendes was trained in law and was involved chiefly in scholarly activities of many sorts. He was associated with a number of faculties and institutes in Rio de Janeiro, being the director of several. Though young, he had already published several books.

The Assessoria was made responsible for economic planning and also served as a board of advisers to the President. Quadros did not want to rely on the Council as the central planning agency since he hoped to achieve a completely fresh approach. Two claimants for economic planning existed in addition to the Council, however. These were the Ministry of Finance and the BNDE. While Mendes did not feel that either of these agencies was the proper home for planning, he did feel that the job of the Assessoria was so complex that the planning function would have to be separated out. Accordingly, the idea was developed of creating a new planning agency which would be outside all of the competing agencies. Quadros was reluctant to do this but was finally persuaded that this was the appropriate course to take. Mendes and the others inter-

ested in institutionalizing planning recognized the long-range
planning possibilities of a planning agency. Moreover, they
realized that the Charter of Punte del Este committed the
Latin American nations to planning as an aspect of the Alliance for Progress.

The decree establishing the new agency, the National Planning Commission (COPLAN), specified that the staff and
facilities of the old Council were to be acquired by COPLAN.
This did not take place. The old agency continued and a new
one was created. This solution had the practical advantage of
maintaining the jobs of the Council staff, while providing new
jobs for appointment by the new administration.

It has escaped the notice of most observers that the directing organ of both planning agencies was virtually identical!
The Commission (i.e., COPLAN) itself is composed of all the
ministers of state, the chiefs of the civil and military cabinets,
the presidents of the Bank of Brazil and of the Economic Development Bank, and the Director General of DASP. This is
also the Council. In addition, COPLAN included the coordinator of the office of technical assistance to the President of
the Republic, the Executive Director of the Superintendency
of Money and Credit (SUMOC), and the Technical Director
of COPLAN itself. The President of the Republic, of course,
was President of the Commission.

Despite the fact that the centers of executive power were
all represented on COPLAN, it did not prove to be a more
vital element in the planning system than it was when acting
as the Council for Development. In the case of COPLAN,
however, the problem of the vacuum of positive leadership at
the top was solved by creating a second collegial body under
the preoccupied cabinet level. Formally, the top body was
called the Deliberative Council of the Commission, and the
subordinate one the Consultative Council. The Consultative
Council was composed of the Technical Director of the Planning Commission, the Assistant Director, and such other persons as the President of the Republic might appoint. The

functions of these two bodies, and those of other officers of
COPLAN, were carefully distinguished and prescribed in the
decree. These distinctions are not important, however, since
the even more basic question of division of function between
the Council and COPLAN had never been clarified at the top
level so the question of function remained confused. Moreover, the Commission never really operated in the form in
which it was created, because the political wheel turned again
before the agency came into operation. In early September
Quadros resigned, Goulart came to office, and the regime was
formally converted into a parliamentary system.

Jânio Quadros' planners had been busy, however, during
the brief period available to them. They created an emergency
plan based chiefly on the directions implicit in the Kubitschek
planning. Perhaps more importantly, they developed the idea
that in addition to having a plan for the duration of the current
administration, it would also be necessary to create a "perspective plan" looking much farther into the future. This idea was
accepted by the next administration and is actually being implemented by the Castelo Branco regime. The most significant
fact about the Quadros period, in terms of planning, is that
despite the relative lack of interest of the President, a planning
staff did organize itself relying chiefly on persons already ex-
perienced in the field, and this staff provided a bridge between
the Kubitschek and Goulart administrations with a considerable continuity of personnel at the technical level.

When President Goulart was finally allowed to take office
under the new parliamentary regime, Prime Minister Neves
issued a decree which continued COPLAN, but on a reorganized basis. The Deliberative Council was retained, but recognizing that it was a mere formality, it was not constituted of
the President of the Council of Ministers (the Prime Minister)
and the Ministers of State. The Consultative Council was converted into a Commission of General Coordination (CCG).
This now became a policy body rather than a technical one,
consisting of those policy level officials actually concerned in

government-wide economic planning, as against sectorial planning in which the Ministers of State would be concerned in their administrative capacity. The CCG consisted of the Minister of Finance, who was chairman, the presidents of the Bank of Brazil and the BNDE, the Director General of the National Treasury, the Director General of the National Labor Department, and the Secretary General of COPLAN itself.

The hierarchical status of the CCG, however, remained ambiguous as established by decree. It was not made clear whether the CCG was in the chain of command over the Secretary General, who was head of the technical staff, or not. The official organization chart issued by COPLAN showed it in an advisory position to the Secretary General. Its functions were only two in number: (a) to give advice on proposals submitted to the Deliberative Council, and (b) to see that the agencies represented harmonized their policies with those of the plan. This implied a nascent implementational function.

The functions of the new planning agency will be discussed below with reference to the implementation of planning. At this point, however, it is relevant to note that the division of labor between the Council and COPLAN remained at issue even after creation of the newer body. In their organic acts, both are instructed to prepare a national plan of economic and social development on a long-range basis. After the reconstitution of COPLAN, both agencies had their proponents who sought to obtain the real central planning function. Leocádio Antunes, the Secretary General of the Council, quite naturally, took the position that *it* should be the national planning center. Since he was also President of the Development Bank, an increasingly important instrumentality of the government, Antunes' opinion carried weight.

Antunes had the support of President Goulart. Others close to Prime Minister Neves hoped that COPLAN, recently created by his decree, would become the central planning agency. The issue was negotiated, and whatever may have been the

stakes in the matter, a compromise was reached.[5] The two
agencies would continue to operate separately. The Council
would be used directly by the President as a unit for special
studies on specific problems which might arise. This is, in fact,
what happened. As late as 1963 the Council was issuing reports under the old official title of the Program of Goals (National Program of Development), though in fact there was no
such program since the end of the Kubitschek administration
in 1960. To COPLAN was assigned the job of preparing the
national development plan. The need to make this decision
was urgent, due to the planning requirement of the Alliance
for Progress. COPLAN was to report directly to the Council
of Ministers rather than to the President of the Republic.

Closely related to COPLAN was a special aspect of planning which was of crucial importance. This was the coordination of the Alliance for Progress programs. Alliance planning
within Brazil involved national, state, and local governments;
regional agencies; private entities; and the U.S. government's
Agency for International Development. A special Brazilian instrument was created for this purpose. This was the Coordination Commission for the Alliance for Progress (COCAP).
COCAP was created by decree of the Prime Minister in May,
1962.[6] This Commission was created subordinate to the Council of Ministers (for formal purposes) *and* to the Secretary
General of COPLAN (for operational purposes). The functions
of COCAP included assisting Brazilian agencies, private or
governmental, in making application for aid, to receive proposals and judge their relation to the requirements of national
planning, to pass on those approved to the appropriate international agency, to pursue the solicitation for the aid with the
international agency, and to follow the utilization of the aid
when received. This is a rational and essential grouping of
functions, but they have not been performed in the centralized

5. Information on this situation was provided by an economist who participated in the discussions, and who must remain anonymous. Partisan and other
considerations were involved.
6. Decree No. 1.040, May 23, 1962.

way in which they were originally visualized. The reasons may be broadly described as "political."

The five members of the COCAP are appointed by the President (formerly being nominated by the Prime Minister and Secretary General of COPLAN). The President chosen for the Commission was Luis Simões Lopes, an eminent leader in administrative reform and education, and President of the Getúlio Vargas Foundation.[7] Other members were chosen from BNDE and the Ministry of Transportation and Public Works. This group took over the work of coordinating requests which had formerly been handled by BNDE under the initial, emergency program of the Alliance. Actually little change occurred, since the staff employed in the job by COCAP included technicians from BNDE and COPLAN even after the change.

The organization of COCAP is important because it represented a theory of how the Alliance planning *should* be done. Specifically, the theory was that the national government should have the power to control all Brazilian requests. This power would be necessary if the Alliance programs were to be in fact fully coordinated with the national plan of development, once created. It must be recognized that 1962 and 1963 were years of political crisis. Insistence on the principle of central control over Alliance programs involved the political question of state sovereignty. The United States Agency for International Development (USAID) had followed the practice of dealing directly with regional, state, and municipal governments in Brazil at various stages of the complex negotiations looking toward completing project agreements. A formal routing of papers through COCAP sometimes occurred, but this did not conceal what was in truth often a direct relationship. Various proposals for a real centralization of decision in this matter eventuated during the second presidentialist cabinet in a vigorous effort to achieve this objective. In practice,

7. This Foundation is a collection of educational enterprises of various sorts, including the Brazilian School of Public Administration and the Brazilian Institute of Economics, a research organization. Both of these have been involved in governmental planning in various ways.

COCAP has only coordinated programs at the national level. COPLAN existed for more than a year before a real national planning effort was begun. It had assembled a staff, which had engaged itself primarily in sectorial economic analysis which had by now become traditional in Brazilian planning. Then, as will be described in detail in Chapter 5, Celso Furtado was appointed Minister Extraordinary for Governmental Planning. He thereupon surveyed both the Council and COPLAN as possible bases for his planning activity, and chose COPLAN as the best suited for his purpose. His position was created by decree, which gave him jurisdiction over COPLAN, though no mention was made of any relationship with the Deliberative Council or the General Coordination Commission. In actual fact, these ceased to operate during the entire period of Furtado's incumbency. He was given specific control of the COPLAN staff, however, as well as the staff of COCAP and the Development Council. He was also made a member of the Council of SUMOC. The political reasons which decree the division between the Development Council and COPLAN still existed, and Furtado made no effort to exercise the authority over the Council in practice.[8] It remained an entirely separate operation.

Just after Furtado's plan, the Plano Trienal, was completed and published in early January, 1963, the parliamentary regime was terminated with a return to the previous presidentialist constitution of 1946. As a result of these developments, Brazil acquired what was in fact its first planning *department*. It now had a planning minister responsible solely to the President of the Republic, with a planning staff under his direct control. The staff had just completed a widely acclaimed national economic development plan, and in terms of its assigned responsibility, it had been a success.

In one of Brazil's recurrent anticlimaxes, the political wheel now turned again.[9] The Minister of Planning retired from his

8. The organic act for the new Minister is Decree No. 1.422, September 27, 1962.
9. The details are told in Chapter 5.

post to return to his job as director of SUDENE. The position of Minister Extraordinary for planning remained vacant, and the signs seemed to point to a return to a plural-headed planning agency on some new basis as a part of the general administrative reform under the leadership of the Minister Extraordinary for Administrative Reform, Amaral Peixoto. This was destined not to occur, however, as will be explained below.

By the end of the Goulart administration in early 1964, certain conclusions respecting organization for planning seemed valid. First, no solution had been found to the problem of institutionalizing leadership in planning. Mário de Bittencourt Sampaio had acted without significant political backing. Kubitschek had then made himself chief planner, and his planning agency was tied to his administration so closely that it could not survive the next political change. Furtado, as technician with the confidence of the President had not even survived the President who appointed him minister. Secondly, no accepted relationship between plan-making and implementation had been achieved. For the most part, "plans" of the central government had not been implemented. We should not conclude that no gains had been made, however. The actual experience of Brazilian central planning organizations is only part of the story. The other part consists of the parallel, but not implemented, proposals about planning institutionalization. These proposals contain the elements which are being hammered into a planning system by the post-revolutionary government as this is written, and we now turn to them.

In 1952 President Vargas became motivated to undertake administrative reform. He appointed a body of experts who drafted a proposal of general reform for the administrative structure of the national government. Included in the proposal were two devices of "coordination." The first was a series of inter-ministerial committees. The second was a Council of Planning and Coordination. The latter entity was based on the conception that planning is basically a matter of policing activities in progress. Toward this end subordinate units of the government would make progress reports on their program every fifteen days. Higher units would evaluate these and make reports every month, and the ministries, in turn, would periodically report to the Council of Planning and Coordination. The purpose of this would be for the central planning organ to be in a position to compare all the programs with the view to eliminating conflict, duplication, and overlapping of effort. This would be done as the problems arise rather than letting them grow into top level conflicts and jurisdictional disputes. A function so conceived is legitimate and necessary. It represents administrative planning in the narrow sense of the kind performed in organization and methods units. The object is efficiency. This proposal did not contemplate planning in the broader sense of policy research and development, social problem-solving, and innovation. Nevertheless, it is the origin of the planning *council* idea, and of placing central planning activity at the presidential level. These two ideas have played an important role in Brazilian planning.

The reform was dropped for a period, but after the death of Vargas, the movement for reform again began to gain momentum. The Vargas proposal was taken up and studied by a whole series of entities including the major political parties, an Inter-Party Commission on Administrative Reform, the Brazilian Planning Association, and a Congressional Mixed Commission on Administrative Reform.[10] These evaluations produced little support for the new planning agency originally proposed. The Inter-Party Commission said: "This organ ought not to be created. Planning and coordination as functions of an organ created for the purpose cannot have a general character. A special agency to plan and coordinate everything, embracing all the administrative domains, would be an unjustifiable complication. A special organ of planning and coordination would not be able to restrict itself to matters of an

10. The absorbing story of administrative reform during this period is told in Presidência da República, Commissão de Estudos e Projetos Administrativos, *A Reforma Administrativa Brasileira* (Rio de Janeiro: Departamento de Imprensa Nacional, 1960), Vol. I, *Reorganização da Presidência da República*.

economic nature. However, planning and coordination in the economic field, can be accomplished to greater advantage by the specialized agency already existing, that is, the National Economic Council."[11]

Ultimately, the Congressional Mixed Commission submitted a shortened and simplified version of the Vargas project to the Congress. In this document, now called the Capanema Amendment, the planning agency was deleted. It had been argued, on the one hand, that the economic planning necessary could be done by the National Economic Council, and, on the other, that the coordinating and policing could be done in the President's immediate office. The fact that neither of these actually happened is perhaps the best commentary on the validity of these ideas.

In 1956 President Kubitschek, still concerned about the elusive administrative reform, appointed a new study-group, this time composed of experts and leaders concerned about administrative reform from a more professional point of view. This was the Commission for Administrative Studies and Proposals (CEPA).[12] The Development Council had just been organized in February, and the new study group recommended that it be continued.[13] It was obvious, however, that the new group had given the matter of planning organization considerable thought. Not only did the report strongly condemn the decisions which led to the removal of the planning agency from the Capanema Amendment, but it developed a number of important ideas about planning which could be taken either as advice to the new Council or as a recommendation for an eventual new planning agency. The judgment was rendered

11. *Ibid.*, Vol. IV, *Relatório Final*, p. 23.
12. President of the Commission was Simões Lopes, President of the Getúlio Vargas Foundation. Among the other members were Professor Benedicto Silva, a leading Brazilian authority on governmental planning, Cleantho Leite, head of the Brazilian Institute of Municipal Administration, Professor Otávio Gouveia de Bulhões, and Roberto de Oliveira Campos. Since the latter two became members of the Castelo Branco ministry, their membership is particularly revealing.
13. *Ibid.*, Vol. I, p. 68.

that Vargas had probably made a strategic mistake when he took a conciliatory attitude toward the removal of the Council for Planning and Coordination from the reform bill. The report then goes on: "We agree that a Council of Planning and Coordination composed of the Ministers of State and presided over by the Chief Executive, perhaps is not the best solution for this problem of administrative organization. Who knows if a single-headed permanent department composed of administrative technicians, researchers, statisticians, sociologists, planners and economists, working as a planning general staff for the Presidency of the Republic, would not be a more rational solution?"[14]

The report of the CEPA then goes on to develop the concept of a "system of planning" which is the first really sophisticated proposal that Brazil had produced. The system would not serve primarily reporting purposes, but would engage in positive planning at all levels in the governmental hierarchy. Agency plans would be developed and the central planning organ would combine these ultimately into a "general organic plan" for the government as a whole. Plans would be based on research and objective knowledge, and would be both short and long range in nature, eventually being divided into phases the first of which would correspond to the annual financial budget. The theory on which this concept rests is indicated in the following statement: "Planning is an intellectual process of selecting objectives and foreseeing and arranging the means necessary to realize, on a predetermined date and in a predetermined place, these precisely defined ends. As such, it is an administrative activity *par excellence*: all the executive agencies ought to have the capacity to discharge it perfectly."[15]

In addition to this, a matter of strategy is involved. The intention is to bring about an improvement in administrative practice throughout the government: "Beyond the creation of a system of institutionalized planning, an object of the fore-

14. *Ibid.*, Vol. IV, p. 29.
15. *Ibid.*, Vol. IV, p. 108.

going recommendation of CEPA is to institute and encourage in our administrative practice the habit of short and long-term planning. The obligation imposed on each chief of service of preparing plans of work periodically, seems to us to present a logical opportunity to promote planning as an indispensable aspect of administration, in all the agencies and subdivisions of the public service."[16]

These ideas represent the real intellectual fountainhead of much of the recent thinking about planning in Brazil. Evidently the Commission itself had developed its thought on the subject considerably between the time of writing the first and last volumes of the report. While the first volume suggested continuance of the Council, the fourth, in listing the five major components of the recommended organization for the President's executive office, included a "Central Department of Planning," without any further details.[17] This proposal brings the line of thought we have traced in the report to its logical conclusion. The theme was soon picked up, as we shall note.

One characteristic of the CEPA concept requires comment. It is clearly based on the underlying assumption that planning is a purely administrative activity. Since planning is to produce governmental policy at the top level, however, there are obvious political overtones in the work. Failure to recognize this fact caused great difficulty when the CEPA idea was later taken up, as we shall see.

The next development occurred in 1962. What proved to be the lame duck Council of Ministers directed its top legal aide (Consultor Geral da República) to prepare administrative reorganization proposals. These were submitted and printed in the *Diário Oficial* in December.[18] The role of this event in the demise of the Plano Trienal is told in detail in the next chapter. While this new proposal was not implemented either, what is important here is its contribution to the devel-

16. *Ibid.*, p. 126-127.
17. *Ibid.*, p. 140.
18. *Diário Oficial*, December 14, 1962, Section 1, Part I.

opment of Brazilian thought about national planning organization. This proposal was based directly on the work of the
Commission of Administrative Studies and Projects. Not only
is this clear from the recommendations themselves, but the
report of the legal counsel specifically states that his intention
was to copy these ideas changing only what was necessary in
view of changes in the situation since the time of the earlier
report.

The leading changes in the situation were the existence of
the new position of Minister Extraordinary for planning, the
development of the Alliance for Progress, and the creation of
several more regional planning and related entities. First, the
new proposal adopted the suggestion of the CEPA report to
create a single-headed department—but now it was promoted
to the status of a ministry. This merely formalized the change
which seemed to have taken place on an ad hoc basis. Secondly, the need had rapidly increased for what is unfortunately
best expressed through use of the vague term "coordination."
It was now clear that a crucial job in any serious national
planning was not only to make an internally consistent plan
out of the programs of the national government, but also to
make this whole effort consistent with the booming planning
activities of a series of regional entities and a new crop of state
plans. Both vertical and horizontal "coordination" was now
needed.

The road chosen to "coordination" was the organizational
device of simply putting the things to be coordinated in the
same agency. The details are treated below in the section on
staff organization. Here we only need emphasize that this
recommendation would produce a planning ministry equipped
to plan with reference to all the programs of the national government including regional agencies. It would also be concerned with state and municipal planning. In terms of function, the new agency would not only plan, but have an
unknown degree of authority to control implementation. This
aspect of the problem is treated below. Celso Furtado, the

planning minister, gave his approval to this proposal. When it was published he was totally preoccupied in making the Plano Trienal and perhaps did not recognize the political dynamite in the proposal. He reports having approved the plan purely on the grounds of the abstract idea that comprehensive, government-wide planning is a good thing.[19] The proposal created immediate opposition when made public on the grounds that it would represent a "super-ministry," which was potentially accurate, and that this would be dictatorial, which is at best questionable.

It was in part a result of this general outcry against the plan that led Furtado to draft his own proposal which he presented to Goulart in March after the regime had reverted to presidentialism.[20]

As administrative theory the Furtado plan was an organizational monstrosity. In essence, it is an effort to combine the single-headed ministry with the plural-headed commission, while weaving into the pattern a complex of interagency committees—all this being related to a set of ministerial planning offices. While this would certainly be more complex in operation than it appears on an organization chart, the proposal pursues its own logic.

A National Development Council was created consisting of the ministers of state and the heads of the civil and military cabinets. The President of the Republic is the presiding officer of the Council. This body would meet once a year to approve the reformulation of the plan. Here resides the political function of decision. Each minister, however, would establish his own planning department to do agency planning. He would then appoint the head of this planning department (or someone else if he so chose) to one or more positions on five interdepartmental committees. These committees had prescribed membership, including not only ministry representa-

19. Interview with Celso Furtado, May 8, 1965.
20. This proposal is in the form of a mimeographed draft, "Projeto de Decreto: Institui o Sistema Nacional de Planejamento e dá outras Providências" (no date).

tives, but also appointees from other key governmental agencies related to the subject of the committee. The five committees were: global planning, sector planning, social planning, regional planning, and coordination of foreign aid programs (i.e., COCAP). Each of these groups would subdivide itself into sub-committees on specific subjects. This system of committees would engage in liaison between the planning staff of the central agency and the various governmental entities. This liaison, however, would be under the coordinative supervision of the Minister of Planning, who would preside at meetings of the five committees. Presumably, this would be technical supervision rather than command. There also would be direct collaboration between the central planning agency and the planning departments of the ministries. One additional feature is of particular interest. The Minister of Planning would be in direct charge of the technical staff of the planning agency, through an Executive Director who would supervise that staff. This would free the minister to serve in reality as a coordinator among the four elements in the situation: (1) departmental planning officers, (2) the central planning staff, (3) the interdepartmental committees and (4) the National Development Council.[21] The minister's role is thus seen to be clearly at the policy level, though he has no final decision in the legal sense. In the proposal as written the super-ministry as a directing and control agency seems to have disappeared.

While this system of planning appears novel, all its elements have been noted before in this study. The ministry derives from actual practice during the few months of Furtado's incumbency. The National Development Council reflects both the existing Development Council and COPLAN. The committees appeared first in the Vargas proposal. The planning departments sprung both from existing practice of certain ministries like foreign affairs and finance, as well as from the proposal of the Commission on Administrative Studies and Pro-

21. This situation can be visualized by reference to the organization chart on page 105.

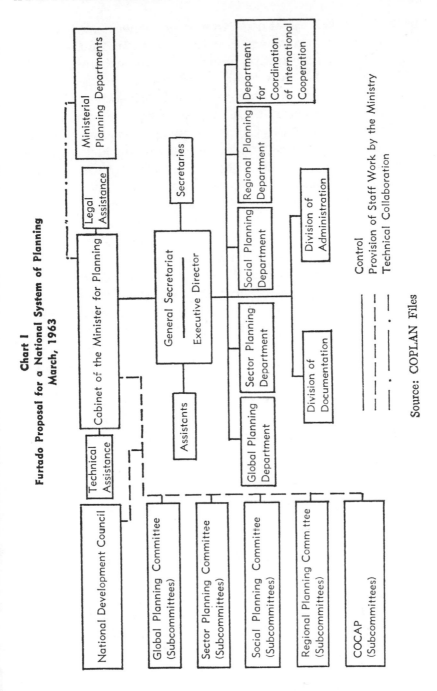

Chart I
Furtado Proposal for a National System of Planning
March, 1963

Ministerial Planning Departments

Legal Assistance

Cabinet of the Minister for Planning

Technical Assistance

National Development Council

Secretaries

General Secretariat
Executive Director

Assistants

Department for Coordination of International Cooperation

Regional Planning Department

Social Planning Department

Division of Administration

Sector Planning Department

Global Planning Department

Division of Documentation

Global Planning Committee (Subcommittees)

Sector Planning Committee (Subcommittees)

Social Planning Committee (Subcommittees)

Regional Planning Committee (Subcommittees)

COCAP (Subcommittees)

———————— Control
— — — — — Provision of Staff Work by the Ministry
— · — · — Technical Collaboration

Source: COPLAN Files

jects. Additional insight came from the experience of SUDENE of which Furtado remained Superintendent. In the then existing political-administrative arena, this proposal appeared to have excellent "fit," everything considered. As presented, however, it was prejudiced by one major consideration. Furtado was relieved from his position in June, 1963, after nine months as Minister as related in Chapter 5. A few days later, July 11, President Goulart signed a decree which eliminated the Minister of Planning and established a new office of Coordination of National Planning in the immediate office of the President. This office lived a shadowy existence for the duration of the Goulart regime.

At this point a major reform of planning machinery was under study as a part of Amaral Peixoto's governmental reform study. The coordinator of the staff work for reform, as well as the leader of the particular work group on planning, was Professor Benedicto Silva who had written the CEPA report earlier. He is directly responsible for the new recommendations for a national planning system. A key idea of this new reform proposal was to establish the planning system pursuant to law rather than decree. It had been noted that the presidential decree was the most tenuous sort of basis for creating permanent planning machinery. The proposal provided for a national council of planning, but unlike that of the Furtado proposal, the new council, also to be composed of the cabinet and a few other top officials, would meet every month. Thus it would become much more deeply involved in the actual planning process. This enlarged the political role of planning at an early stage in the process. The new proposal also differed from that of Furtado in not providing for the complicated system of interministerial committees. Top level deliberation would occur only at the level of the Council itself. Like the other proposal, the Silva project provides for a Secretary General of planning who would be head of the technical staff, and would be located within the office of the President of the Republic. At the ministerial level there would also be a planning staff, but a new idea was added. Each ministry would have its own planning council composed of the minister and top department heads and other officials of the ministry. Here again, in each ministry, a channel for political influence was to be opened up. The philosophy of this proposal is the same as that of the previous CEPA report. Actual initiative for innovation was intended to reside both at the presidential level, and at the cabinet level, so that a genuine two-way exchange was expected in the decision-making process. The proposal was never implemented.

The various proposals for planning machinery discussed above are highly relevant to the new planning machinery created by the Castelo Branco government, particularly because the new Minister of Planning was Roberto Campos, a member of the Kubitschek commission which produced the CEPA report. Within days after the establishment of the new revolutionary government under the *Ato Institucional* and the designation of Castelo Branco as President (April, 1965), he had appointed Campos Minister Extraordinary for Planning. Campos presented to the President two possible plans for the organization of the new planning establishment. One consisted of an arrangement similar to the Council for Development. The other would establish a ministry. The strengths and weaknesses of both were described to the President, including the dangers which could readily be foreseen in the "super-ministry" idea.[22] Castelo Branco's response was decisive and immediate. He preferred the ministry without any such embellishments as a political policy council. The President's view of the planning process dictated this decision. Branco was selected for the presidency in part because he was a "non-political" general, adhering to the general notion that military men should be professional soldiers rather than politicians. He believed that planning, both for military operations and for the government generally, was a technical staff function. He wanted a profes-

22. This event was described in an interview with José Nazaré Teixeira Dias, the first Chief of Cabinet for Campos, August 4, 1965.

sional planning staff, which he felt was a highly important part of the governmental machinery, deserving cabinet status. Accordingly, a new Ministry Extraordinary of Planning and Economic Coordination was created by decree.[23] Internally the new ministry was fluid in its organization, reflecting at any one time the current task assignments to the staff, as the Program of Action was prepared and implementational methods devised. An extremely close, but informal, relationship existed between Campos and Otávio Gouveia de Bulhões, the new Minister of Finance, based on past associations.

While the purely technical ministry seemed satisfactory for the purpose of preparing plans, it did not contain a built-in capacity for communication with the interests in and out of government vitally affected by central planning. Accordingly the President established a formal instrumentality for this purpose, the Advisory Planning Council (CONSPLAN).[24] The decree establishing CONSPLAN gave it the power to advise, and to initiate suggestions. Further, it was authorized to create work groups and assemble experts to study specific problems. Clearly, however, it was intended not only as a source of advice, but also to serve as a channel through which the government could inform and convince the interests represented, while at the same time involving them in the decision process.

The make-up of the Council is an innovation in the Brazilian planning experience, since it formally brings interest group representatives into relationship with governmental planners. The Council includes:

4 representatives of labor
4 representatives of industry
1 member of the National Economic Council
4 professionals including two economists, one sociologist, one engineer, and including among the four at least two university professors

23. Decree No. 53.914, May 11, 1964.
24. Decree No. 55.722, February 2, 1965. In the Portuguese, Conselho Consultivo do Planejamento.

3 representatives of companies, and state or regional organizations
    of planning or economic development
1 representative of the mass media

The President of the Republic, or his indicated minister of
state, presides over the Council. As in most Brazilian public
bodies, every member has an alternate—the sanction of losing
group representation in case of absence from the meeting is
traded for the opportunity to provide more people with a "position."

All members are appointed by the President of Brazil. The
eight members representing labor and industry are chosen from
lists presented by the national labor unions and trade associations through the Minister of Labor and Social Welfare. The
National Economic Council elects its member, presumably
subject to approval by the President. The representatives of
states, regions, and development companies are selected from
lists presented by these entities (which are not defined)
through the Ministry of Planning. Other members are the free
choice of the President. These arrangements clearly do not
guarantee a representative body, though they make it possible,
depending on the selections made from the lists by the President. Terms of the Council are two years and extendable for
another two years, as compared with the five-year term of the
President. Expenses of the Council are to be borne by the Ministry of Planning. While the scope of the Council's advice is to
cover both short and long-range planning, as well as implementation, it is clearly subject to substantial control by the
government.

The Council did, in fact, provide its criticisms of the Program of Action. Several of these were published by CON-
SPLAN, in some cases along with a reply to the criticism by
Minister Campos who is the designated Executive Secretary
of CONSPLAN.[25] One of the members of the Council, Pro-

25. Conselho Consultivo do Planejamento, *O Debate do Programa de Ação*
(Rio de Janeiro: Secretária Executivo do Conselho Consultivo do Planejamento, Ministério do Planejamento e Coordenação Econômica, 1965).

fessor Antônio Dias Leite, became the leading critic of the Program of Action as time went on. Among his various criticisms was the assertion that CONSPLAN was not serving its role as an input into the planning process. Since, for a time, CONSPLAN seldom met, he employed the press for periodic sharp attacks on the Program. This may be in part why CONSPLAN became more active during the last year of the Branco regime, 1966. CONSPLAN was convened to provide Campos the opportunity to answer the charges made by Leite. In addition, it was called into session more frequently beginning in June, 1966, to announce the beginning of work on the ten-year plan, to inaugurate work groups for that purpose, and to review plans for administrative reform.

In terms of actual operations, the planning ministry of Roberto Campos is organized in virtually the same fashion as the Furtado ministry, with a single planning director at the top who reports directly to the President. The advisory function attached to the Campos ministry is new. During the Furtado period, however, the minister actually contacted the same groups that are now represented on the advisory group in an informal fashion, as the pressures of the day might suggest.

It is well to note that both ministries have operated under crisis conditions demanding quick formulation of plans. The departmental form of organization is eminently suited to this task. Both ministries, however, developed their own plans for a permanent system of planning and implementation. As plans, these two schemes were significantly different, recognizing that such differences sometimes dissolve in practice. The Furtado proposal has already been described, and included a National Development Council consisting of ministers of state, tied in with a series of interdepartmental committees. The Campos proposal for a permanant ministry was consistent with the concept of the existing extraordinary ministry by providing for a minister directly subordinate to the President.[26] The only dif-

26. The discussion here is based on the status of organizational planning

ference would be that the new agency would be a regular statutory ministry on a par with the other cabinet ministries. The Furtado proposal leaned in the direction of early participation in the planning process by a minister-level planning council. The Campos proposal would leave planning initiative to the technicians. In either case, of course, the President would be in direct control insofar as he chose to be.

Probably the more significant difference between the two proposals concerns the arrangements for internal organization of the ministry and for implementation of planning. Here it becomes even more clear that the Furtado plan admitted a larger role for politicians in the earlier stages of the planning process, while the Campos approach contemplated a more purely professional planning process. We now turn to internal organization of the planning agencies.

INTERNAL STAFF ORGANIZATION

In considering this subject several pitfalls must be borne in mind. Since Brazilian government typically operates with various categories of persons other than full-time employees—consultants, part-time employees, full-time employees who work part time, and employees who work occasionally or not at all —it is difficult to conceptualize the real pattern of organization. In addition, a high level of fluidity in assignments typically exists. It is not a question of a specific employee necessarily holding a specific "position." One result of this situation is that official organization charts tend to represent functions or areas of responsibility rather than stable working units of people. In this discussion we will try to maintain clarity as between functional responsibilities of the agency and the actual roles of people in organization.

The first national planning agency in any permanent form was the Council for Development. The organizational changes

as of August, 1965. The project had not been submitted to Congress by July, 1966.

of this agency are too numerous to record here. We will discuss organization of the staff during its last active period, 1963.

Under the Council was the Secretary General, a policy-level officer engaged in various other activities in the field of public affairs in addition to his work with the Council. Under the Secretary General were the two top technicians. One of these, the Executive Director, was in charge of all the administrative and service activities for the staff. In addition, he supervised four work groups known as "Executive Groups," charged with studying the problems of specific industries—automotive manufacturing, shipbuilding, heavy materials, and moving pictures. These four were the remnants of a much larger number of work groups which produced the Program of Goals. The other top level technician was in charge of five more work groups, assigned to studying the developmental problems of particular river-basins or regions, and in one case to problems of municipal development.

The best idea of the variety of work of the staff since 1956 can be gained from reading the list of reports published by various work groups.[27] Initially these were components of the Program of Goals itself. More recently a great variety of reports have been published on such subjects as regional studies, studies of specific industries, the agrarian question, the uses of electronic computers, education, progress reports on the Program of Goals, tax reform, banking reform, and the Latin American Association of Free Commerce.

In brief, the work procedure was to receive directives from the President of the Republic as to problems needing study. These were then assigned to a work group constituted for the purpose. When the study was finished, the personnel were assigned to the next problem.

These studies of rather specific problems represent micro-planning efforts in areas where there is no regularly constituted planning agency capable of undertaking the job. The most

27. See Presidência da República, Conselho do Desenvolvimento, *Lista de Publicações* (February, 1963).

ADMINISTRATION 113

notable development arising out of this approach was the fact that the planning studies began to move away from mere assembling and analysis of data with recommendations. In several cases considerable fieldwork was done in which the planners interacted with the people in the industry or area in question. They became involved in drafting legislation, consulting, installation of recommendations, and the training of personnel for the new activities. During the process, and on an informal basis, the work groups held what amounted to hearings at which they monitored the opinion factors relevant to the problem in the area concerned. In these ways, the work of the Council was comparable to the techniques worked out in the "small watershed program" of the Tennessee Valley Authority in the United States.

One of the areas of work, to cite an example, was a pilot study of developmental problems in a rural community area in the state of Ceara. The study arose from the question of how best to apply the funds of federal origin which under the Constitution have to be delivered to the *municípios* in this area. There was a suspicion that these funds were in fact being dissipated on projects of little value for the development of the area. Accordingly a Work Group of Municipal Studies was created in the Council, which did a preliminary study on the basis of which it established in the area of Ceara a study group with representatives not only from the Council staff itself, but also from key groups in the district under study.[28] As the study progressed, the approach taken assumed that to answer the initial problem question, it would be necessary to perform a thorough planning study of the area. Thus a technique to

28. The representatives invited to participate included persons from The National Service of Assistance to Municipalities, SUDENE, the Rural Social Service, The Development Bank for the Northeast of Brazil, The Council for Technical Assistance to the Municipalities of the State of Ceara, the University of Ceara, the Ceara Section of the Brazilian Association of Municipalities, the Northeastern Association of Credit and Rural Assistance, The National Department of Works Against Drought, The Technical Office for Agriculture, and the Economic Council of Ceara.

apply to studies of municipal development generally began to take form.

Because of the somewhat peculiar position of the Development Council, with a legally defined mission similar to that of the parallel agency, COPLAN, it became free to develop its own program. It chose not to compete with COPLAN, but adjusted to the new conditions by exploiting what was until then a new approach to central planning—the problem-solving approach. This involved no macro-planning, no coordination function, no programming responsibilities, and no reporting or implementing responsibility for some pre-established plan. Properly exploited, the approach of the Council could be a highly valuable function in planning, of a kind frequently overlooked in national planning efforts, focused as they necessarily are on construction and implementation of national plans. Similar sorts of studies and related activities are typical of state planning in the United States provided on the basis of technical assistance to localities and regions without their own planning facilities. Brazil's subsequent proposals for structuring the system of planning generally neglected this approach on the theory that somehow local, state, and regional plans would be prepared and then coordinated at the center. Given the sparsity of planning resources in Brazil, however, the technical assistance approach from the central government provides an alternative pending the time when local entities can in fact develop planning establishments and plans. The Campos ministry ultimately attacked this problem, however, as will be described below.

The COPLAN staff, meanwhile, had followed a very different style of organization. Its organization chart as of early 1963 was truly magnificent in its conception. Under the Secretary General were five departments or sections plus two program coordinators. The departments included global planning, public finance, documentation and statistics, technical assistance, and agency administration. Most of these are the usual service departments for planning. The Global Planning Department, however, was the key section which integrated all the work of the other portions of the agency into one national plan. The two coordinators were responsible for sectorial and regional planning respectively. Under the regional coordinator were coordinators for the North, Northeast, Center-South, South, and Center-West areas of the country. These are the traditional regional devisions for planning purposes. In addition the Regional Coordinator supervised the work of the Regional Co-ordination Commission on which were represented the regional planning agencies. The Coordinator of Sectorial Programming would supervise, under this plan, seven other coordinators of natural resources, energy, transportation, agriculture, industry, communications, and social affairs. Each of these was divided into Divisions to a total of thirty-eight, on a commodity or functional basis, for example: iron ore, ports, diesel motors, air transportation, fishing, and so on.

This conception of planning organization is well ordered to produce an economic plan which is based primarily on the various economic sectors. A problem arises, however, when noneconomic areas of planning and programming are poured into this mold. The effect is to consider them as "sectors." This problem appeared chiefly in the fields assigned to the coordinator of "Social Sectors." The subdivisions of this area were social security, education, housing, water supply and sewage, social assistance, science and technology, and public administration. Many would argue that the relevance of plan-ning for education or for public administration, for example, lies only in small part in the economic effects of these activities within the economy. They are tremendously important, how-ever, because of their relevance to economic development in the long range. There are, in fact, schools of thought that hold that each of these is the fundamental consideration in sound economic development, but not because of the effect on the economy in the next three- or five-year period. Typing these aspects of planning into the sector analysis pattern probably has been one of the causes of de-emphasis on these very crucial areas of planning. To relegate educational and administrative planning to the same organizational status as diesel motors, for instance, seems to be somewhat shortsighted. The dominance of "economic" planning in Brazilian governmental planning will be a subject of further discussion in the final chapter.

The organization of COPLAN outlined above was never really implemented, though it was the agency's intention to do so. The many organizational divisions are greater in number than the total number of personnel of the agency, professional, clerical, and casual. In early 1963 the operating units to which staff were actually assigned included the Global Planning Department, the Documentation and Statistics Department, the Administrative Section, the Transportation Coordinator, and a few scattered persons in other areas. As in the Development Council, the staff was highly fluid. When Furtado went to work on the Plano Trienal, many persons were recruited for COPLAN. Others were set to work in their own agencies, wherever technicians, economists, or planners were to be found. As the planning was completed, these borrowed personnel returned to their regular jobs. The ease of this sort of shifting of personnel was an advantage when planning had to be done on a crash basis. On the other hand, it inhibits the development of a permanent planning system due to attrition of the staff in the periodic lulls which characterize Brazil's planning experience.

The Furtado proposal presented to President Goulart in March of 1963 and never implemented is of special significance in the history of Brazilian planning organization because of its contrasts with the proposal of the Campos ministry of 1965. Different philosophies of the planning process are represented to a significant degree. (See organization chart, page 105, of this chapter.) The proposed agency structure is very simple. Under the Executive Director fall five substantive departments and two service divisions. The departments are global planning, sector planning, social planning, regional planning, and international cooperation. The divisions are documentation and administration. This is substantially the plan of the existing COPLAN, except that social planning now moves from a position within sector planning to a status parallel with it. In terms of current planning theory, this is a clear advance.

Let us consider the relationships which the Furtado proposal establishes between the various elements in the planning system. The main outlines of the planning process involve a planning chronology substantially as follows. First, by the last day of December each year, the individual agencies of government would be required to submit to the Secretary General of Planning their proposals for capital investments for the following period. There is no mention in the proposal of whether *program* plans would be submitted as well. Presumably they would be, if intended for any impact in the national development plan. These submissions would come from the planning department of the agency concerned. The Secretary General would assemble the plans relevant to the field of action of a particular subcommittee of the interdepartmental committee system, and submit them to that committee. According to the wording of the proposal, the subcommittee would put these "into permanent form." To take this literally would conflict with the rest of the procedure, and we suppose this really means that the subcommittee could make recommendations as to the way of integrating these proposals, perhaps even preparing the document. However, it is the relevant department of the planning staff that now makes its evaluation of the proposals, transmitting this to the full committee having jurisdiction over the subject. The full committee would approve the proposal for integration into the global plan. It would then go back to the Secretary General, and presumably, at least in its general policy aspects, to the global planning committee for review. When the entire plan was completed, it would go through the minister to the National Development Council, which is to say, to the President of the Republic and his cabinet, for adoption. This would occur once each year as the plan would be reformulated.

Several features of this process are worth special note. First, the role of the subcommittee could be especially significant, despite the fact that it appears in imprecise form in the draft of the proposal. We assume that this role would have to be advisory to the planning staff technicians. However, since the subcommittee would be composed of planners representing various governmental agencies, the central staff would *immediately* begin to get feedback on its own ideas. Moreover, if the central staff and agency representatives could agree at this stage, this would go a long way toward getting the agreement of the full committee at the approval stage, since *some* of the members of the subcommittee would also be on the full committee. As this early step would be entirely conducted by technicians, any disagreements would have the maximum chance to be resolved, through additional studies, collecting more data, or applying more refined analytical techniques. Where the difference of opinion proved to rest on nontechnical factors, such as a directive from the parent agency, at least the problem would come to light at a very early stage in the planning process, and strategies could then be devised to meet the situation. This comment assumes sufficient political stability and maturity at the cabinet level so that positions taken there would hold firm from the beginning to the end of the planning process. This problem is dealt with at length in another portion of this study, but there is a real question as to the validity of this assumption in the Brazilian milieu.

A second significant point is that this process would tend to compel planning in the agencies prior to central planning, if they would hope to get a share in whatever capital investment funds might be available. They would have to raise questions and take positions at an earlier point than has previously been the case. So what we really see is a process in which policy decision occurs at the beginning, in the individual agencies. Then a technical step occurs as planners in the agency planning departments and the central planning staff prepare the proposals. Then another policy review occurs in the full committee, and the decision taken there is formulated into the plan by the staff technicians of the central planning agency. Final decision is taken at the cabinet level. By this time, however, the process has provided an opportunity for a political and technical mix at each stage of the planning process. We might fairly conclude that this planning procedure would produce, by its very nature, a high level of consensus and commitment.

A related point, however, is that the process of producing this level of commitment is both complex and slow. It is not something that could be accomplished in two months, nor could it produce a plan at the end of that time to which everyone is committed. Rather, there would have to be a truly continuous process throughout the year every year. It would surely take some time to gain such a degree of commitment to planning as an integral part of the decision process.

The Furtado proposal for a planning system has two earmarks. First, it is designed to emphasize the process of innovative planning within the agencies of government. Secondly, perhaps reflecting the negative reaction to the super-ministry idea, it contains no definitive machinery for implementation. On the second point, a system of agency reporting to the planning ministry is provided as well as a directive to the DASP to maintain close liaison with the planning agency during all stages of budget preparation; but the only lever of the planning agency would have been advice to the National Development Council. The strength of the proposal is the degree of political participation and commitment that is built into the plan-making process. Whether this would be enough to insure implementation without a central control agency is the question. The theory of the Furtado scheme was that planners did not have to be implementers.

The Campos proposal, developed during the summer of 1965, was significantly different. Campos was willing, and Castelo Branco was anxious, to establish a professional planning and implementation process. With a more stable, military-based regime at his back, Castelo Branco could perhaps afford less political clearance during the early stages of planning, and combine this with central implementation controls. At any rate, this is the basis for the Campos proposal.

The basic organization is a model of hierarchical rationality (see chart on page 121). A Minister of Planning and Economic Coordination, assisted by his personal staff, would direct the ministry. He would operate at the political level as a regular member of the cabinet. Under him would be the Secretary General presumably the professional staff director. All units of the ministry would be under the jurisdiction of the Secretary General, and there would be three basic units. These include coordination of budget and finance, coordination of sectorial planning, and long-range planning. In addition, the administrative units of the ministry would be under the Secretary General. This proposal would formalize what was already taking shape in the extraordinary ministry. The long-range planning office already existed as the Office of Applied Economic Research (EPEA). Various sections for sectorial planning had participated in creating the Program of Action. What was to be added, however, was a real innovation in Brazilian planning. It was proposed to add budgeting and financial control to the ministry.

To tie together budgeting and planning would be a revolutionary move in Brazilian national administration. It would, in fact, constitute a major step in the direction of establishing again the values of rational administration of the variety termed "diffracted" by Fred Riggs.[29] The major previous effort to do just this occurred during the Vargas dictatorship. The rise and decline of the DASP indicates the great difficulty in achieving this goal.[30] Brazilian planning which lived a feeble life in the DASP during the end of the Vargas era, was now to take over from the DASP the budget process itself.

29. Fred Riggs, *Administration in Developing Areas: The Theory of Prismatic Society* (Boston: Houghton Mifflin, 1964).

30. Gilbert B. Siegel discusses this portion of Brazilian administrative history comprehensively in "The Vicissitudes of Governmental Reform in Brazil: A Study of the DASP" (Ph.D. dissertation, University of Pittsburgh, 1964).

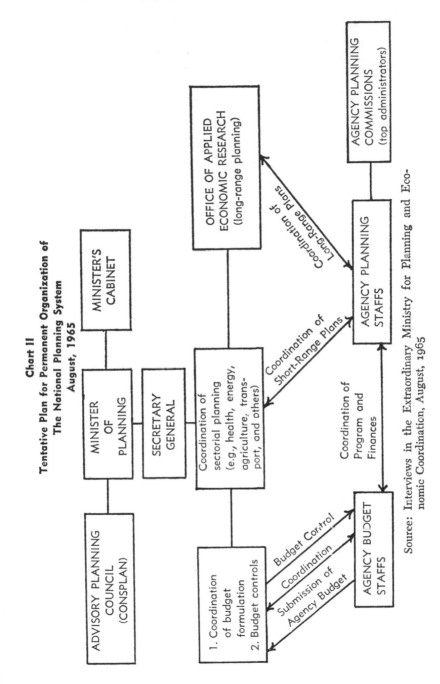

Chart II

**Tentative Plan for Permanent Organization of
The National Planning System
August, 1965**

ADVISORY PLANNING
COUNCIL
(CONSPLAN)

MINISTER
OF
PLANNING

MINISTER'S
CABINET

SECRETARY
GENERAL

OFFICE OF APPLIED
ECONOMIC RESEARCH
(long-range planning)

AGENCY PLANNING
COMMISSIONS
(top administrators)

Coordination of sectorial planning (e.g., health, energy, agriculture, transport, and others)

1. Coordination of budget formulation
2. Budget controls

AGENCY PLANNING
STAFFS

Coordination of
Long-Range Plans

Coordination of
Short-Range Plans

Coordination of Program and Finances

AGENCY BUDGET
STAFFS

Budget Control

Coordination

Submission of
Agency Budget

Source: Interviews in the Extraordinary Ministry for Planning and Economic Coordination, August, 1965

The administrative planners within the Campos ministry recognized that the new proposal would involve a thorough reorganization of governmental practice. It was to be combined with reorganization within each ministry itself. Each ministry would establish a planning section and a budget section. Within the ministries, however, these would not be merged in one agency, but would be parallel. The planning process is envisaged as follows. The planning section of each ministry would work out its long-range plans in collaboration with the long-range planning department of the planning ministry (EPEA). Annual planning would also be done by the ministry planning sections, and in so doing, they would submit plans in their sector to the Ministry of Planning office for sectorial coordination. Short-range sector plans having been coordinated at the national level, they would then return to the ministry planning offices for programming. At this point the ministry budget office would take over and create a program budget for the coming year, which would be submitted to the budget office of the planning ministry for coordination into a national program budget. Once the funds became allotted, administration of the budget would also rest with the same office of the Ministry of Planning, rather than in the Ministry of Finance as previously the case.[31]

Officials of the Brazilian planning ministry view the process outlined above as similar to indicative planning on the French model. The fact that plans would originate from below rather than in the central agency is the basis for the contention that the new planning system would not represent the "super-ministry" in a new form. It should be noted that relations of the governmental agencies with the Ministry of Planning would occur at three stages or cycles during the planning process. Long-range plans, short-range programs and budgets would be

31. Budget reform was already underway before this proposal was submitted to Congress. The Castelo Branco government attempted to apply budget ceilings for the first time in the 1965 budget. The 1966 budget is a demonstration program budget. The plan is to convert to a definitive program budget for the year 1967.

presented. The crux of the process rests on the precise function of the ministry at these three points. If this function includes addition, modification, and veto of plans, central control is assured. If these powers are not vested in the central ministry, it could hardly be more than a vast technical assistance agency, valuable as that might be. There seems little doubt that it is the intention of "the Revolution" to employ central planning as a firm tool of achieving its goals. The Ministry of Planning is intended not only to plan, but to insure implementation. This approach to planning has long been advocated by Roberto Campos as his published writings will attest.[32]

In addition to incorporation of implementation in the central planning agency, the other major contrast of the Campos proposal to the Furtado project concerns the political-technical mix. Campos' plan provides for a purely technical process up to the point when "the plan" is completed within the Ministry of Planning with two qualifications. First, the advisory function of CONSPLAN is a channel through which outside political pressures could be expressed when and if the minister so desires. Secondly, each minister could, if he chose, channel political decisions into the planning process before his agency sends its plans to the Ministry of Planning. In Brazilian government, with its frequently changing cabinets and the insulation of the minister from subordinate technicians, this second possibility would not seem a likely one. We can conclude, then, that the Campos proposal establishes an essentially technical planning process. Whether the Furtado proposal with its early mix of political decisions with planning, or the more purely technical project of Campos is more suited to the Brazilian politico-administrative system will be discussed in the final chapter.

While this discussion of planning organization has neces-

32. See especially "A Transição do Planejamento Para a Administração" in Roberto de Oliveira Campos, *Economia, Planejamento e Nacionalismo* (Rio de Janeiro: APEC Editora, 1963), p. 46-51. Campos has held these views for years. The item cited is undated, but the footnotes indicate that it was originally written about 1952 or 1953.

sarily led to comment about implementations of plans; several other dimensions of implementation have not been touched. These will now be examined.

IMPLEMENTATION OF PLANNING

The great problem of Brazilian planning is not how to prepare good plans, but how to implement them. Far too little attention has been given to the relationship between "good" plans and implementing processes. Since most would agree that a "good" plan is one which can be implemented to a significant degree, it is apparent that the evaluation of plans is in part a function of available administrative capacity to implement them. A discussion of plan implementation, then, would require a complete evaluation of Brazilian administrative competence. Since an extended analysis of this subject is impossible here, we will be content to comment on selected aspects of Brazilian administration which are directly relevant to plan implementation.

A considerable literature has recently begun to appear concerning implementation of plans in developing countries. Much of this deals with what must be done to have an effective system of implementation. So much must be done, it would appear, that one wonders whether it is even possible to speed change in a society through planning. The requirements are no less than fundamental administrative reform and reorganization, following fundamental changes in the political order, based on rapid increases in educational levels associated with changes in basic social values, attitudes, and traditions. In short, effective implementation depends on the presence of conditions which do not yet exist, and which it is the object of planning to bring about.

While recognizing the partial validity of this frustrating circularity, we may still assume that some potential for plan implementation exists, and that this potential may be exploited in the near future. Our object, then, is to identify the nature and extent of this potential in Brazil and relate this to planning implementation practices of the present time.

The administrative obstacles to plan implementation have been dealt with most effectively by Waterston and Gross.[33] Gross utilizes three major categories of obstacles including deficiencies in natural and human resources, resistance to plans by interests affected, and defects in planning by those responsible for carrying it out. We shall concentrate on the last of these categories, which reflects at least in part the first two.

Waterston lists backward personnel practices, dilatory procedures, archaic financial controls, lack of coordination, problems of organization, and inadequate administrative service to the private sector.[34] Gross adds overcommitment, *projetismo*, document orientation, underevaluation, overevaluation, and administrative myopia.[35] Every student of Brazilian administration will recognize immediately that each of these obstacles is prominent in Brazil, with the probable exception of overevaluation.[36] Brazilian personnel administration is characterized by patronage appointments, excessive job security, low pay, low performance levels and advancement by ascription rather than by achievement. The exceptions are few enough that the generalization stands on a firm basis. Dilatory procedures abound. The sign of status is a heavy backlog of work which no one else can do, together with a long waiting line in the outer office. These can be achieved by failure to delegate, casual attendance to duty, low output, and failure to communicate within the organization. When financial resources are

33. Albert Waterston, *Development Planning: Lessons of Experience* (Baltimore: Johns Hopkins Press, 1965), Chapters 8 and 9; Bertram M. Gross, *Activating National Plans*, Occasional Paper, Comparative Administration Group, American Society for Public Administration (Bloomington: International Development Research Center, 1964), pp. 2-23.

34. Albert Waterston, *Development Planning*, Chapter 8.

35. Gross, *Activating National Plans*, p. 12 *et seq.*

36. Numerous examples are to be found among the writings of Brazilian and foreign scholars. See, for example, Nelson Mello e Souza and Breno Genari, *A Experiência Brasileira do Planejamento Governamental* (Rio de Janeiro: Escola Brasileira de Administração Pública, 1963); and Gilbert Siegel, "The Vicissitudes of Governmental Reform in Brazil."

much less than appropriations, the budget becomes meaningless. Financial "control" is not relevant, and the ability to secure an allotment of funds is measured by political influence. Lack of coordination is vividly displayed in the history of the Development Council and its competitor, COPLAN. The difficulties of both Brazilian and foreign businessmen in obtaining routine service from such governmental agencies as the customs service and the post office is notorious. Corruption is a recurrent theme in Brazilian administration, if we may use the term in its Anglo-Saxon context. At the top level lurid exposés have been published in Brazil, most notably with reference to the Vargas, Kubitschek, and Goulart administrations. At the bottom of the administrative hierarchy the prevalence of petty bribes and kickbacks has spawned the institution of the *despachante*—a businessman whose service is to cut through administrative red tape through judicious use of money, influence, or favors. The use of the *despachante* is so prevalent that governmental agencies employ them in their dealings with other governmental agencies.

The point in citing administrative "obstacles," however, is not to point the finger of criticism at a "backward" administration. Rather, it is to emphasize the great similarity of Brazil's administrative practice to that described by Fred Riggs as characteristic of prismatic polities generally. Despite the clearly prismatic characteristics of Brazilian administration, efforts have been made to make planning more than a shadow-play. These efforts have been more unsuccessful than successful, which is hardly surprising in view of the obstacles cited above. However, we cannot lose sight of certain solid achievements in implementing plans, however controversial the plans themselves. One can list the achievement of most of the Kubitschek goals, including most dramatically the construction of Brasilia. Cities, highways, and hydroelectric dams do not get built without public planning. The programs of SUDENE in the Northeast have had undoubted impact. While it is too early to evaluate implementation of the revolutionary government, it is not too early to report that it has made far greater strides than any previous government in consciously establishing machinery, laws, and procedures for plan implementation. Our task, then, is to review the efforts to create implementational machinery for planning and formulate an idea of the potential which may exist for central measures to implement national planning in a political system such as Brazil's.

Among the multitude of writings on one or another aspect of plan implementation, two stand out as efforts to take a comprehensive view. The first of these, by Saul Katz, proposes a systems model for plan implementation which includes the interrelated set of interaction systems presumed necessary to implement plans.[37] The set of systems is so comprehensive in scope that it comprehends all of public administration plus a portion of politics. It is too elaborate for our purpose. The second, by Bertram M. Gross, employs a set of categories for classifying the processes of implementation which is particularly appropriate as a framework for our commentary here.[38] In the basic processes of implementation he includes (1) mobilizing influence, (2) the application or use of influence, (3) coping with conflicts, and (4) employing strategy.

The mobilization of influence in behalf of national planning is hardly separable from mobilization of influence behind any and all of the political goals of the regime in Brazil. The Program of Goals was a source of political strength for Kubitschek, just as Kubitschek's winning of the presidency was a source of

37. Saul M. Katz, A Systems Approach to Development Administration, Papers in Comparative Public Administration Special Series No. 6 (Washington: Comparative Administration Group, American Society for Public Administration, 1965). The systems include manpower, finance, logistics, participation, legitimate power, and information. The systems have sub-systems, and each has the administrative functions of decision, specification (programming and assignment of responsibility), communication and control. Even more useful for planning administrators is his Guide for Modernizing Administration for National Development (Pittsburgh: Graduate School of Public and International Affairs, University of Pittsburgh, 1966). This study was prepared for the O.A.S. Development Administration workshop in Buenos Aires, November, 1965.
38. Bertram M. Gross, Activating National Plans.

strength for the Program of Goals. The SALTE Plan had only limited political support either within or outside of the administration, and its success was circumscribed accordingly. Goulart's struggle to achieve sufficient political support within and outside of the government for a viable administration failed miserably, and the Plano Trienal was first a tool and finally a casualty of that struggle, as the next chapter will describe. The strength of the alliance which sustains the revolutionary government of Castelo Branco, including the top military officers, a substantial segment of the bureaucracy including the key agencies of financial management, large landowners, and much of the urban and industrial classes, was sufficient to give the Program of Action an excellent start. The successful passage of much of the program requested by the President through the Brazilian Congress during the first year and a half of the revolutionary regime indicates this. To emphasize such points in detail would require a dissection of the entire Brazilian political system which we are not equipped to do in this study.

The remaining three processes of implementation, however, may be described more specifically in terms of planning. The use of influence, as employed by Gross, includes persuasion, pressure, and the promotion of self-activation. There are many forms of persuasion, and most of them have been slighted by Brazilian planners and administrators who view the whole administrative enterprise in mechanistic rather than in human terms. Planning processes, regarded as technical, have typically been performed without a concurrent process of achieving commitment of potential implementors through constant consultation during the planning process. Such a procedure would have been regarded as "political" and not professional. Persuasion boiled down to a matter of persuading the President of the Republic what he should sponsor, and relying on his persuasiveness with other political actors. Yet persuasion was virtually the only tool of implementation during the early history of Brazilian planning.

The need for systematization of the processes of consultation were noted above in discussing the proposals for new planning machinery during the last fifteen years. It was Celso Furtado who most fully recognized a need for a variety of kinds of consultation. He recognized this as a result of his harsh experiences as Minister of Planning. When the Plano Trienal was completed, it came under attack from various quarters. Furtado was dispatched to explain the plan and to persuade the objectors, both in the labor movement and in the industrial community of São Paulo, that it was necessary for the development of Brazil. These efforts were in vain. The Furtado proposal for planning machinery, however, sought to rectify the lack of consultation through use of interministerial committees and other means. Recognizing for the first time that planning somehow was related to budgeting, Furtado's proposal directed that, "To the end that the proposed budget reflect the policies of the plan of development, the Director General of the DASP will maintain permanent articulation with the Ministry of Planning during the elaboration of the budget."[39] The door for persuasion was to be kept open. The Campos proposal does not include any formal provision for intragovernmental persuasive activities. This is not to say that they are not in fact employed. The relationships between the planning and finance ministries and the development bank are derived from a long history of cooperation, and from ready-made channels for consultation. However, a wide field is still open in which such activities as proposing plans and goals, convincing by "showcase" examples, or by using the techniques of planning education and propaganda, could be exploited. Consultation with interests outside the government has been provided for through CONSPLAN as described above.

While no strong trend toward the use of persuasive influence has been noted, the same cannot be said of the use of pressure, the second form of influence. A number of the forms of pressure seem to be increasingly accepted as a basis for plan implementation. Gross distinguishes increasingly strin-

39. "Projeto de Decreto," Article 20.

gent types of pressure: bargaining, manipulation, command, and use of force.

We can immediately recognize that a different attitude toward the use of these techniques applies as between the private sector and the governmental hierarchy itself. Moreover, we may note that even when government sponsors a developmental activity it may frequently attempt to provide that it be administered independent of normal governmental controls so that it is subject to bargaining and manipulation rather than command and use of force. This is the case with the two types of Brazilian government corporations: government authorities (*autarchias*), and mixed corporations (*sociedades de economia mixta*). The former is purely governmental. The latter combines private and public ownership.

Brazilian implementation of national planning by the private sector, and to a degree by the governmental corporations, relies more on bargaining and manipulation than on coercion. As between these two, bargaining has proved difficult in a political arena in which the bargainers are not highly organized. Such bargaining as occurs tends to be interpersonal rather than interinstitutional. As such it is also largely invisible and not subject to research. Manipulation, however, has been systematically invoked in behalf of plan implementation. Incentives and deprivations are applied as an indirect manner of achieving desired behavior, while basic reliance remains on the market mechanism.[40] The stimuli used in Brazil are not unique, and include such things as control of the money supply, the use of subsidies, and tax incentives, for example. When a stimulus becomes strong enough, it is virtually a command, and the two categories merge into each other. Coercive measures to achieve plan goals in the private sector include taxation, control of the exchange rates, control of profit remittance abroad, maximum salaries, and price control, to take the more

40. See a discussion of the use of the market mechanism in national planning in Charles E. Lindbloom, "Economics and the Administration of National Planning," 25 *Public Administration Review* (December, 1965), 274-83.

prominent examples. Such measures are not self-enforcing and their effectiveness depends on the ability of the government to enforce them. Dollar-cruzeiro exchange control has often been relaxed. Taxes have frequently remained uncollected. The Furtado plan foundered, at least in part, because of the opposition to the way these controls were to be applied, and others were honored more in the breach than in the observance. The Castelo Branco government, however, has been more energetic and successful in the administration of controls of these kinds.

The more interesting issues of implementation, however, relate to the very important governmental sector of development plans. However sensitive the administration must be in dealing with the private sector, might it not deal forcefully within its own area of competence? There is considerable reason to believe that intrabureaucratic pressure politics is not so different from that of "private" interests. In any event, the Brazilian government has found it difficult, even through coercion, to insure implementation of plans for which it is responsible, either in the central government or in the regional entities of that government such as SUDENE. The SALTE Plan administrator was in constant competition with the Minister of Finance. During Furtado's incumbency a certain rivalry existed between the Ministry of Finance and the planning agency. This was in part responsible for antagonism to the proposed "superministry." When Campos became Minister of Planning, however, this problem no longer existed, and it was at this point that real attention could be given to the desire for intragovernmental implementation based on a firm system of controls.

The notion of central control of planning was not original with Campos, and has been traced above in terms of administrative organization. At this point it is necessary to emphasize the key role of budgeting and budgetary control as an instrument of implementation of national policy. Coercion of more than a hundred agencies of the Brazilian national government, in the interest of plan implementation, is normally viewed in terms of control of money. The SALTE Plan was a sham since it was a plan with no relation to the funds necessary to carry it out. The Program of Goals was as effective as it was primarily because President Kubitschek made sure that funds were allotted to his favorite projects, such as the construction of Brasilia. Furtado planned to systematize the control of money. In January of 1963 COPLAN was engaged in preparing for the allocation of budgeted sums through divisions of implementation to be created within the planning agency.[41] This intent was never carried out for reasons to be shown below. The Vargas proposal of the fifties was based on the concept that implementation consisted essentially of central review of plans originating from below for the purpose of removing conflicts and inconsistencies and for setting priorities. It was only later that the idea of central macro-planning led to recognition of a need for central initiative in plan-making and implementation using a system of budget controls. During the Furtado period both the idea of grass roots initiatives arising from the ministries and regional agencies, and the idea of central macro-planning, were very much in the thinking of the organizers of planning activities. No definite conclusions were reached as to the proper balance between centralized and decentralized approaches, however. Consequently, it was difficult to devise implementation machinery until it became apparent whether it would merely coordinate submitted projects at the center through some form of veto over inconsistent parts; or whether it would retain the initiative, create a plan, and supervise its execution.

The "super-ministry" plan, which was based on the CEPA report was not specific as to implementation measures, but it seemed to propose central initiative and coercion. It said that the central planning agency would approve plans, coordinate activities in the various sectors of federal administration, plan and *execute* the policy of the federal government for regional improvement and *other plans for internal* policy which may be established, and guide and supervise the banks for regional

41. Interview with Guilherme A. Pegurier, January 30, 1963.

economic development. This is a big order, but the report had little effect on the course of events.

It was only with the Campos ministry that a clear idea emerges as to precisely how national plans are to be implemented. Some hint of this is given in the decree establishing the revived ministry.[42] Like most decrees delegating authority to a Brazilian governmental agency, the present one is not specific. It does, however, authorize the Ministry of Planning to direct and coordinate the revision of the national economic development plan in "cooperation" with the ministries and other agencies of the national government; to "coordinate" through general, regional, and sectorial plans the programs and projects drawn up by the governmental agencies including independent authorities, mixed corporations and subsidized enterprises; to "coordinate" foreign aid; and to "coordinate the preparation and execution of the General Budget of the Union and of the other agencies. . . ."

What this language means is not clear from the decree itself, but may be judged by the plans for implementation procedures to be recommended to Congress as a step in creating a new and permanent ministry. These plans have already been described above. A four-step process is at the core of the procedures envisioned: governmental agencies would submit plans within the general framework of the long-range perspective plan of the country; these would be integrated in the Ministry of Planning, approved, and returned to the agency of origin; the agency would then submit a program budget consistent with the plan; and finally, when approved by the Ministry of Planning, this budget would be controlled by the ministry itself. In short, once the agency's program advanced to the stage of an acceptable program budget, the Ministry of Planning would supervise execution through budgetary controls.

Viewed purely as a formal process, the implementation of planning would be much like the procedure for budgeting in

42. Decree No. 53.914, May 11, 1964.

the United States, except that a perspective plan would have been prepared to serve as a guide by a central planning agency. There is no assurance whatever that the process as it will actually occur will be similar to budgeting in the United States, however. The contemplated procedures fit the model of classical, rational bureaucracy. Decisions would move up the chain of command for review and determination at the center, and these determinations would control decentralized effectuation of the decisions—subject to central constraints to insure implementation according to plan. We can assume that this would work in Brazil to the degree to which Brazil in fact has the kind of rational, hierarchically organized bureaucracy that the model of Max Weber envisions. This is not the kind of bureaucracy that presently exists in Brazil. On the contrary, the Brazilian bureaucracy clearly has prismatic characteristics.[43]

While national policies and the laws that implement them can be determined at the center, the complex process of indicative planning and of responding to sensitive cues from a central budget office would require a high level of sophistication at all levels of the hierarchy. This implies well-trained and professional administrators, the delegation of authority and responsibility, effective in-service training programs, full-time employment, and recognition of capacity and achievement in personnel decisions.

The frequent absence of these qualities in Brazilian administration might merely mean that the quality of implementation and of planning would be low. On the other hand, the use of the bureaucracy for political maneuver, and the constant pressure for rapid development under which every administra-

43. See Siegel, "The Vicissitudes of Governmental Reform in Brazil"; Mello e Souza and Genari, A Experiência Brasileira do Planejamento Governamental; Robert T. Daland (ed.), Perspectives of Brazilian Public Administration (Rio de Janeiro: Brazilian School of Public Administration, Getúlio Vargas Foundation, and University of Southern California, 1963); Juarez R. B. Lopez, "Some Basic Developments in Brazilian Politics and Society," in Eric N. Baklanoff (ed.), New Perspectives of Brazil (Nashville: Vanderbilt University Press, 1966). This point is further expanded and documented in the final chapter.

tion must operate, might be expected to combine to make planning in fact a matter of essentially central initiative and coercion, at least during a transitional period of "administrative development." Bureaucratic weaknesses might well be counteracted, where they occur, through central preparation of plans which are not "compulsory." That is, instead of standard types of budgetary controls and related systems of reporting, a budgetary incentive system might be created by which the observance of centrally established plans, priorities, and performance standards would produce rewards for the agency in question. Rewards could conceivably include higher pay (by classifying personnel into "professional" categories), the addition of new functions transferred from other agencies, more adequate space, equipment, clerical assistance, and the other kinds of benefits which all organizations seek. Using such an approach, hopefully the area of good plan implementation would rapidly expand building on islands of strength, wherever these could be found.

Such a strategy would not only give priority to plan implementation as against maintenance of sinecure-filled agencies, but would be the major incentive toward government-wide administrative development. This approach would be as applicable to regional entities and to independent agencies as to the ministries. In some degree it could be adapted to encourage states to undergo administrative development.

The techniques described above would not overcome "political" difficulties, nor would any other. They would depend on a very effectively administered central control agency —presumably the Ministry of Planning. They would require the creation of performance standards and of effective working relations with central auxiliary agencies, notably the Ministry of Finance. The presently close collaboration of the two ministries makes this seem plausible for the first time. Perhaps the greatest danger would be the growth of a new central control bureaucracy within the Ministry of Planning itself. Even should this ministry avoid the dangers of red tape, it would face the problem of maintaining intellectual leadership in plan-making in the best sense, while at the same time maintaining the routine operation of the incentive system. It is difficult to cultivate system, order, fairness, and routine without sacrific-ing imagination, creativity, and vision. Only gifted leadership can perform this wedding.

Gross's final category of "using influence" is promoting self-activation. We have come very close to discussing this possi-bility in recommending an incentive system of planning imple-mentation as a form of coercion. However, it is worth considering self-activation as such. One might take the posi-tion that in Brazil this should be the basic strategy, and it might be an effective one. What has already been done along this line? Very little has been done when we view the record. In relation to some of its studies, the Development Council, abolished by the revolutionary government, held local meet-ings similar to public hearings on some of its proposals in local communities. These activities were very limited in scope. Some encouragement has been given to the establishment of planning units in the ministries, such as that which has oper-ated in the Ministry of Foreign Affairs for some years. We have noted that proposals to create planning units in subordi-nate governmental agencies have been a feature in several recent plans for a system of planning.

In general, however, no substantial effort to promote initia-tive in decentralized planning had been launched up to the time of the Campos ministry. In the summer of 1965, how-ever, a new activity was added to the ministry which could be of utmost importance. A Regional and Municipal Planning Division was created within the ministry. A new breed of planner was appointed as director of the new division—a gen-eralist, noneconomist planner.[44] The objective of the new unit is nothing less than to implant a nation-wide "integrated"

44. This development was described by the first director of the division, Mr. Harry Cole, who was originally trained as an architect, and later had experience in town planning in Great Britain and in the United States. Inter-view, August 4, 1965.

regional, state, and local planning system in Brazil. At least initially, there are no levers available other than persuasion to apply pressure toward this end. A developing line of thought within the division, however, is that ultimately the availability of federal funds for implementing plans in local areas may be made dependent on the establishment of a system of comprehensive planning in the area in question. Essentially this is the same technique that is used in the urban renewal program in the United States.

The Regional and Municipal Planning Division's first job is seen as selling the doctrine of comprehensive—as compared with economic—planning. Comprehensive planning would include physical, economic, social, and sectorial planning. The emphasis is being put on the establishment of planning institutions locally, rather than on the content of plans. The intention is to strengthen the hand of local planners and technicians vis-à-vis local politicians. The strategy is to begin the program by working with the smaller state governments. Large states have political strength to make their demands felt at the national government without assistance, and they already have planning agencies in operation. The most profitable field to till, then, seemed to be the smaller and weaker states.

The actual work of the ministry in this field involves personal contact activities of a promotional nature, the preparation of a manual on comprehensive planning, and the preparation of legislation which would give priority in federal aid to projects in local areas that meet certain planning criteria.

An expansion of the work of this division could satisfy three of the major needs for any national program intended to stimulate local planning initiative. These include: (1) the rendering of technical planning assistance, including the loan of planners, to local agencies, (2) the training of regional and local planners, and (3) central research, clearinghouse, and informational activities. With the additional stimulus of a centrally administered incentive system, local planning could begin to emerge from its present undeveloped state.

A SUMMATION

What have we now said about the administration of planning in Brazil? Brazil has rushed, within a relatively few years, from sporadic, fragmentary planning efforts to the development of centrally constructed macro-economic plans. The problems of implementing these plans have been so great that only a minimum of results has been achieved. As a reaction to these frustrations, proposal after proposal has been made to "organize" planning in some permanent and systematic way. The predominant tendency in all these proposals has been to establish a strong national, central planning agency which would create a national plan and insure its implementation using the methods of rational bureaucracy. The problem is that the Brazilian bureaucracy does not have the characteristics which fit this model, and this is the chief difficulty in administering Brazilian planning. A natural response to this situation would be to "decentralize" planning, not only within the national government, but to regions, states, and cities. The difficulty here is that the inadequacies of Brazilian administration, from the planner's point of view, are even more marked at the periphery than at the center, with some exceptions. What is to be done in this dilemma?

At the present juncture of Brazilian planning, the solution has been to employ both approaches at the same time in a mixture in which central plans, centrally administered, predominate. The absence of a tradition of effective central personnel controls and performance budgeting make this solution a difficult one.

What has already been implied at various points in this chapter is that while the hard task of remodeling national administration along lines of the classical-rational model is being attempted, certain alternative approaches may be even more productive than the present one. Specifically, the use of *incentives* rather than *controls* might achieve more within the national government itself, pending the time when sophisticated control systems might be developed. We are tempted to suggest that certain nations are psychologically more receptive to control than to incentives, while others respond more to incentives while rejecting coercion. If there is any truth in this, certainly Brazil falls in the latter category.

Moreover, a greater emphasis might well be placed on the promotion of decentralized planning, also using incentives as the lever. This could involve expanding the activity of the Division of Regional and Municipal Planning. In particular, it would require a broad attack on the training of planner generalists, as well as more economists and other specialists. This approach would stimulate local initiative and participation, create a clientele for central planners, and build on islands of strength. To some degree this possibility has already been recognized. The planning ministry is already talking in terms of copying the French system of indicative planning. Regional planning has achieved substantial successes, notably in São Paulo, Guanabara, and the Northeast.

Some of the implications of following this kind of advice, however, are highly political and partisan in nature. National plans have political as well as rational-technical functions. In order to relate these clearly partisan factors to the planning process in Brazil, the following chapter is devoted to a detailed discussion of the politics of the Plano Trienal, with some added comparison of political ramifications of the Program of Action during its first year.

5

POLITICS AND
BRAZILIAN PLANNING

THE GOVERNMENTAL CONTEXT OF PLANNING

A national development plan is an effort to allocate values authoritatively for a society, either directly or indirectly. Since this is one of the common definitions of politics it would appear that governmental planning is political in nature. This chapter views planning in Brazil within its political context. More specifically, the process of central governmental planning is viewed as a dependent variable with the political system as an independent variable. The question is then posed, what are the characteristics of the political system which have produced the kind of planning experience which Brazil has enjoyed? Insofar as this question can be answered, we can study the compatibility of planning with its political environment, given any particular set of planning goals.

To initiate this inquiry we will review the ways in which the Brazilian political system has been viewed. We can then suggest the implications of these views for the planning process. What should Brazilian planning be like in terms of these models? Following this, we will explore the political course of planning during the last two administrations as a case study and draw conclusions.

John Friedman has dealt directly with the subject of the relevance of political system characteristics to planning.[1] Friedman constructs a nine-cell matrix of political systems using economic-technological development as one dimension and political organization as the other. Economic-technological

1. John Friedman, *The Social Context of National Planning Decisions: A Comparative Approach*, Occasional Paper, Comparative Administration Group, American Society for Public Administration (Bloomington: International Development Research Center, 1964).

development is transitional, transitional with a modern sector, or modern, following Brian Berry.[2] Political organization is that of a reconciliation system, a modernizing autocracy, or a mobilization system, following David Apter.[3] Friedman deals with the planning context of reconciliation systems having a transitional economy with a modern sector. Brazil falls into this cell, along with Ireland, Mexico, Argentina, Venezuela, Chile, Uruguay, Malaysia, Israel, Lebanon, Greece, Turkey, Colombia, Iceland, and India. In discussing the Latin American examples of these systems, Friedman lists the style of planning which presumably results from the social context of these specific planning environments, including: (1) a high level of governmental involvement, (2) an uneven distribution of planning capabilities, (3) focused planning (in contrast to comprehensive planning), (4) short-range considerations dominant in planning, (5) a low level of deliberate coordination, (6) use of noncoercive implementation techniques, and (7) vagueness of goals.

It is not difficult to infer that a high level of governmental involvement is a political response to a high level of expectation for development. Presumably shortage of planning expertise, spot planning, and short-range planning reflect existing technical and political under-development. Low levels of deliberate coordination, noncoercive methods, and vague goals stem from the existence of a reconciliation system rather than one of the authoritarian varieties.

Others have viewed the situation in similar terms using different system dimensions. Alfred Diamant presents a rather bewildering array of seven matrices using two dimensions of his own (political system goals and political system style)

2. Brian J. L. Berry, "Basic Patterns of Economic Development," in Norton Ginsburg (ed.), *Atlas of Economic Development* (Chicago: University of Chicago Press, 1961).

3. David E. Apter, "System, Process, and Politics of Economic Development," in Bert F. Hoselitz and Wilbert E. Moore (eds.), *Industrialization and Society* (UNESCO: Mouton, 1963), pp. 135-158. A more definitive statement by Apter is now available, *The Politics of Modernization* (Chicago: University of Chicago Press, 1965).

along with four dimensions from Banks and Textor: economic development status, political modernization in terms of periodization, political modernization in terms of historical type, and political leadership.[4] If we look at Brazil's placement in these matrices, the results are surprising. Diamant is interested solely in movement regimes, a category into which Brazil does not fall. We should not be too surprised, then, if some of Diamant's peripheral cells contain peculiar bedfellows. Brazil is characterized as a limited polyarchy with developmental goals, which seemed eminently reasonable until the establishment of a military dictatorship in October, 1965. It later appears in the economic status of "intermediate" development among countries with development goals, along with only three others: Colombia, Mexico, and Uruguay. Next it appears again as a country of intermediate development among countries with a "limited polyarchy" as political system style together with only South Africa and Uruguay. We next find Brazil characterized as a development-oriented country in which the struggle between the modernizing and the traditional elite has long since been settled in favor of the modernizing elite. Twenty-one countries fall into this category. Thirty-three countries are called developmental and also offshoots from European countries, as distinct from autochthonous and tutelary situations. All of the Latin American countries necessarily fall into the European offshoot category, though some are termed underdeveloped rather than developed. Brazil next falls with thirty-one other countries into a group with developed economies and advanced periodization. Finally, in terms of political system style and political leadership (presumed to be distinct dimensions), Brazil is called a limited polyarchy with moderately elitist leadership together with only one other country—Viet

4. Alfred Diamant, *Bureaucracy in Developmental Movement Regimes: A Bureaucratic Model for Developing Societies*, Occasional Paper, Comparative Administration Group, American Society for Public Administration (Bloomington: International Development Research Center, 1964); and Arthur S. Banks and Robert B. Textor, *A Cross-Polity Survey* (Cambridge: The M.I.T. Press, 1963).

Nam! The total impact of this presentation for one interested in Brazil drives one to the conclusion that Brazil's regime has something in common with virtually all the other countries of the world outside the Communist bloc, but is quite unlike any other in its total pattern. In order to escape the highly generalized characteristics listed by Friedman and the conflicting cues found in the Diamant matrices, we are able to turn to the Riggs theory of prismatic society.[5] The prismatic society may be compared with the transitional society except that it refers to the degree of specificity in the functions of societal structures rather than to progress from one stage to another. In the present world most transitional societies would also be prismatic. Riggs's model of prismatic society is readily understandable when it is placed in a position between the two more familiar models, the fused (traditional or folk) and the diffracted (or modern and industrialized). In short, the prismatic society has some of the characteristics of the fused society, and some resembling the diffracted society. Each of these types of society has its corresponding bureaucratic style and structure. For Riggs the bureaucracy of the fused society is the "chamber" which performs bureaucratic functions as well as the other elite roles of the society. The diffracted society has its "office," which is roughly the classical Weberian bureaucracy with its rationalized and specialized structure and processes. The prismatic bureaucracy is called the "sala" which is the model Riggs develops in detail.

The prismatic bureaucracy, or sala, says Riggs, exercises greater power than the bureaucracy in either the fused or diffracted society, since it operates in the absence of political controls which are provided by the kingship in the fused society or the political institutions of the diffracted society. Prismatic political institutions are formalistic rather than effective as control instruments. Given this assumption, it follows that administrative efficiency varies inversely with the weight of

5. Fred Riggs, *Administration in Developing Countries: The Theory of Prismatic Society* (Boston: Houghton Mifflin, 1964).

bureaucratic power, since efficiency is the result of performance subject to sanctions. If there are no effective political control systems, or sanctions, there is no motivation toward efficiency. The sala, then, is more relevant as a ladder by which to achieve elite status than as a tool for achievement of formal goals. These remarks are only enough to suggest the import of the Riggs model. What is of direct concern to us are the characteristics of the sala model of administration.

Risking oversimplification, we take the liberty of summarizing seven key characteristics of the sala. The first of these is price indeterminacy. With reference to administration, this means that salary and service levels in government are not fixed, but vary according to the status of the beneficiary. A second is the existence of recalcitrant clienteles. Due to the lack of sanctions on administrators to insure performance of services, the clienteles are forced to apply direct pressure to expedite the securing of services—or to secure them at all. This condition, along with price indeterminancy produces the climate for what would be termed institutionalized corruption by the standards of the diffracted society. Bribes are regularly expected for the performance of services, and a whole profession of virtual bribe-givers is supported by the consumer in order to apply the financial incentives to the bureaucracy. A third characteristic is communalism and nepotism in recruitment. Since positions in the public service are sought more for the access to power which the positions give than for the salaries associated with them, appointments to positions in the sala are made on the basis of family and communal relationships rather than the prospect of service to be rendered by the appointee. Appointees come from groups outside the administration which share common communal symbols of identification and which tend to create "clects" within the bureaucracy which seek to expand and compete with rival "clects" based on different family or communal identifications.

A fourth characteristic of the sala is the selective application of the rules. Rules, like prices, services, and recruitment, are applied selectively according to the status and identifications of the individual concerned and his ability, through his own "clect" connections, to gain exemptions from the rules. A lack of interagency coordination is a fifth characteristic. Since the bureaucracy contains competitive elements within it which compete for power, the incentives in the system promote exclusiveness rather than cooperation. Service incentives are absent. A sixth characteristic Riggs terms poly-normativism or normlessness. The presence of conflicting and overlapping norms such as ascription v. achievement produces a confused cynicism on the part of the clientele respecting administration. The manifest or formal norms are *not* implemented in fact, due to the presence of conflicting traditional norms which are implemented in the sala. A final characteristic is the disengagement of authority and control. Despite the presence of relatively great power within the sala, outputs cannot be efficiently achieved. The formal centralization of authority is overcome by the consequences of the factors noted above—in effect, by a lower echelon veto of top policy. The response to this situation is frequently an effort to further centralize the formal institutions of authority. This response is foredoomed to failure since only the formal situation is changed by reorganization. The basic values and loyalty-disloyalty patterns remain. These seven characteristics of the sala are, quite clearly, highly interrelated aspects of a single situation, rather than independent variables.

It is apparent that Friedman's description of planning in Latin American polities has a high degree of fit with the characteristics of the sala model. The high level of government involvement in planning and development activity is a necessary response to rising expectations. A significant part of this response is the creation of central, that is formal, planning institutions. The manifest function of these institutions is to plan and implement plans, chiefly through "non-coercive" techniques. The intervening difficulties, however, produce limited results. Due to the sala pattern of recruitment, limited plan-

ning capabilities are not effectively employed. As a result of
the disengagement of authority and control, long-range and
comprehensive plans are not implemented and focused planning is the result, based on short-range or even emergency
considerations. Coordination is not effected due to the tensions
existing in the sala. The basic condition of poly-normativism
produces a vagueness of planning goals.

Our question now is, "to what extent does the history of
Brazilian central planning display the relationships just set
forth drawn from current analyses of planning and administration in developing countries?" We approach this question by
presenting a case history of Brazilian central planning during
the Goulart administration, with additional comment as to subsequent developments where relevant. Conclusions based on
the case history will be reserved for the concluding section.

GOULART'S APPROACH TO PLANNING

When João Goulart succeeded Jânio Quadros to the presidency in September, 1961, there existed certain preconditions
which disposed him toward the creation of a specific national
plan. The most obvious of these is precedent. More or less
systematic planning had been attempted since the time of
Vargas at the national level. Regional planning had an even
longer, if confusing, history.[6] State planning had already
achieved a new vogue.

A second precondition was the political utility of a plan.
As a reform-oriented president, Goulart needed a program.
Having suddenly come to office with the surprise resignation
of Jânio Quadros, no ready-made program was at hand. The
Jânio program was available, but suffered from various liabili-

6. A considerable literature is developing on regional planning in the Northeast of Brazil. See, for example, Albert O. Hirschman, *Journeys Toward
Progress: Studies of Economic Policy-Making in Latin America* (New York:
Twentieth Century Fund, 1963); Stefan H. Robock, *Northeast Brazil: A Developing Economy* (Washington: The Brookings Institution, 1963); and additional studies in progress.

ties so far as Goulart was concerned. Moreover, several recent plans had proven political assets. Kubitschek's plan was clearly successful from a political point of view. This became quite clear after his announced candidacy for the presidency in 1965, when he stated that he would run on the basis of a similar new Program of Goals. Carvalho Pinto, then Governor of São Paulo, had been dramatically successful with his Plan of Action for that state. Mauro Borges had profited by a plan in Goiás.

Finally, Goulart came to office facing substantive problems which cried for solution. Several obviously required technical attention as a basis for solutions. The most intense of these was an increasing rate of inflation, closely followed by demands for agrarian reform; recurring crises in the supply of such staples as meat, milk, rice, sugar, and beans; the deepening problem of urban slums; and unrest in the drought areas of the Northeast.

President Goulart came to office in September of 1961. Despite the fact that planning was clearly desirable from these several points of view, it was not possible to begin immediately. An even more pressing imperative was to attain the degree of political stability necessary for governing, and this proved a difficult task. The details of Goulart's accession to power were told in Chapter 2. He had been permitted to take office by sufferance of a divided military after a compromise establishing a parliamentary system. Once the immediate threat of violence had receded, Goulart struggled for a restoration of the presidency on the pre-existing constitutional basis. It took over a year, until the plebiscite of January 6, 1963, to accomplish this constitutional repair. Only after the campaign for reforming the Constitution was far advanced could the problem of *program* gain sufficient priority for action. At the time, Goulart's perception that restoring the powers of the presidency was so important as to justify giving it a year of the five-year term was widely challenged. Later events soon raised the question whether even the restored presidency was strong enough to implement a reform program of the scope which Goulart undertook.

In any event, the stage at which planning could receive attention was reached in September of 1962. On September 28, a decree was published creating the position of Minister Extraordinary for Planning, and Celso Furtado was appointed to the post, charged with the preparation of a three-year plan for the Goulart administration.[7] Two considerations made the production of a plan particularly important at this time. The first was the imminence of the plebiscite on presidentialism to be held in January. Publication of the plan was timed a week before the election so as to strengthen the presidentialist vote.[8] President Goulart felt he already controlled the vote of the left wing. The plan was intended to gain support from the middle class. It was only with considerable strain on the usual procedures in such matters that the plan was ready in time to serve this purpose. When it was presented to the Council of Ministers on December 18, Furtado hoped for a thorough study of the plan by the Council. The President of the Council (equivalent to prime minister), Hermes Lima, however, sought immediate approval by the Council and transmission to the President—and this is what happened.[9]

The second factor which made preparation of the plan a high priority matter was the Brazilian perception of the attitude of the U.S. government. Under the Alliance for Progress, financial aid and other assistance was to be made available on the basis of a national plan. While there was provision for emergency aid on some projects before completion of a plan, the bulk of the money would presumably begin to flow only after a plan was produced. At this point Brazil was extremely sensitive to the criticism from various official and unofficial

7. Decree No. 1.422, September 27, 1962.
8. In some quarters it was charged that the plan was made solely for this purpose. See, for example, "Adeus aos Planos," *Correio de Manhã*, January 23, 1963. Furtado confirmed that the plebiscite was regarded as the deadline for the plan.
9. *Jornal do Brasil*, December 19, 1962.

U.S. sources to the effect that the Brazilian government was unstable, and its economic problems were not under control. The importance of this factor in the mind of President Goulart was underlined by a minor drama which occurred during December. Furtado and his staff worked under pressure to complete the plan. A sixty-day limit had been prescribed by the decree creating Furtado's post. After a remarkable effort, the 450-page plan was completed in two volumes on Saturday night, December 15th. Early Sunday morning Goulart, in Brasilia, called Furtado who had been working in Rio. Furtado explained that the plan had been finished hours before, and now he was going to take a much earned rest. Goulart urged him, however, to use his Sunday making a summary of the plan and to bring it to Brasilia. By two a.m. on Monday, a fifteen-page summary was completed, and Furtado flew to Brasilia to present it to the President. As it turned out, the summary of the plan was needed for discussions with the Attorney General of the United States, Robert Kennedy, who lunched with Goulart and Furtado that day. While no official explanation of the Kennedy visit as other than a social call was ever made by either government, it is widely known that in fact the occasion was used to present Brazil's plan in an effort to counteract the pessimistic statements about Brazil expressed by President Kennedy a few days before.

While the plebiscite and the U.S. attitude were important factors, they were by no means the only reasons for preparing the Plano Trienal. This becomes more clear on exploring the nature of the commitment to the plan of the two chief actors, João Goulart and Celso Furtado. By the time of his appointment as Minister of Planning, Furtado already had formed his theory of economic development, his procedure for planning, and his role in plan execution. In all of these experiences, Furtado carefully preserved his image as a professional planner and administrator rather than a politician. He constantly attended professional conferences throughout the world and produced a stream of books and articles which have been translated into many languages. After he left the government, Furtado continued his research and scholarly interest in planning and development in the United States and France. The commitment of President Goulart to planning is of a very different order. His career as a politician has already been reviewed. Suffice it to say that in virtually every major public speech during early 1963 he repeated his commitment to planning as a basis for his reform program, and to the Plano Trienal in particular. Goulart acquired a basic understanding of what the plan contained through a series of meetings with Furtado while the plan was in preparation—two or three sessions a week. When Goulart received the completed plan, aides reported he was exultant.[10] The following exchange was reported in the press: (Furtado) "Mr. President, I am not a politician. I am a technician. This is the plan of a technician. I will only be able to collaborate in its execution if political influences can be avoided. In any other event, the government will be able to find many politicians more effective than a technician like me." (Goulart) "I have never wanted so much to do anything as to attempt the implementation of this plan just as it is. I am going to try. Is it possible that nothing serious can be accomplished in this country?" Two days before the January plebiscite, when queried about his moves in the event the vote went for a return to presidentialism, Goulart replied that he would immediately constitute his cabinet for the purpose of giving effect to the Plano Trienal.[11]

Despite the enthusiasm of the President and his chief planner, however, there were already signs that a battle was shaping over the role of planning in the new administration.

A SUPER MINISTRY: THE STRUGGLE FOR PLANNING LEADERSHIP

The role of planning in government is a very simple concept to grasp. Essentially it is a question of applying reason to

10. *Ultima Hora*, December 19, 1962.
11. *Jornal do Brasil*, January 4, 1963.

public problems. But the role of *planner* is a complex concept, and it is by no means well defined in Brazil. While it is recognized that the planner must be a technician, there is no generally recognized theory as to his degree of responsibility for gaining political acceptance and for implementing the plan. Furtado became chief planner for the administration, however, with a personal theory of planning well developed. His aspiration for SUDENE was his aspiration for the nation. He sought to be a technician with respect to devising the plan, a tactician in securing allies for the policies required, and an administrator of the plan-implementing agency.[12] Strung through his prolific writings can be found numerous statements which relate to his view of the role of the planner (Furtado frequently uses the term "economist" in place of "planner"). For example: "It is necessary to keep technical activity and political command closely united. . . . The experience that we had in the Northeast, with technicians totally disconnected from political party activity, teaches us a lesson. This lesson is that technical action does not make sense if it occurs in isolation. In other words, technical action, in our generation, necessarily has a social dimension."[13]

When applied at the national level, the implications of the Furtado approach ramified widely. Here was the conception of a central point which would combine the intellectual basis for policy formulation with the governmental authority to insure the implementation of policy through an agency of planning and action—of which SUDENE was the prototype. At the national level this central organ of action was necessarily central not only to the national government itself, but also to regional planning and state planning as well, in order to insure a "comprehensive and coordinated" approach.

With the appointment of Furtado as Minister Extraordinary for Planning, this theory was not long in taking definite shape

12. See Hirschman, *Journeys Toward Progress*, pp. 66-91, for a description of the way in which Furtado performed these roles in the Northeast.
13. Celso Furtado, *A Pre-Revolução Brasileira* (Rio de Janeiro: Fundo de Cultura, 1962), pp. 61-63.

in specific terms. The admittedly interim decree establishing planning, in addition to directing that a national economic and social plan of development be prepared, prescribed "coordination" of the "plans and activities" of the regional planning agencies already created under federal law, and "coordination" of all the plans for foreign economic and financial aid and technical assistance.[14]

The term "coordination" in the decree is nowhere defined. This activity could range all the way from informational clearinghouse functions to hierarchical supervision. In any event, the issue was not a serious one, since SUDENE and the São Francisco Valley Company were already under the supervision of Furtado who retained his position as Superintendent of SUDENE.

The September decree was followed in November by a further development of the central planning and control agency idea which left little doubt as to the meaning of "coordination." This was Article VII of a proposed governmental reorganization law published in the *Diário Oficial* at the direction of the Council of Ministers.[15] The report accompanying the proposal states that it carried the approval of Celso Furtado and the Director General of the DASP. The proposal says: "The responsibility for planning, coordination, and control are conferred on the Ministry of Development and Planning *which also will care for execution of regional and national development policy.*"[16] The proposal extends the supervision of the new ministry far beyond that of the original decree to include

14. The regional agencies included: Superintendência de Plano de Valorização Econômica da Amazônia; Superintendência de Desenvolvimento de Nordeste; Commissão de Vale de São Francisco; and Superintendência de Plano de Valorização Econômica da Fronteira Sudoeste de País. The Departmento Nacional de Obras Contra as Secas, a part of the Ministry of Public Works, was not included. This agency has a long history of political competition with SUDENE, and is well entrenched in the Northeast.

15. *Diário Oficial*, December 14, 1962, Section I, Part 1. This contains the proposed law and the report of the Consultor Geral da República, Gilvan de Queiroz, who had been directed to prepare it. In his report, Queiroz states that the proposal was in essence a copy of the work of the reorganization commission which reported in 1951.

16. Italics added.

all the activities of the various sectors of federal administration. It specifically covers "planning and execution" of policy of the federal government which concerns "regional economic improvement, recovery, and development, and other plans for internal policy which may be established." Specific areas of authority mentioned are drought programs, sanitation, aid to the Indians, the statistical system and the census, assistance to municipalities, regional banks, and the territories. The agencies connected with these activities would have been transferred to the new ministry, and in addition the National Economic Development Bank, the Central Brazil Foundation, the Getúlio Vargas Foundation, and of course the National Planning Commission and the Council for Development. The last two were already under Furtado's jurisdiction under the September decree. In addition, the proposal prescribed a Department of Planning and Coordination in each of the seventeen ministries which the reorganization would establish.

The reasons for developing this proposal and publishing it at this precise time, two weeks before unveiling of the Plano Trienal, are obscure. There is no evidence that the proposal was a serious one. Furtado reports that it was part of a political intrigue being conducted from a point close to Goulart for the purpose of reducing Furtado's influence.[17] Even if this was not the real motive of the move, this was its chief effect.

The proposal was read as an effort to create a "super-ministry" which would be the control center for the entire administration with its agent, the Planning and Coordination Department, in each ministry, and direct supervision over much of the rest of the administration. Only the *autarquias* and mixed enterprises were untouched, and through control of economic policies even these would presumably be subject to much influence from the new ministry. This proposal resembled nothing so much as the technique of Vargas in centralizing control over the bureaucracy through creation of the DASP. It was much more frightening, however, since the controls of DASP

17. Interview with Celso Furtado, May 8, 1965.

were chiefly administrative in character. The proposed ministry was explicitly designed to control *program*.

The response to this rather offhand proposal was immediate. Though there was little if any discussion of who the new minister might be, either assumption presented problems. If Furtado, riding the crest of initial enthusiasm over the new plan, were to be minister, a self-professed technician would assume the prime post of political power next to the presidency. Should he not be placed in this post, it would fall into the field of political contention with the danger of being staffed by a person who might use the bundle of centralized powers for objectives other than those of rational planning—even, it was suggested, for sustaining a new dictatorship.

It became known that within Furtado's agency, COPLAN, studies were being made of the possible structure and functioning of such a ministry. While the nature of these plans for the new ministry of planning were never made public, they did include at one stage the idea of planning units per se for global and sectorial planning, and in addition, implementation units which would supervise execution in the ministries and other agencies, as well as in the regional planning agencies.[18]

The plans for a super-ministry, while never formally recommended or adopted even within the planning agency itself, were obviously widely discussed within the cabinet, and the negative reaction was bitter. Even before publication of the Plano Trienal, which called for creation of a national planning *system*, the lame duck cabinet was expressing concern over the super-ministry, charging that it would establish a dictatorship, and that it would return a virtual prime minister despite the fact that a plebiscite to eliminate the parliamentary system was expected to be successful within the week, as proved to be

18. Interview with Anton Pegurier, Secretary General of COPLAN, January 18, 1963. Within the COPLAN staff the conception was that the chief weakness of Brazilian planning to date was in the field of implementation. This was conceived to include a process apparently very similar to the kind of budget allotments and pre-audit familiar in United States administration. This was never adopted as a part of the planning function, though the "plan of containment" represents the same idea in vestigial form.

the case.[19] During early January the same theme was expanded
and repeated. It was feared that neither San Tiago Dantas,
nor Carvalho Pinto would accept the Ministry of Finance in
the new cabinet if its powers were to be so summarily atten-
uated in favor of a new ministry of planning. It was suggested
that there was something undemocratic about plan implementation being in the same hands as plan making. This theme
was given a "theoretical" basis by Almino Afonso, leader of the
Brazilian Labor party (PTB), who shortly became Minister of
Labor, when he asserted that plan making was purely technical, while plan execution was political in nature.[20] Afonso
publicly recommended that the Minister of Finance be charged
with execution of the plan, and he hoped Dantas would get
the job.

January was a period of uncertainty about the future of
the planning ministry project. Prior to the plebiscite the press
reported categorically that Carvalho Pinto, recently Governor
of São Paulo, had been offered the post as Minister of Planning.
Some said this was merely to influence the vote. After the
election, however, Pinto gave a major statement to the press
in support of the need for planning, and specifically favoring
the concepts of the Plano Trienal. He did not mention the
ministry proposal.[21] If he was running for the job, he was unsuccessful. A few days later, after a meeting between Goulart
and Amaral Peixoto, head of the Social Democratic party
(PSD) and recently appointed Minister Extraordinary for Administrative Reform, the main outlines of an administrative
reorganization were proposed which contained no ministry of
planning whatever. A new Ministry of Interior, however, was
proposed, which would contain some of the implementational
responsibilities formerly attributed to the Ministry of Planning,
including the coordination of the regional agencies. The press
attributed to Furtado the suggestion that two ministries be

19. *O Globo*, December 29, 1962.
20. *Jornal do Brasil*, January 3, 1963.
21. *Correio da Manhã, O Globo, Tribuna da Imprensa,* and *Jornal da Bahia*, January 10, 1963.

formed, one for planning, and one for development.[22] Immediately following these announcements, the press lamented that the new cabinet just being formed would evidently lose the services of the only three ministers committed to planning, naming Furtado, Calmon (Finance) and Ribeiro (Education). The respected *Correio da Manhã* noted that apparently planning had gone out the window only seventeen days from the publication of the Plano Trienal.[23]

Certainly it was clear that the administration would not push ahead with the super-ministry idea, but neither did it abandon planning. Instead, the day after the editorial, the new Minister of Finance was named. He was San Tiago Dantas who soon became the intellectual leader of the cabinet. Dantas was a respected, moderate-nationalist, lawyer and professor. He was a senator from the Brazilian Labor party, and had served as foreign minister during the interlude of parliamentarism. Within a few days a remarkable transformation had occurred within the administration. In place of Furtado, who had constantly been in the public eye with explanations and defenses of the Plano Trienal, Dantas became the new spokesman. It was quite evident that he had undertaken a full commitment to carry out the plan, including the implementational responsibility. This was the image he created, and this is precisely what he did. He spoke for the plan not only in Brazil, but became its proponent abroad. In this he received the full cooperation and support of Furtado, who now remained behind the scenes, reverting to his technical role. Dantas accepted and advocated the theory that execution and planning should be organizationally separate.

Furtado, for his part, seems to have recognized that a policy decision had been made. Yet he still saw the need for a rationally structured system of planning, and on March 3, he delivered to the President the result of his studies on the subject, now somewhat revised. This proposal has been discussed

22. *O Globo*, January 17, 1963; *Jornal do Brasil*, January 22, 1963.
23. *Correio da Manhã*, January 23, 1963.

in detail in Chapter 4. In essence it provided a planning system in which there would be heavy political participation in the plan formulation stages. The dream of a purely professional planning-and-implementation agency now seemed dead. Brazil was not ready to transfer unprecedented power to a professional staff, and it was the cabinet, representing the chief centers of partisan political power, that gave the *coup de grâce*. The very structure of the cabinet itself had evidently been influenced by the issue over the proper role of the planner. The implementation of planning descended firmly into the hands of an avowed politician, the Minister of Finance.

PUBLIC RESPONSES TO THE PLANO TRIENAL

When the Plano Trienal was announced at New Year's, it was immediately subjected to criticism, much of it violent. At first this originated from right-wing, banking, and industrial groups, the radical left holding its fire. Soon, however, the radical left jumped into the fray with a bitter attack against the plan. The administration and the planners gauged the criticism, and took certain compensatory measures which modified some features of the plan. The attack from the business interests seemed to decline, while that of the left became more bitter. Within a few months the positions of both sides had shifted considerably. Early critics of Dantas and Furtado were now defending them against the attack from the left.

This shifting of positions of both the right and the left, is an example of an initial reaction to the proposed plan on the basis of preconceived images, followed by a later more mature response based on the actual contents and application of the plan itself. The action began well before the plan was officially announced. In Brazil major political decisions are commonly signaled in advance, either directly through favored press outlets of the administration, or indirectly through a participant who speaks at his own option for purely personal reasons. In the case of the Plano Trienal, both of these things occurred.

Two weeks before the plan was announced, information and misinformation as to the contents of the plan began to filter into the newspapers. Each journal tended to see in the plan what it hoped would be there, with the exception of the daily *O Globo*. This journal from the start feared the worst, and attacked Furtado and the plan with bitter venom well before any information whatsoever on the contents of the plan had become available.[24] This attack, of itself, served to help the leftists define their position as generally supportive to the plan and Furtado.

An early report stated that the plan provided for a program of development exclusively relying on Brazilian resources. While it is true that the plan did emphasize the self-help approach, it retained a place for a certain amount of foreign aid. However, the inaccurate report immediately found favor with the leftist nationalists who had long sought an end to foreign investment and aid, calling them imperialist exploitation. When the plan was more widely understood, the leftist position rapidly changed. When the initial leftist image first appeared, the right became even more vindictive in its attack, not on the yet unborn plan so much as on its author, Furtado. The *Tribuna da Imprensa*, formerly published by Brazil's most notorious anti-Communist, Carlos Lacerda, said: "Mr. Celso Furtado is today one of the greatest barriers to good relations between Brazil and the United States, for three reasons: (1) He is incapable, in spite of his fame as a genius; (2) he is disloyal and thinks not of the country, but only of his own ambition for power; (3) he is a Communist, and only works for his scheme to solidify a Communist apparatus in the Northeast."[25]

24. Typical of the attack is the following statement: "If Mr. Furtado wants, as in fact it appears, to prepare a totalitarian revolution on the left through the pre-revolution in progress, at least he ought to do it without doing such violence to the simplest principles of economic analysis." *O Globo*, November, 28, 1962. The author of the anti-Furtado campaign of *O Globo* was Eugene Gudin, an economist who maintained a steady battle against all things of the left. He attacked Furtado personally, as well as opposing governmental planning as such.

25. *Tribuna da Imprensa*, December 18, 1962.

By the eve of its unveiling the opposition to the plan seemed to be deepening. The leader of the National Democratic Union (UDN), Herbert Levy, said his party would fight any statist aspects of the plan, and suggested that in this his party had the support of a considerable segment of the PSD. The leader of the PSD was Amaral Peixoto, Minister of Extraordinary for Administrative Reform, who expressed reservations about the plan, being particularly concerned about the powers of the planning agency.

The *Jornal do Brasil* scooped the press by printing verbatim the official summary of the plan on December 30. It was formally revealed by President Goulart the following day.[26] Within a very short time, the initial images began to shift. Rightest forces never really contradicted their former protestations in so many words, but their attack slacked off. Dramatic change came from the left, however. Within a month of publication of the plan, the transformation was complete and the plan was anathema to anyone with "true sympathy for the masses." The signal which was definitive in this transformation was given by the venerable but still dynamic Communist, Luis Carlos Prestes. The plan, he said, contained no concrete measures against spoliation of the masses. It must be fought. The plan catered to the interests of foreign capital. It limited salaries. It was public knowledge, he went on, that the Goulart administration had initiated conversations with the International Monetary Fund, the United States ambassador, and the United States Department of State. As a consequence, he asserted, the imperialists would be the real behind-the-scenes decision makers for Brazil, in exchange for credits.[27]

The radical left now followed the Prestes line with enthusiasm. These forces included the General Labor Command (CGT), the unofficial central headquarters of organized labor dominated by the radical, Communist-connected left; the National Student's Union (UNE), subsidized by the government

26. *Jornal do Brasil*, December 30, 1962.
27. *Jornal do Brasil*, January 31, 1963.

160   BRAZILIAN PLANNING

and led by Communists; and the Nationalist Parliamentary
Front (FPN), a group of leftist members of Congress. These
groups formed themselves into a "Popular Mobilization Front"
(FMP) which also included the military group of officers and
sergeants supporting General Osvino Ferreira Alves. The FMP
was not launched solely to fight the Plano Trienal. Rather, it
had formed as the result of other tensions, most notably the
crisis within the military in which Generals Osvino and Kruel
were the principal antagonists. The FMP was intended to join
all the radical leftist forces in support of various leftwing causes
then current. The Plano Trienal was only one of these issues.[28]
The leader of the FMP was Leonel Brizzola, Federal Deputy,
former Governor of Rio Grande de Sul, left wing nationalist,
and brother-in-law of the President.

The real battle was conducted less in general terms—for or
against the plan—than in terms of specific issues. The latter
will now be reviewed briefly, for the purpose of establishing
the nature of the governmental response to each of the demands made upon it.

The wage increase. The greatest pressure brought against
the plan was used to breach the 40 per cent limit on the increase in salaries for civil and military personnel. This limitation was simply a part of the general plan of containing
governmental budgetary expenditures in the interest of controlling inflation. To pay more would simply mean printing
more paper money and further inflating the cruzeiro. First
signs of trouble came with the formation of the new presidentialist cabinet. The PTB was reluctant to accept the post
of Minister of Labor, which it was expected to hold, since this
post would normally carry with it the responsibility to use its
close connection with organized labor to hold to the administration's containment policy. Finally the leader of the PTB,
Almino Afonso, accepted the post, but made no effort to re-
strain labor's demands. When Dantas was appointed Minister

28. The organizational manifesto of this group is found in *Tribuna da
Imprensa*, April 24, 1963.

of Finance, he asserted that the ministries of Labor, Finance, Planning, and Industry and Commerce would act jointly to carry out the Plano Trienal. Very soon he was omitting the Ministry of Labor in similar statements. Virtually as soon as the new cabinet was formed, the CGT came out for a 70 per cent salary increase. Nevertheless, in early March, Goulart sent the 40 per cent increase proposal to Congress, within the spirit of the Plano Trienal. This was at a time when negotiations were in progress with the United States and the International Monetary Fund, both of which were concerned about an anti-inflationary policy.

A month later it was widely rumored that the government was about to change its opinion on the pay increase. What had happened in so short a time? It is true that the pressure from the CGT and labor generally, including various sectors of the PTB, was continuing. More than this, however, President Goulart was passing through a crisis seemingly having nothing to do with financial policy. Leftist General Osvino had come into serious conflict with rightist General Kruel who was Minister of War.[29] During the ensuing crisis the sergeants of the Brazilian Army, who had been organizing themselves slowly and quietly for political action, leaped to the defense of General Osvino in various public ways. Military discipline was applied, however, and the sergeants became less vociferous. The significant point is, however, that they continued their political interest on a permanent basis, and joined other forces of the radical left in the FMP, as related above. Thus the military crisis gave added stimulus to the left wing coalition, which immediately took up the pay increase issue. On this question the sergeants, along with other military associations, could legitimately express themselves since it affected them directly.

On May 2, the day following an outpouring of sentiment

29. The events in this controversy are told in Robert T. Daland, "Four Months of Political Strife in the Military," in Frank Sherwood (ed.), "The Dynamics of Government and Administration in Brazil" (MSS in the School of Public Administration, University of Southern California).

on the pay increase question during Labor Day festivities in which Goulart was heavily involved, Dantas announced the new policy. It would be possible, he said, to allow 60 per cent increases to the civil and military employees if the same law provided for a non-inflationary source for the money. Dantas suggested a compulsory loan to be administered in connection with the income tax. He said this was agreed to with the full support of the ministers responsible for the Plano Trienal.[30] There now followed a wave of sentiment, frequently from sources formerly critical of some phases of the Plano Trienal, fearing that the plan had been abandoned, and demanding that there be no retreat. The administration countered, as in every other case, with the theory that the plan never had been rigid, and only minor modifications were being introduced to reflect changed conditions.

The Chamber of Deputies acted rapidly, voting an increase of the entire 70 per cent demanded by an overwhelming margin of 169 to 56. Even the amended conditions laid down by Dantas, then, were not met. He continued to defend the action, however, and finally announced that part of the additional 10 per cent added to the agreed-upon 60 per cent increase could come from the consumption tax where collections were running considerably higher than originally estimated.

One would think this was a complete victory for the pressure group supporting the pay increase, but there is more to the story. The military were unhappy with the precise schedules of increase which were announced, and were even more unhappy with the slowness of making the increase effective. Accordingly, as soon as the second presidentialist cabinet (and the fourth during Goulart's two and a half years in office) was formed, dramatic new developments occurred. A meeting of sergeants and second lieutenants had voted an ultimatum to the President and Congress demanding final action on the pay increase within ten days. Paratroop forces had threatened to stage a mass jump over Brasilia to back up the ultimatum,

30. *O Globo*, May 2, 1963.

and words were spoken comparing the fall of the Bastille to the fall of Brasilia. The situation rapidly cooled when the new Minister of War, Jair Dantas, acted swiftly and forcefully, jailing a number of the leaders of the meeting. In view of these events, it seems evident that the 40 per cent ceiling would have been, in truth, much more than the Goulart administration had the potential to insist on.

Instruction 239. The Brazilian government controls by decree the official rate of exchange between the cruzeiro and the dollar. Regulations controlling this rate, for various purposes and at various times, are complex. In general, however, at the time of publication of the Plano Trienal the official rate was 475 to the dollar.[31] When Brazilian commodities were exported and sold for dollars, the exporter received this official 475 cruzeiros for each dollar. This means that if the official rate was to be increased, the exporter would receive more money for his product. In April the agency responsible for controlling the exchange rate, the Superintendency for Money and Credit (SUMOC), did raise the exchange rate from 475 to 600 cruzeiros to the dollar in an order known as "Instruction 239." Dantas justified this on the grounds of necessity to stimulate exports, thus producing a more favorable balance of trade. Groups from both the left and the right of the administration attacked the new instruction on the grounds that it was inflationary. The left argued that the increased payments to exporters would enrich the vested interests at the expense of the masses. The right insisted that there would be no economic gain since exports would not be stimulated by the measure.[32]

The stance of the two groups opposing Instruction 239 was

31. There was also a free market rate for transactions which did not employ the regular banking system. This rate was substantially higher than the controlled official rate, but was not available to exporters.
32. *Tribuna da Imprensa*, April 24, 1963. These opinions are reported in the *Conjuntura Econômica*, organ of the Brazilian Institute of Economics of the Getúlio Vargas Foundation. Supporting opinions came from the conservative National Economic Council and the Guanabara Commercial Association. Among other things it was argued that since the official rate was raised, exporters might hold back exports expecting a still higher rate to come later.

different. The leftists were opposing the Plano Trienal, in part, because they attributed Instruction 239 to the plan. Dantas, in fact, claimed it was at least consistent with the plan. The right, however, was saying that the new instruction was a first sign that Dantas was abandoning the plan, with the implication that the plan ought to be preserved after all. The relevance of this episode for planning lies in the fact that the economic effects of the rule were not really clear. This is not to say that the political problem for the administration would have been solved with complete and accurate data. However, with a more complete understanding of the technical elements involved, the strategies of the actors could have been based on real instead of imagined issues.

Ceilings on credit and prices. The manufacturers and bankers liked controls no better than labor or the exporters. Limitations on both credit and prices, they said, were preventing them from investing in expanded facilities, and thus tended to prevent them from reaching the goals of the Plano Trienal in their sectors. The first industry to complain in these terms was steel, notably the great mixed-enterprise at Volta Redonda, the National Steel Company (CSN). Its prices had been pegged by the government at the existing level, just as a 20 per cent increase was about to be adopted by the company. Not only would this endanger financing of the enterprise, but since other wholly private steel companies were not affected by the price control, the effect was to subsidize the customers of CSN, it was said. The automobile industry, the largest consumer of steel, was likewise feeling itself injured by the credit restrictions of the Plano Trienal. Under the circumstances, therefore, they sought an audience with Dantas, and informed him that if the regulation was not changed, orders would fall by 70 per cent, and that production had already fallen by 30 per cent. Similarly Ford had released 300 employees, and Willys was planning to release 1,500.

Shortly thereafter, Dantas took the position that credit limits could be increased after all, because the estimates of the Plano

Trienal were not entirely accurate, and new information allowed a change of policy. SUMOC soon issued the necessary order. Furtado defended both the salary ceiling increase and the new credit ceilings as within the spirit of the Plano Trienal.

The plan of containment. As soon as the Plano Trienal was adopted in January, a plan of containment was drawn up limiting the various ministries and other governmental agencies to expenditures which were less than those which had been appropriated for the fiscal year. The purpose of this was to reduce total outlay, and remain within the debt limit, which was established at 300 billion cruzeiros in the Plano Trienal. After the first three months under the plan, Dantas announced that new economic trends allowed an increase in this limit to 316 billion cruzeiros. Part of this was attributable to the larger than expected collections from consumer taxes. Part of this increased income therefore could be used toward the salary increases but, in addition, part would be used to increase the amounts to be spent on health and education under the plan.

The question immediately arises, did these five "adjustments" represent a serious abandonment of the Plano Trienal? The question can hardly be answered in objective terms, because of the lack of any meaningful standard of measurement. It must be recalled that these five alleged breaches in the plan took place, or were about to take place, only three months after the plan "went into effect." At this point, President Goulart met with Dantas and Furtado to evaluate the results of the first three months under the plan. The reports of the meeting are contradictory. Reports attributed to sources close to the President alleged that he was considering modifying the plan since it had not achieved the desired results.[33] Official reports of the meeting, however, stated that the results were satisfactory, and that while inflation had not stopped, it was under control and would be less than during the previous year.[34] Such a statement was undoubtedly necessary for politi-

33. *Jornal do Brasil,* April 30, 1963.
34. *Ibid.,* May 1, 1963.

cal reasons. However, in realistic terms it is hard to believe that even the most perfect plan would achieve any such dramatic results in a short three-months period, especially while being bitterly fought from all sides. By the end of June, when both Dantas and Furtado left the cabinet, inflation of over 30 per cent was already recorded for the first half of the year. If this same rate continued, the total inflation for the year would be more than the previous year, rather than less as had been promised under the plan.

By now the wheel had turned full circle. The very voices which had begun by charging Furtado, and later Dantas, with statism were now condemning them and the Goulart administration for abandoning the Plano Trienal and the road to stability. They claimed that the planners were responding to political pressures while justifying their actions as adjusting the plan to new realities and finding "new trends" in the data.

DEATH OF THE PLANO TRIENAL

To recapitulate, by the end of January 1963 the new cabinet had been formed, and the new policies under the Plano Trienal had begun to be put into effect including limitation on salary increases, limitations on government spending, price ceilings, limitations on credit, elimination of certain government subsidies, and further devaluation of the cruzeiro. The attack which now developed against selected parts of the plan such as the 40 per cent limitation on salary increases for military and civil servants and the change in the exchange rate, stemmed from the very political sources upon which the Goulart administration itself rested. The "objective, rational, scientific" plan for the economic development of Brazil, it appeared, ran counter to important economic commitments. These were represented in the cabinet by Almino Afonso, Minister of Labor, and in the President's household by his brother-in-law, Deputado Leonel Brizzola, former governor of Rio Grande de Sul. Both privately and publicly these men and their associates kept the Dantas-Furtado policies under attack. When President Goulart gave a major address to the workers on Labor Day (May 1) their leaders organized parades with great banners carrying out the theme: "Down with the Plano Trienal!" This was, in part at least, in support of their 70 per cent wage increase demand. It was now becoming quite evident that Goulart would yield to these pressures.

It is instructive to note Furtado's interpretation of what had happened to this point. He notes that since Goulart initially had the political support of the left in Brazil, the Plano Trienal was intended to serve as a means of gaining support of the middle class for the administration. As soon as the plan was announced, Furtado's job was to meet with representatives of industry, banking, the labor unions, and the military in order to explain the need for planning in general and the Plano Trienal in particular. To him this was not only loyalty to Goulart and to his own plan, but was a part of a larger mission to "sell" the importance of planning techniques and institutions.

It was his failure to convince the bankers and industrialists of the merit of the plan that ultimately led to its demise, according to Furtado. As soon as it became apparent to Goulart that he was not getting support for the plan from these interests, he concluded that the bid for middle class support—including support of the middle-class-controlled press—had failed. Thereupon the critics of the plan from his own forces to the left realized that Goulart himself was becoming ambiguous as to the merits of the plan, and they took the opportunity to resort to the streets to oppose it in the May 1 rally. The plan now became more a liability than an asset to Goulart, and he allowed the campaign to "get" Dantas and Furtado to run its successful course.[35]

What happened next is not clear as to detail, but it is quite

35. Interview with Celso Furtado, May 7, 1965. See also Furtado's broader commentary on politics of planning in Brazil, "Political Obstacles to Economic Growth in Brazil," 41 *International Affairs* (April, 1965), 252-66.

clear as to result. Reports circulated that Dantas and Furtado gave President Goulart some sort of ultimatum: presumably that the attacks on the financial policies of the administration by sources close to the President would have to stop, or they would leave the government.[36] On all sides fear was expressed that the Plano Trienal might be abandoned or seriously modified. Both Dantas and Furtado, however, gave no public sign of disagreement with the President. In fact, they appeared to yield on the policies described above. They further emphasized that the plan itself was not rigid, but flexible; that it set forth only basic directions; that its projections were subject to constant change as new data came in; and that its means could change as long as the ends remained in view.[37]

Despite this effort to gloss over the breach, the end was already near. The press began to demand cabinet reform for the purpose of solidifying support behind the Plano Trienal and retaining the confidence of the United States and international investors.[38] Early in May, Goulart denied that he was considering any such move. By the end of June he had replaced every member of his cabinet.

The causes for the change, called "cabinet reform," are complex and go beyond the immediate concerns of the Plano Trienal. Goulart had just been through a severe crisis in the military forces with the contenders split along a right-left axis. The leftist forces in that struggle were the same which had been attacking the Plano Trienal during the crisis over financial policy. In addition, Goulart's major preoccupation was with agrarian reform, and he was not getting the cooperation in the Congress that he needed to advance this program. Being pushed and pulled in various directions, seeming to change his positions on vital matters with each change in the political wind, being violently attacked in the press for two-faced be-

36. Based upon a mass of press commentary and rumor; see the following: *Tribuna da Imprensa*, April 24, 1963; *Jornal do Brasil*, May 3, 1963; *Correio da Manhã*, May 1, 1963.

37. *Jornal do Brasil*, April 28, 30, 1963.

38. *Jornal do Brasil*, May 4, 5, 12, 18 and 31, 1963.

havior and vacillation, it is possible to explain his actions on
the basis that he felt it necessary to re-establish the fact—in his
own mind, at least—that he was the center of power. In any
event, after protracted negotiations, a completely new cabinet
was installed in office by the end of June. Gone were the leftists who had attacked the Plano Trienal. Gone were the planners. Gone were those who had remained neutral. At one
stroke, Goulart had solved his problem among the military
commanders, eliminated Dantas who was by now a liability,
and increased his own maneuverability by creating vacancies
in the cabinet.

The new question was, had Goulart thrown out the baby
with the bath? Throughout the period, he had professed himself in firm support of the general policies of the Plano Trienal.
Dantas had said, on leaving his post, that his policies would be
carried on without him by the new administration. Furtado
had taken his leave gracefully, announcing that his mission was
completed (presumably plan *making*) and that he would therefore return to his regular job at SUDENE. Now, he said, the
second phase of implementation would begin, once the long
awaited administrative reorganization could be completed.

A new factor in the situation was the appointment as Minister of Finance of the well known planner-statesman, Carvalho
Pinto. Carvalho Pinto was a professor of tax law, former judge,
Secretary of Finance for São Paulo under Jânio Quadros, and
successful governor succeeding Quadros in São Paulo. He was
highly respected and a political moderate. On assuming office,
Pinto said: "I am a man preoccupied with planning and planning will count in my administration."[39] Goulart implied,
rather indirectly, that the administration would continue under
the guidance of the Plano Trienal. The official line became
clearer when Carvalho Pinto said that the Plano Trienal would
be adapted to the present situation of the country, but that he
would not hesitate, if he judged it necessary, to modify the

39. *Jornal do Brasil*, June 21, 23, 1963.

financial policy previously laid down.[40] The political status of
the Plano Trienal had now clearly changed. Once the basic
policy guide of the government with the full support of the
President, the Minister of Finance, and the Minister Extraordinary for Planning, it was now a piece of technical work to
be applied when and as convenient, still without specific implementing machinery. The real question was not the future
of the Plano Trienal, all but interred. Rather, it was whether
the new government would create a new system of planning
and a new global plan.

The Plano Trienal had a shorter life than most of Brazil's
national plans—only five months. Yet its short life is no measure of its contribution. Much of it was resurrected in the next
plan. More than this, it was the first really professional plan
that Brazil ever had. A serious effort was made for a time to
put it into effect and to create for it real institutions of implementation. Unlike the previous "plans" of Brazil, it was more
than a paper document. Its failure teaches us much about the
problems of creating a real national planning system.

INTERNATIONAL PRESSURES

Events which have been discussed in the last two sections
are more completely explained on the basis of international
politics. It is obvious that some element which affected these
happenings is still missing if we consider the following chronology already described: (1) The Plano Trienal is created as
a technical document; (2) the administration accepts it
hurriedly, almost grasping as at a straw; (3) upon announce-
ment, the plan comes under immediate and vicious attack from
several quarters; (4) modifications are almost immediately
adopted on key points; (5) the planners defend the modification as consistent with the original plan; and (6) they are
immediately removed from the cabinet, and a new financial
policy is adopted by their successors. It is not too difficult to

40. *Jornal do Brasil*, June 24, 1963.

explain this sequence of events if one additional dimension is added—international pressures.

The question of international pressures on Brazilian policy itself is a political issue in the country. The question is, when does "foreign aid" become "pressure" or "interference"? The answer to this question varies with the political point of view of the respondent. Cutting away the emotionalism usually associated with this question, the plain fact is that foreign governments do not give aid except with certain conditions attached, to insure that some of that country's goals will be implemented along with those of Brazil. If the interests of the two countries involved overlap sufficiently, there is a basis for giving the "aid." In the nature of things, each country will attempt to maximize the attainment of its goals, yielding as little as possible to any conflicting goals of the other country.

Brazil has received various types of "aid" from several countries. A major portion of this has come from the United States over the years, particularly in the form of loans of various sorts and military assistance. In the post-World War II period, two new factors developed which are directly relevant to the story of the Plano Trienal. One of these is the growing program of aid for developing countries provided through United Nations sources; the other is the creation of the "Alliance for Progress" program as a joint activity of American states.[41] The Alliance was created in August of 1961 with the signing of the Charter of Punta del Este. In signing the charter, along with other members, Brazil agreed to create machinery for long-term development planning and to prepare such plans.

The fact that the "Alliance" was widely billed as a partnership, both in North America and South America, tended to blur the fact that what it really involved was a grantor-grantee relationship in which the grantor stipulated the conditions which the grantee must meet in order to get the money or other aid as the case might be. It is very easy to overemphasize this point. Once the aid was formally given and accepted,

41. See the account in Chapter 2.

a real partnership situation could and did develop, with success which varied from project to project. At the point of
giving the money, however, conditions were insisted on. This
gave real point to the criticism widely heard, especially from
the radical left, that the United States and the International
Monetary Fund were dictating Brazilian governmental policy.
While there could be no direct dictation of policy, there were
statements as to minimum conditions that had to be accepted
and implemented by the Brazilian government if it wanted the
aid in question. Aid did not have to be accepted, nor did it
have to be given. Yet the financial difficulty of the government
was so great by 1962 that there existed great temptation to
yield on some of the conditions in order to get the aid. This
temptation can very easily be described as "pressure."

In the case of the Plano Trienal, for the first time, there
seemed to be an opportunity to get substantial amounts of
foreign aid, particularly in the area of non-loan forms of assistance which previously had been available chiefly in the field
of military assistance. To oversimplify, it can be said that there
were two major conditions which were mutually understood
within the Alliance for Progress program, and implicitly recognized by the International Monetary Fund (in which the
United States government has a substantial influence). One of
these was the procedural requirement of the Punta del Este
charter that an over-all development plan of basic reforms had
to be prepared by governments seeking aid.[42] The presenta-

42. There was established in the Alliance a category of "emergency aid"
of grants and loans during the period before a plan would be completed.
Numerous projects were initiated under this heading. The distinction between
this and long-range aid was not widely understood, and confusion was created
as a result. In addition, the procedures which quickly developed for allocat-
ing this type of aid involved "requests" from Brazilian governments and private entities, which were submitted to authorities of the U.S. Agency for
International Development for approval or rejection. Unfortunately the procedures for granting long-range aid ultimately assumed much the same pattern. Procedures of a truly "partnership" nature would have involved granting of lump sum aid funds, and delegating other aid decisions to an
international body which would constitute the awarding agent. Some such
change in the structure of the Alliance was the chief issue involved in the

tion of such a plan served various purposes, but in particular the purpose of providing the information on which to judge conformity to the second criterion. The latter was an insistence on a stable economic policy. In Brazil this meant a strict anti-inflationary policy. This was the real condition for most forms of foreign aid. The reasons for this condition were eminently logical, and can be summarized under two chief headings: (1) control of inflation is necessary to insure that the sums of money spent actually produce the results for which they are intended, rather than being diluted by a rocketing price spiral; and (2) inflation must be controlled to insure political stability so that governments which receive the aid will continue to exist under conditions which make it possible to carry out development programs which are scheduled. There is an assumption here that economic and political instability are related.

While both of these consequences—stable economy and political stability—seem to outsiders to be obviously in the interest of Brazil or any other country, this conclusion is by no means accepted by all wings of Brazilian political thought with equal intensity. As in most developing nations, there are important groups whose great fight is to destroy a vested-interest-protecting stability in order to achieve basic goals of changing the existing social and economic order. Tolerance or need for stability varies from group to group of the politically active. The United States, seeking basic reforms in Brazil as much as Brazilians themselves, sees the process of reform as employing the relatively calm procedures of legislation and administration as they have developed in the United States in the last hundred years (in every area except race relations). It hopes those processes will be used by the countries receiving aid.

Brazilians, on the other hand, feel that the traditions of Western Europe and the United States, already highly developed in the economic sense, are not necessarily the best for

Kubitschek-Camargo assignment to make recommendations for revisions in the "Alliance."

Brazil. Specifically, there is a strong sentiment that the high value placed by U.S. economists on inflation-control conflicts with the even more desperate need for a continuing and ever-increasing rate of economic expansion. It has already been pointed out that such measures as price controls, credit controls, and exchange controls may serve as limits on the amount of expansion in the sectors affected, and that the problem is to achieve some compromise between two competing goals. The history of the Plano Trienal shows clearly that Brazil under Goulart placed a higher value on development than on the control of inflation, as compared with U.S. policy. This feeling proved to be so strong that important amounts of foreign aid were endangered by the Goulart administration in order to adhere to this national value judgment. We shall now review some of the chief incidents which support this conclusion.

Well before the Plano Trienal was completed, there were many signs of interest in its effect on obtaining foreign aid. The rumor was already out that San Tiago Dantas, not yet Minister of Finance, would undertake a mission to Washington to negotiate with American and international authorities on this subject. During the fall, the parliamentary cabinet was discussing the Calmon Plan, presented by the then Minister of Finance, which allegedly had been formulated under the influence of the International Monetary Fund (IMF). The leftist newspaper *Ultima Hora* asserted that the IMF had no place in the as yet undivulged Plano Trienal. *O Globo*, to the right, directly contradicted this, saying that Calmon's principles were copied directly in the plan.[43] On December 13, President Kennedy made statements to the press which were interpreted as questioning Brazil's economic stability and the future of its aid programs. His brother Robert, the Attorney General, hurried to Brazil for an unannounced purpose, presumably so that this "misimpression" could be directly corrected by President Goulart and planner Furtado.[44]

43. *Ultima Hora*, December 19, 1962; *O Globo*, December 28, 1962.
44. This event was described earlier in this chapter.

The most dramatic event during the fall of 1962 was a statement of the Minister of Labor, João Pinheiro Neto, who alleged that the IMF was exercising an economic dictatorship in Brazil, and that two of its chief agents were Roberto Campos, Ambassador to the United States, and Otávio Bulhões of the National Economic Development Bank (BNDE). This attack on two high officials of the government of which he was a part brought Neto's removal from office. The ironic nature of this development became clear only after the revolution of 1964 when these same two men became the ministers of planning and finance respectively, under the government of Castelo Branco.

As soon as the plan was released, Ambassador Campos reported that it was under study in Washington. Evidently it had arrived there on or before its publication date in Brazil. From this time forward speculation and rumors filled the press as to the reaction of the U.S. government to the plan. Interest immediately centered on Dantas' prospective trip to Washington. It became quite clear that now Brazil had an important stake in the outcome of the mission. Dantas himself said as much in a major statement on assuming the post of Minister of Finance.[45] A few days later a team from the IMF visited Furtado, reportedly collecting data for its routine annual report, it was carefully announced.

The plans for the crucial Dantas mission were announced at the end of January. First the U.S. Undersecretary of State for Economic Affairs would hold meetings with Dantas and others in Brazil. Then Ambassador Campos would pursue negotiations in Washington in order to insure that there was a sound prospect for success in definitive agreements. Only then would Dantas go to Washington, probably in March. This timing would also allow a little time to observe what steps toward implementing the Plano Trienal the Goulart administration would take.

By the time Dantas went to Washington, March 11, there

45. The text of his message is found in *Jornal do Brasil*, January 25, 1963.

were reports on all sides that the United States government was greatly impressed with both Dantas' competence and the energy with which he and the Goulart administration had set into motion the Plano Trienal. The tone of these reports is conveyed in a statement of Walter Lippman widely reprinted in Brazil:

If we study the agreement just worked out in Washington between the Brazilian Finance Minister Dantas and Mr. Bell who now manages foreign aid, we are bound to marvel at the political courage of the Goulart government. To end the inflation and to re-establish its international credit-worthiness, the Brazilian government has adopted a program which only a very strong government, strong in its hold on popular support, would dare to undertake. The Goulart government is going to raise tax collections by 25 percent. It has eliminated the subsidy of wheat, which had doubled the price of bread. It has eliminated the subsidy of petroleum products, which has raised the price of gasoline. It has increased commuter railroad fares five times over. It is cutting down the expansion of bank credit to a third of what it has been. It is freezing government employment and is trying to freeze government pay. It is an astonishing program. Yet it is said that the Goulart government, which is left of center, is strong enough to carry out the program. We must hope that it will be, and surely the Administration has been right in deciding to help it. For it would be hard to name any item in our whole global foreign aid program which, if it succeeds, will do so much good.[46]

The only things that marred the prospective negotiations with the U.S. government were the ever-critical voices of a few members of the U.S. Congress who hoped to use Brazil's need as the lever with which to gain complete restitution for American companies whose properties had been confiscated by Leonel Brizzola when he was governor of Rio Grande do Sul.

The favorable attitude of the U.S. government, however, was not matched by the IMF. Dantas reported that three major problems were causing difficulty. The IMF was insisting

46. From the *Washington Post*, March 28, 1963, reprinted in the *Brazilian Bulletin*, April 1, 1963.

on: (1) the containment of inflation within one year rather than three; (2) freeing the exchange rate from control; and (3) pegging salaries at existing levels.

When Dantas flew back to Brazil with U.S. Ambassador Gordon on March 27, he carried with him the agreement that the United States would supply about 400 million dollars in grants and loans of various sorts. This part of the mission had been a total success. Negotiations continued, however, with the IMF.

As a result, some but not all of the pressure to make the Brazilian inflation control program look good was removed. The United States agreed to supply an immediate total of 84 million dollars. The remainder, however, was conditioned on compliance with two major requirements: (1) implementation of the basic inflation-control policies of the Plano Trienal as listed in the agreement, (2) successful negotiation by June 1963 for credits of 100 million dollars from Japan and Western Europe. In addition to these requirements, an effort was to be made to obtain from the IMF credits for a refinancing of Brazil's foreign debt. With this in view, the IMF agreed to a deferral of the payments due it in March pending the sending of an IMF inspection team to Brazil.[47]

In view of the changes (which have been described above), in the policies foreseen in the Plano Trienal, any strict interpretation of the agreement would have cut off the more than 300 million dollars of U.S. aid not already paid to Brazil. In this fact, it is suggested, lies the key to the otherwise puzzling chronology of events listed at the end of the last chapter. The Plano Trienal had to be created in order to seek foreign aid. It had to be constructed on a technically competent and sincere basis to be convincing. Thus Furtado, the planner, and Dantas, the tactician, politician, and diplomat, were assigned the job. They were personally, fully, and sincerely committed

47. The text of the agreement is contained in an exchange of letters between Dantas and AID administrator Bell, dated March 25, 1963. It is reprinted in full in the *Brazilian Bulletin*, April 1, 1963.

to it. The President was committed as well, insofar as political pressures by which he felt himself bound permitted. Yielding in some degree to these pressures, it was still necessary to rationalize the changes as consistent with the plan. Furtado and Dantas cooperated in making these rationalizations in the interest of the plan, that is, in order to get the foreign cooperation essential to the success of the plan itself. They were kept in office, despite the increasingly severe pressures for cabinet reform. Many of these pressures were not directly related to the plan itself, such as the crisis in the military, and could not be disregarded indefinitely. Eventually it became clear that the negotiations with the IMF would not be successful, though there was still hope for the European credits. At this point, Dantas and Furtado became expendable.

It was in the circumstances described above that the much demanded new cabinet was formed. However, there was still concern about the interpretation of the agreement with the United States. It was necessary to continue to speak of the Plano Trienal and to have a Minister of Finance committed to a planning approach and to follow the "general lines of policy" of the previous minister. Carvalho Pinto was a man who met these qualifications. He was appointed Minister of Finance in the new cabinet and immediately announced a new financial policy. In essence, the new policy made explicit the trend already underway since early May: more emphasis on stimulating development, less on control of inflation.

The chief points of the new program included: (1) austere administration, (2) a "realistic" development policy, (3) *gradual* control of inflation, (4) banking reform, (5) tax reform, (6) selective credit policy to aid farming and promote social justice, (7) administrative reorganization, (8) elastic foreign exchange policy, (9) expansion of foreign trade, and (10) improvement of planning and the execution of planning. These points are more properly goals than policies; as goals they were also contained in the Plano Trienal. According to information supplied by officials of the Ministry of Finance, policies to be employed in seeking to achieve these goals would differ from those of the Plano Trienal in four ways: (1) the request for funds from the IMF would be dropped, rather than risk a probable refusal; (2) credit restrictions would be loosened; (3) more paper money would be issued; and (4) the compulsory loan attached to the pay raise would be "altered."[48]

It is difficult to assess the net effect of the international pressures. Certainly they accounted for a variety of political maneuvers, stratagems, and considerations of timing, as recounted above. It is possible that they may have accounted in some degree for the anti-inflationary policy written into the Plano Trienal and energetically launched by Minister Dantas. But they were not sufficient to alter the long-time directions of Brazilian policy to tolerate inflation and rely on economic growth to solve the problems of the country. It remained to be seen if the new cabinet could find a solution to Brazil's foreign debt problem other than the one suggested at this juncture by Leonel Brizzola and the radical left, simply to announce a unilateral moratorium on all foreign debts!

POLITICS V. PLANNING: GOULART AND THE REVOLUTION

With the virtual abandonment of the Plano Trienal the Ministry of Planning disappeared. On July 1 Carvalho Pinto took office as Minister of Finance in the new cabinet. Pinto was a former governor of São Paulo, noted for his successful planning in that state. The responsibility for planning now moved into the Ministry of Finance itself. Pinto could accomplish very little, however, in view of the inability of the government to enforce any effective financial controls. The administration lived from one economic crisis to another, announcing stop-gap regulations from time to time as immediate conditions seemed to warrant. The rate of inflation in-

48. *Brazil Herald*, July 3, 1963; *Jornal do Brasil*, July 5, 1963.

creased dramatically. Wages were rising rapidly along with prices, and Brazil found it impossible to obtain funds for scheduled foreign debt payments falling due.

Only in late October did Carvalho Pinto come out with anything resembling a financial program.[49] The new goals were the old goals, including reducing bugetary deficits, channeling investments into economic infrastructure, increasing tax collections, controlling inflation, and of course rescheduling foreign debts.

In the same month, an office for "coordination" of planning was created in the office of the President itself, headed by a well known economist and administrator, Diogo Gaspar. The purpose of this office was to collect project plans for public works from the various agencies of government and combine them into a list of capital projects—reverting to a much earlier planning approach. In terms of organization, the new situation was identical to that first employed by Jânio Quadros with planning residing in the Assessoria.

Rumors now began to circulate that Carvalho Pinto was seeking release from his position since his advice on fiscal policy was not being taken. Specifically, the government decided to authorize a "13th month salary"—like a Christmas bonus—to federal employees, and to tie salaries to the increasing cost of living index. These actions widened the breach in the inflation control effort.

In November Carvalho Pinto further detailed his program, apparently as a last effort to effect a semblance of financial stability. In December he resigned and his successor, Nei Galvão, a banker from Rio Grande do Sul, took his place in the cabinet. Galvão soon overturned some of Pinto's hold-the-line policies and announced his new program, which emphasized the renegotiation of foreign debts and the giving of preferential treatment to exporters as a means of acquiring foreign exchange.

49. *Correio de Manhã*, October 26, 1963; *Diário de Notícias*, October 25, 1963.

The new minister was no more successful than the last, however, and the financial affairs of Brazil continued to deteriorate as one crisis came upon the heels of the last. Additional controversial policies were initiated, including the establishment of a government monopoly on the import of petroleum. Minimum wages were increased by about 100 per cent (depending on the region of the country) by presidential decree on February 22, 1964. The alarming growth of unrest over price increases brought the establishment in February and March of a new system of price controls, initially on clothing, fabrics, shoes, and pharmaceuticals. These controls were to be rigidly enforced by severe police methods. Other new shifts in financial policy attempted both to keep incomes up and prices down, in an almost self-defeating circularity. Some of the Carvalho Pinto policies, such as the extension of a compulsory loan to the government by certain businesses, began to be reconsidered. By February, it became apparent that the government, perhaps in desperation, was about to take new and drastic measures.

It is not possible in this study to recount the intriguing story of the onset of the March Revolution. Yet the Revolution is so intimately tied with the failure to achieve the objectives of the Plano Trienal and with the course of planning subsequently, that it is impossible to disregard it entirely. It was apparent to any observer in February that a great change was brewing in Brazil. The following words were written in February, 1964, by Professor George Bemis, a USAID contract professor then living in Brazil:

In attempting to give an overall assessment as to the character of recent, present and anticipated governmental developments in Brazil at this point in time, there appears to be much evidence that events are approaching a major turning point. . . . It appears quite likely that the month of March may represent a basic transformation in strategy. Brazil in its reform movement may be at the end of what might be called a preliminary stage of exploration, orientation and organization and may be entering upon a more dynamic stage of combination, decision and action.[50]

Bemis was not referring to an imminent military takeover, but rather to the expected adoption of radical nationalist policies by the administration of President Goulart which was precisely the course of action which the military decided to prevent, as events soon proved. On March 13 Goulart held a mass meeting in central Rio de Janeiro which proved to be an act of committing the administration to the immediate and vigorous prosecution of a range of both well defined and poorly defined "basic reforms" before a crowd of 200,000 persons. Even more colorful than the usual Brazilian political extravaganza, the ceremonies were punctuated on three occasions by specific news releases. The first announced that the President had just signed the decree authorizing the expropriation of certain privately owned lands for the purpose of agrarian reform. The second announced the expropriation of all privately owned oil refineries. The third stated that the President would sign a strict rent control decree the following day. The last speaker of the evening was the President himself.

A wave of unrest immediately followed the March 13 meeting. The President was said to be infringing illegally on the powers of Congress, and there was talk of impeachment among well-known politicians. The match which finally ignited the Revolution was a direct attack on military discipline supported after the fact by the President himself. Two weeks after the March 13 meeting, a large group of sailors and marines mutinied as a result of their commanders' efforts to limit their political activities. The mutineers were taken into custody momentarily, but almost immediately amnestied by the President as a general strike was threatened in their behalf. The amnestied sailors and marines staged a noisy victory march, after which the President himself made a belligerent defense of the men

50. George W. Bemis (ed.), *From Crisis to Revolution* (International Public Administration Series No. 1) (Los Angeles: University of Southern California, 1964), p. 220.

in an address before a group of non-commissioned officers. This was Good Friday.

By Monday, following Easter Sunday, the revolution was planned and set in motion. It later developed that it had been in planning for some time, but the deadline was moved up as a result of the events of March. On March 30 Governor Magalhães Pinto of Minas Gerais issued a manifesto proclaiming the revolution and the establishment of a revolutionary capital at Juiz de Fora in his own state. Most of the key civil and military leaders of the country either joined the revolution immediately or proclaimed their adhesion within a matter of days. President Goulart fled the country, having been unsuccessful in getting support from any major military force. The event was virtually bloodless.

The revolution could have been posited on the explicit constitutional basis that its purpose was to restore the Constitution which had been breached by Goulart and his adherents. The Constitution itself provides for this kind of action by the armed forces, which are authorized to guarantee the "Constitutional powers, law, and public order."[51] In fact, something quite different was happening, which was directly relevent to planning.

The relation of the Revolution to economic planning and development is suggested in the revolutionary decree itself.[52] The *Ato Institucional* carefully states the constitutional theory in which it is based, namely, that there are two constituent powers: election and revolution. When the normal constitutional processes failed to remove a government which set out to "bolshevize" the country, the Revolution was employed to achieve this end. The powers of the Revolution are exercised directly by the Supreme Revolutionary Command (Commando Supremo da Revolução) consisting of the three commanders of army, navy, and air force. This Supreme Command does not

51. *Constitution of Brazil* (1946), Article 177.
52. *Ato Institucional*, published April 9, 1964. Since the revolutionary regime later issued a second *Ato Institucional*, the one to which we refer here is now designated *Ato* number one, and the later *Ato* number two.

have to act through Congress, Courts, or other instrumentali-
ties. The continuance of the Constitution of 1946 is simply an
act of the Supreme Command, which it can at any time modify.
The *Ato Institucional* (or any subsequent act) takes prece-
dence over the existing Constitution.

Students of Brazilian military intervention are accustomed
to the exercise of constituent power by the military; but they
had always found that the military intervenes to set affairs
back on the desired path, and then retires from the scene to
let the constitutional system operate on its own until the next
crisis might arise. This pattern was not repeated in the Revolution of 1964. In short, the Supreme Command views itself as
retaining authority to govern, while delegating most of this
authority to the regular governmental institutions including
the Congress and the President. That the Supreme Command
had not released control was not apparent immediately following the re-establishment of the Presidency and the Congress
shortly after the revolution took place.

Why did a new pattern occur with the 1964 revolution?
The manifest reason is clearly signaled in the *Ato Institucional*
itself. The reason for issuing the *Ato* is said to be, ". . . to
assure to the new government to be established the means
indispensable for the work of economic, financial, political, and
moral reconstruction of Brazil so as to be able to confront
directly and immediately the grave and urgent problems, on
which depend the restoration of internal order and the international prestige of our Fatherland."[53] While the 1946 Constitution was retained in most respects, the powers of the President were increased by the *Ato*, ". . . toward the end that he
can fulfill the mission of restoring economic and financial order
in Brazil and to take the urgent measures needed to drain the
communist infection, whose pus already had infiltrated not only
the top leadership of the Government but also its administrative branches."[54] Significantly, in both clauses, the restoration

53. *Ibid.*
54. *Ibid.*

of economic and financial order—that is development planning —is listed *before* the political objective of getting rid of the Communists in government. That this emphasis was no accident became certain only during the course of the succeeding year and a half.

To make economic development the major positive goal of the Revolution was to convert it from a mere change in government to a long-range governmental program in the sense of the Egyptian or Mexican Revolutions.[55] Accordingly, the formulation of the new set of development plans after the establishment of the new regime becomes of crucial importance. Until the end of the Goulart administration the development goals of Brazil had to be subordinated to the survival and enhancement drives of the regime in power. The Revolution from the outset proposed to subordinate the political contest to the requirements of development planning. At this point, this assertion must remain a hypothesis rather than a statement of fact. The ensuing pages will contain evidence relevant to this thesis.

POLITICS AND THE PROGRAM OF ACTION

The immediate creation of a new national plan after the revolution of March, 1964, dominated the subsequent course of politics. The plan itself and its organizational mechanisms have already been described in this study. Despite certain differences as compared with previous plans, the Program of Action (PAEG, Programa de Ação Econômica do Govêrno) affected key groups in the population in much the same fashion as had the Plano Trienal. What political factors, then, allowed PAEG to live and then to prosper while the Plano Trienal was done to death in its infancy?

We can consider each group that had attacked the Plano

55. It is for this reason that we shall continue to capitalize "revolution" in this study in order to distinguish the long range movement from the brief military coup which established it.

Trienal. In 1962 a highly organized and well financed radical nationalist left existed in Brazil. This group dissolved with the revolution. Some of its leaders had their political rights removed by the new government. A great many more disappeared during the first days of the revolution, including a majority of the hard core professional Communists. It was this precipitate abandonment of Goulart by his erstwhile political cohorts which made the military phase of the Revolution so easy.

While the activist leaders had disappeared, the followers remained in the military forces, the unions, and the governmental agencies. These were the groups where the rank and file were the most concerned about the policy for containing salary increases, which was a key part of PAEG. Continued demands were made that public salaries be raised. The administration repeatedly asserted it would *not* raise public salaries during 1965. As the year wore on, however, a study group was appointed to recommend necessary salary increases. Following its recommendations, the administration announced increases in three stages, beginning January 1, 1966. A reported movement among army colonels to fight the salary policy of PAEG was officially denied. Whatever unrest existed among civil and military personnel produced no effect on government policy.

The case for an increase in the minimum wage was argued persuasively by the representatives of labor.[56] They argued that labor was itself a major resource for development which must not be depleted in value. The general principle of tying wages to the rate of inflation was strongly advocated. No efforts were made to take the case to the streets, however, and the government did not yield.

The real key to the acceptance of any plan in Brazil is the

56. See especially the statement of labor's representative on CONSPLAN, Salomão Vieira Pamplona, in Conselho Consultivo do Planejamento, *O Debate do Programa de Ação* (Rio de Janeiro: Secretária Executivo do Conselho Consultivo do Planejamento, Ministério do Planejamento e Coordenação Econômica, 1965), pp. 115-120.

business community. Celso Furtado's failure to "sell" the São Paulo industrialists and the Rio bankers was the signal to the nationalist left to give it the *coup de grâce*. Those who want easy credit like the PAEG no better than the Plano Trienal, due to its tight credit restrictions. The National Confederation of Industry condemned the plan in March of 1965, despite reports that some key industrialists favored the plan. Other businessmen, however, were more favorable. Exporters tended to approve it since it sought to stimulate exports. The government proposed a tax exemption scheme for companies holding the line on prices. This measure elicited support, especially from retailers. As a net result, business was split on the plan and realized the benefit in holding the line on wages.

During 1965 and 1966 it was becoming increasingly apparent that the Revolution's candidate for president, to succeed Castelo Branco on March 15, 1967, was the Minister of War, General Costa e Silva. In May, 1966, Costa e Silva gave a speech making general statements about his views on government policy. This was greeted with considerable enthusiasm by the National Confederation of Industry whose spokesman interpreted the remarks to mean that the new president—none doubted that he would be duly elected—would continue inflation control at a slower pace, employ means toward the old goals more favorable to industry, and consult with industry on both planning and execution of government policies. The stance of Costa e Silva tended to calm the opposition of the business community, insofar as it existed.

The Program of Action was subjected to the most severe attack from the partisan politicians who had survived the purge and remained in opposition to the revolutionary regime. The perennial critic of the government, Carlos Lacerda, launched a major statement on TV during May, 1965.[57] Lacerda took a position reminiscent of Hayek, that comprehensive planning is inconsistent with a democratic society. The state should be less, not more, active in the economy. Economic policy should

57. *Jornal do Brasil*, May 19, 1965.

rest on opportunism, though some measures to stimulate economic growth might be undertaken by government. His chief
criticism, however, was the most common one heard throughout Brazil—that the PAEG had not worked. He cited failure
to curb inflation, and the rise in unemployment, the unfavor-
able balance of payments and the budget deficit. A few days
later Campos answered Lacerda in a major TV address, noting
the literary and political skill which went into the Lacerda
statement but attacking Lacerda point by point on economic
grounds. In July the National Economic Council approved the
plan. Lacerda soon became less active in politics, but the criticism he launched continued. The second Institutional Act had
reduced the political parties to two. Of these the opposition
party, the MDB, attacked not so much the PAEG as such, but
rather the behavior of the Planning Minister himself in the
details of execution of the plan. He was charged in the Congress with misuse of the funds of FINEP by favoring foreign
consulting firms over Brazilian firms in the studies supported
by this fund. To the renewed charge of *entreguismo* (selling
out to foreigners) was added the charge that Campos had con-
cealed information from the Congress and even falsified information. An investigation by Congress was demanded, but the
vote was lost in the lower house of Congress by 101 to 16.[58]

The most serious attack on the PAEG came from the
economists, though they differed among themselves as to what
the Brazilian economy was really like.[59] The most virulent and
tireless critic was a member of CONSPLAN, Professor Antônio
Dias Leite. He affirmed that PAEG was not properly made,
since there had not been democratic consultation with
groups concerned outside the government. CONSPLAN, which
was supposedly to perform this function, had not worked, and
there was not enough real consultation. Secondly, he held that
because the plan did not conform to the reality of Brazilian
economics (as he viewed this reality), it had not worked.

58. *Jornal do Brasil*, June 16 and 17, 1966.
59. *O Debate do Programa de Ação*.

Specifically, inflation had not been controlled as much as the plan had predicted, economic growth had been less than predicted, and labor had not participated sufficiently in the benefits of the economy.

During the extended debate over these points Leite used the press as a forum and Campos, Bulhões, and Branco used TV and other public forums to make the defense. The most heated exchanges occurred during the summer of 1966. During this time considerable controversy existed over what the data actually was. The lack of a really accurate index of inflation and growth contributed much to becloud the issue. When it was all over, however, the government had admitted that the PAEG's aspirations had not been completely fulfilled in terms of inflation control and growth, but that substantial progress had been made. Even the sharpest critic would have to admit that the indicators were slowly becoming more favorable. While the spokesmen for industry had been saying that the program represented a "shock treatment" which should be reduced in intensity, Professor Leite was saying that measures attempted had not produced results fast enough. The natural defense was to note that economic renovation takes time, and that to achieve the goals immediately would in fact be a "shock treatment" which the country could not stand.

As the debate continued, the press, at times critical of economic policies, seemed to mellow. The moderate *Jornal do Brasil* editorialized that a country psychologically prepared to accept the sacrifices inherent in development will secure development; that during previous administrations development had been accompanied by gross corruption, while this was not true of the present regime; that while the *Jornal* did not subscribe to the monetarist position (ascribed to Campos), it did feel that the PAEG represented an appropriate compromise among the available alternatives.[60]

The government's spokesmen, not the least eloquent of whom was the President himself, blanketed the country with

60. *Jornal do Brasil*, May 27, May 29, June 7, 8, July 3, 1966.

explanations of the policies in force. A major document was issued late in June in defense of the PAEG.[61] New figures were released suggesting that the *real* income of workers in São Paulo had increased by 8 per cent instead of decreasing as Professor Leite had alleged. This data was based on a sample survey from a universe of 890,000 workers in São Paulo—one of the earliest uses of this technique for public relations purposes by the government of Brazil. The creation of the funds described above was emphasized. Figures of the Getúlio Vargas Foundation just available showed that inflation for January to May of 1966 was 21 per cent in contrast to 27.3 per cent during the same period of the previous year (despite an increased rate of inflation for food). The following figures for growth were released:

PER CENT AND PER CAPITA INCREASE IN REAL
DOMESTIC PRODUCT
1962-1965

Year	Per Cent Increase in Real Domestic Product	Per Capita Increase in Real Domestic Product
1962	5.4	2.2
1963	1.6	−1.8
1964	3.4	0.3
1965 (est.)	5.0 to 5.5	1.7 to 2.2

Source: *Folha de São Paulo*, June 25, 1966.

During this period, as the government was pointing to these and other signs of progress under the plan, it began seriously to tool up for creation of the ten-year plan. On March 21, 1966, Castelo Branco installed the work groups for the new plan before a meeting of CONSPLAN. He said that one purpose of the plan was to prevent the periodic strangulation of the planning process which had always resulted from changes in government. He said the new plan would be more efficient than previous plans, it would be used to give all groups in the population a consciousness of national goals. The PAEG had

61. *Folha de São Paulo*, June 25, 1966; and *Diário de Notícias*, June 26, 1966.

diagnosed the ills of the country, he went on, but the ten-year plan would now attempt to cure them.

The work groups were intended to coordinate all governmental levels as well as private activity. They included groups on: general planning, agriculture, social development, industry, infrastructure, regional planning, and macroeconomics. The press generally approved the idea of a ten-year plan, noting that it could be the basis for the new administration of Costa e Silva when he came to office. By June the work groups were beginning to make their reports. On June 25, CONSPLAN met to discuss the ten-year plan being created (Professor Leite did not attend the meeting). On this occasion it was announced that all the structural reforms of the PAEG had now been installed. The government appeared to have moved well along the road toward consultation, and had striven to create a more realistic and positive image of the planning approach to economic development in Brazil. At this writing it would appear that planning as an institution had grown stronger during the Castelo Branco government. It had received the firm support of the President. Whether the controls imposed by Campos had made him so unpopular that with the advent of the new regime in 1967 he would be expendable was not yet clear. He had solid accomplishment to his credit in addition to controlling inflation and promoting economic growth. He had reorganized the economic machinery of the government. He had converted a budget deficit into a surplus. The balance of payments was now positive instead of negative. Foreign aid was again beginning to flow more freely.

The impression that planning was the foundation stone of the Revolution is reinforced when we go back to trace the political events which are the context of the planning developments just recited. The Castelo Branco government regarded political reforms as part and parcel of the over-all recovery of Brazil under the Revolution. That is, political stability and control were viewed as basic to economic recovery. The political opposition, notably in the PSD and PTB parties, needed to test their strength. The period of summary removal of civil rights had ended with the expiration of the original decree in October, 1964. The question was, would there be a return to politics as usual?

In the Congress the Revolution had been well served with the enactment of a host of reform measures. The first electoral test was the São Paulo mayoralty election. Would it be held as scheduled for March, 1965? The military leaders were split on the desirability of permitting the election to occur. Castelo Branco tipped the balance in favor, however. The election proved reassuring. The victory was won by a general, though his opponent had the support of Governor Adhemar de Barros, who was later stripped of his political rights. The Revolution itself was not an issue in the election.

With this peaceful example before the regime, Castelo Branco immediately announced that the elections for governor in eleven states would be held on schedule on October 3, 1965. There was no doubt that the state elections would constitute a test of the revolutionary program at the polls. Opposition leaders now set about procuring candidates who would challenge the Revolution.

The next seven months proved to be a crucial watershed in Brazilian politics. They determined whether the Revolution would submit itself to the requirements of democratic politics in electoral and congressional arenas, or whether it would persist in its politico-economic program regardless of Congress, courts, and electorate. During the period clues were given by the regime time and again. As early as February 14 Castelo Branco had asserted publicly that the Revolution was "definitive and irreversible."[62] This theme was repeated and embroidered constantly during the next months by Branco, and significantly by Minister of War Costa e Silva. The Minister became embroiled in a dispute with the Judiciary—still a stronghold of Goulart appointees—over civil and military juris-

62. *Boletim Informativo* (Washington: Brazilian Embassy, February 15, 1965).

diction. The Supreme Court was telling the generals to go back to the barracks. Costa e Silva assured the court that the military would not stray from its duty to the "supreme" ideals of the Revolution.

When fears were expressed that the statements of the regime might mean the October elections would be voided, Costa e Silva assured the country that the winners *would* be inaugurated, whomever they might be. Then he added, the armed forces would not permit any threat to the institutions of this Revolution from any source.[63] In August the President asserted that the government would not permit the use of the elections to destroy national "tranquility"—especially by "counter-revolutionaries."[64]

The provocation for statements of these kinds was the candidacy of certain politicians regarded as strongly anti-Revolution. Costa e Silva was constrained to say—on the same day that the President spoke: "The Army repudiates candidacies imposed by communizing and anti-revolutionary forces which are utilized by corrupt and subversive elements."[65] The ministers of navy and air force made similarly strong statements backing up the President and the Minister of War.

Within days the candidate of the Brazilian Labor Party for governor of Guanabara (Rio de Janeiro) was removed from eligibility by the Regional Electoral Court on the technical grounds of lack of residence requirements. Residence had only recently been required by a new law sponsored by the Revolution. The candidate, General Lott, lived a few miles outside the state. Early the next month Paes de Almeida, the anti-Revolution candidate in Minas Gerais, was similarly withdrawn from the election by the Supreme Electoral Court (overturning a previous ruling by the Regional Court in Minas Gerais). With the election a few weeks off, both candidates were replaced with persons, possibly less objectionable, but also tending to oppose the Revolution.

63. *Boletim Informativo*, April 29, 1965.
64. *Boletim Informativo*, August 9, 1965.
65. *Ibid.*

As the election approached, frenzied activity took place among revolutionary leaders in an effort to create a solid front as between the various civilian and military leaders. There was apparently growing opposition to the regime stirred especially by the onset of elections. A proposed meeting of all "revolutionary" leaders was never held. Rather, individual conferences with the President took place. Juracy Magalhães, the ambassador to Washington, was recalled to "coordinate" the political affairs of the Revolution. Within a month the decisions which presumably were made during these sessions were announced. In the meantime, ever-stronger statements were made, until election day, that the regime would prevent counter-revolutionary action by military force if necessary.

The election was quiet, but proved a disaster for the Revolution. In the key states of Guanabara and Minas Gerais the anti-Revolutionary candidates won easily. The same happened in some of the other eleven states. No more than one or two of the eleven governors elected had any clear identification with the Revolution.

The President now conferred with his military ministers. The decisions previously arrived at, and perhaps new decisions, were now made explicit. A series of constitutional reforms to further strengthen the regime would be proposed to Congress, but the governors-elect *would* be permitted to assume office. General Costa e Silva made it clear that Castelo Branco had insisted on this last point. The reforms included a variety of new powers, plus election of the President of Brazil by Congress instead of popular election.

Congress appears to have stiffened its position as a reflection of the October 3 election. Castelo Branco sent the reforms to Congress October 13. In a few days it became clear that Congress might not accede. The regime now kept its long series of promises. Just before Congress was about to vote, on the morning of October 26, Castelo Branco went on the air in a national television hookup. He announced that the Revolution must do what is necessary to consolidate the political, economic, and financial order. After pointing out that the Revolution legitimates itself by itself, he decreed a new Institutional Act Number Two; on the grounds that, ". . . the country needs tranquility in order to secure its national recuperation, its development, and the well-being of its people."[66] The next day the President in a major speech expanded fully on the theme.

The new constitutional instrument provided for:

1. Constitutional amendments at the proposal of the Senate, Chamber of Deputies *or* of the President, and ratification by absolute majority in the Chamber and the Senate.
2. Legislative initiative on financial matters in the Chamber of Deputies *or* by the President.
3. Increase in size of the Supreme Military Court to 15 Justices; and of the Federal Supreme Court to 16 Justices (an increase of 5).
4. The President is empowered to decree a state of siege for up to 180 days, and to suspend stated civil rights during this time.
5. With the advice of the National Security Council, the President is empowered to suspend political rights, for a ten-year period, and to remove from office officials of federal, state, or municipal governments (thus restoring the temporary power exercised under the first Institutional Act).
6. Existing political parties are terminated. New ones can be formed, with sufficient support in the Congress, under the terms of a law already enacted on July 15, 1965 (Law 4.440).
7. The next President of Brazil to be elected by the Congress on a date set by the President, but no later than October 3, 1966, the incumbent being ineligible to succeed himself.
8. The act itself is capable of being modified or added to at any time by the President through a "complementary act" (ato complementar). During the Vargas regime, these were known as "decree-laws."[67]

66. *Boletim Especial* (Washington: Embaixada do Brasil, October 27, 1965).
67. Up to January, 1967, such acts had been issued in a steady stream to a number of 31. They continued to detail the newly forming formal political structure.

Reaction to the new assumption of power was anything but violent. Of the press, only the conservative *Correio da Manhã* and the leftist *Ultima Hora* editorialized against it. Campos asserted that the new Act would contribute decisively to implementation of the Program of Action. As if to confirm this assertion the Rio stock market responded to the Act by an upsurge of transactions and a stabilization of prices.

One complementary act followed another during the next months. The President constantly replayed the theme that the new powers were necessary for tranquility, recovery, and development. He noted the accumulation of foreign exchange, a 1965 growth rate of 5 to 6 per cent, the decreasing emissions of paper money, and the prospect of complete monetary stabilization in 1966.[68]

These events clearly underline several points of contrast between the politics of the Plano Trienal and of the Program of Action. The same interests opposed both plans for the same reasons. The Branco regime, however, staked its life on firm adherence to its program and made this clear by constant repetition. The military leadership was solidly behind the President on the program, unlike the case of the previous regime which had never won the support of the military. The President and the Ministers of Planning and Finance acted as a team, and probably as a result of their long records of public service, were more effective in winning over much of the business community. The big difference, however, was one of strategy. The Goulart regime employed its plan as a political tool. The Castro Branco government made the plan for economic recovery and development its prime goal which justified the political reforms undertaken as means to achieve that goal. Which government *really* was most concerned with basic social reform is a moot point. Goulart set out to change the structure of society—if only as a means of acquiring powers. He failed in both. The revolutionary government merely sought tranquillity and economic development. That this path

68. *Boletim Especial*, November 12, 1965.

might produce basic social reform is a possibility which cannot be evaluated at this writing.

BRAZILIAN PLANNING AND THE POLITICAL SYSTEM

The political "system" of Brazil is characterized by a great
variety of highly politicized elements; but these elements are
not structured into a relatively permanent pattern. Both physical and cultural diversity are extreme in Brazil. The range
between primitive subsistence patterns and a highly industrialized civilization is also extreme. Add to these features promoting diversity a federal political constitution, and it is not
difficult to understand why Brazil does not have political institutions which can efficiently perform the function of aggregat-
ing diverse interests.

The political elements include interest groups, political
parties, bureaucratic clects, family groups, and regional groups.
Each of these has its own dominant personalistic leader. Each
avoids any permanent alliance which would dilute the primary
loyalty. A consequence of this basic political situation is an
inability of the "system" to produce dominant political support
behind any one national policy or leader through the mechanisms of the democratic process of elections and related be-
haviors as envisaged in the Brazilian Constitution. Since the
democratic impulse is strong in Brazilian culture, the formal
political institutions exist. Presidents and Congresses are
elected. A large bureaucracy occupies governmental offices.
But in reality nothing glues the system together.

The president is normally the most powerful political figure
in Brazil, yet he must spend virtually all of his time, energy,
and influence on the single job of trying to assemble the power
to govern. He must exploit the full patronage of his office to
"buy" the support of the leaders of other political elements.
There is no basis for a program, for even program must be
bargained away in order to remain in office. Program is totally
subordinated to factional competition. Most presidents have

not even succeeded in remaining in office to fill out their term, to say nothing of conducting a program. Vargas was removed twice. The Populist leader, Jânio Quadros, with overwhelming electoral support, only lasted seven months. Goulart did not succeed in filling out Quadros' term of office. Only Kubitschek was elected to serve a full term in recent years (being inaugurated only by the narrowest of political margins). The fate of Kubitschek, however, seems to prove the point. He was stripped of his political rights and forced into exile by a later government on the grounds of actions he took while in office which were the essential means of maintaining his political position.

The relevance of this to planning is quite clear. The one political focus in Brazilian politics is the presidency, and any "plan" which he may sponsor is no more than his own personal commitment. Mechanisms for creating truly national political goals do not exist. However valid the plans of the professional planners, their force depends on the political force of the president, who has very little to spare. A formal central planning institution is meaningless except as an adjunct of the presidency. It is true that "development" is a national goal in Brazil, at least in the literate sectors of the population. Yet no consensus has been achieved on the means toward this end.

If it is impossible to have a central plan in a real sense due to political fragmentation, might it yet be possible to administer such a plan if it could be achieved? What is the potential of the bureaucracy to remain neutral in the political struggle, and carry out a politically neutral, that is technical, plan? The fate of each successive plan gives us a clue to this. The bureaucracy is a façade within which the same fragmentation and diversity of political allegiance exists as within the rest of the political system. The struggles over establishment of a central planning and implementing agency with real teeth show the threat to established vested interests which any implementing agency would have. Politics was deeply involved in the decision on planning machinery.

Even if a central control agency should somehow be created, the ability of the bureaucracy to administer any new planning programs is subject to question. Even the traditional housekeeping functions of law and order, tax collection, customs collection, and postal service are subject to the worst kind of administrative lapses. The truth is, the majority of the Brazilian bureaucrats do not administer programs. They occupy positions of privilege. Achievement is not an objective, but promotion is. Persons who enter the bureaucracy with the motive of public service are constantly frustrated in trying to do their job, normally by their superiors.

In this kind of a bureaucracy—really a welfare and patronage payroll—the capacity for positive administration simply does not exist. Plans cannot be implemented if they require interagency cooperation and coordination.

All of the generalizations just made must be qualified in one important respect. The military forces *do* provide a stable institution with a capacity for performance. As an aggregator of interests, however, the military has never been effective, since its political participation has always been sporadic. The revolution of 1964 seems, in short perspective, to be a dividing point in Brazilian politics. The military has become a permanent, full-time participant during the past two years. The significance of the PAEG is precisely that it *is* the program of the Revolution. The Revolution is justified on the grounds of the importance of the regime's economic program. The role of planning has been reversed. That is, planning was formerly one of the political tools of an administration, however sincere the planners themselves, as technicians, may have been. Under the Revolution, the political activity of the regime has been turned to the service of the plan. The seriousness of this change only became clear in October of 1965 when the Revolution found it necessary to add greatly to its self-assumed powers in order to carry out its program. Political parties were dissolved, and an effort is presently being made to construct a new party system that will serve the aggregative function which the old one did not. With the creation of only two parties, a preponderance of active politicians flocked to ARENA, the party of the Revolution, from every political direction except the radical left. The opposition, MDB, remained small, demoralized, and divided. Its adherents from the extreme left and the extreme right did not make easy bedfellows. Its most crippling aspect is the lack of certainty as to the degree of freedom it will be allowed by the Revolution. Subversion against the regime had become a rather broad concept by 1966. Even Lacerda had become, through choice, politically quiescent. The most prominent potential presidential opponents of the revolution had been eliminated through deprivation of their political rights, including both Juscelino Kubitschek and the Governor of São Paulo, Adhemar de Barros. The MDB felt so impotent that it left Costa e Silva unopposed in the election for President on October 3, 1966. On this occasion Costa e Silva was elected by Congress as expected. The Revolution had so carefully constructed the new electoral arrangements, and had so judiciously used its powers of intervention in state and local government and of withdrawing political rights, that the continuity of the Revolution seemed inevitable.

To the charge that this course was dictatorship, the answer was that it would take until March 15, 1967, to restore Brazil to political and economic health. This was the date set for the inauguration of Costa e Silva. A radical right existed in the country and within the military which felt that the period of rule by fiat should be extended for several years. During the last half of 1966 a new constitution was in the making, presumably to return the country to a constitutional system with the beginning of the new presidency.

While this restructuring of the political system is being attempted, the actual work of "planning" goes on in much the same fashion as before. We are in a position to evaluate the Friedman–Riggs expectations as to the style of planning which the Brazilian system should produce. Their formulations suggest for Brazil: (1) a high level of governmental involvement, (2) the development of formal central planning institutions which perform their manifest functions with only limited success, (3) imperfect utilization of available planning capabilities, (4) short-range and focused planning rather than comprehensive planning, (5) a low level of interagency coordination, (6) the use of noncoercive means, and (7) polynormativism leading to vagueness of goals. This result is seen as characteristic of prismatic administration (Riggs) in a society which is making the transition to a modern economy (Friedman) and which is a reconciliation system rather than a mobilization system or an autocracy.

It is abundantly clear that all of these expectations are apt with respect to Brazil up to 1964. The level of governmental involvement has continued to increase, however ineffective it may have been. The central planning institution has little affected the course of development, though it produced planning documentation. Planning resources were wasted in that much fine research has been done without equivalent performance by the bureaucratic implementers. In addition, the planners tended to move up into political and dangerous positions, thus prejudicing their professional utility. Short-range and focused planning has been the rule, within the rough guidelines set forth in three- to five-year plans. Interagency coordination has been notoriously absent. Despite the existence of proper plans, Brazil has been bedeviled by vagueness of goals, specifically on the question of structural reforms. The Goulart government wanted to change the institutional structure, especially in the area of agrarian reform. The Branco regime has not sought rapid agrarian reform, but has moved very quickly to reform political institutions. It is difficult to say that noncoercive means have been used. Goulart tried expropriation, and the present government uses compulsory loans and similar devices.

The political problem of Brazilian planning may be summarized as follows. Planners have attempted to employ the concepts of the classical, rationalistic bureaucracy with its hierarchy of authority, its achievement orientation, and its emphasis on trained professionalism. Central planning has been attempted as the way of speeding development. The failures of planning are due to the fact that the classical bureaucracy does not exist in Brazil. No system of central planning with a high level of government involvement can be effective unless there is a bureaucracy subject to central control. Through this bureaucracy, controls over the economy can be established.

It has been the strong hand of the Brazilian military, which *is* a hierarchically responsible entity (despite the breaches of hierarchy during the Goulart regime), that has made the PAEG productive to a degree. The Congress has been encouraged by the military to enact necessary measures. Others are issued by presidential decree. The austerity which the PAEG has required of the country *did* produce the reaction which was produced by the Plano Trienal. The political expression of this reaction, however, has been neutralized completely by the regime through the Institutional Acts and Complementary Acts. Whether central planning can become effective under the new conditions depends on whether the military can and will produce successful changes in the political and administrative structure. If the military-based regime can move on from political reconstruction to creation of some semblance of the Weberian bureaucracy in the sense of initiatives at the center controlling outcomes at the periphery, the model of planning being attempted in Brazil could prove effective. Whether this will occur cannot yet be seen. In the meantime an alternative to the central planning approach exists, and will be discussed in the next chapter.

6

PLANNING IN AN UNSTABLE
POLITICAL SYSTEM

There is a sense in which the concepts "planning" and "political system" are antithetical. If we direct our attention to empirically derived descriptions or models of the political system we see an interlocking set of parts and processes. We conceive of the actors in the system as engaging in activity calculated to achieve their goals. Various demands are made on the system, various accommodations are made among the actors, and certain outputs occur. The strivings to change system outputs or to maintain existing output patterns is an endless activity known as politics. If the system is a democratic one, however we wish to define this quality, the outputs of the system are also "democratic," that is, correct. The individual actors may plan their own strategies very carefully, but *system* outputs properly flow from the free play of the political marketplace. The play of the actors can be purely selfish so long as they stay within the rules which bound the particular system.

If the political system in question is a nation, what possible role could planning play? Would not planning interfere with "free politics?" The answer to this question is not a simple one. If we may assume that the actors, operating within the rules, achieve consensus on goals, there is a role for planning since this is a way to bring expertise to bear on complex problems. That is, the actors know what they want, but the planners know best how to get it. If, on the other hand, we assume that the actors cannot achieve consensus on goals, or on the essential means for achieving goals, there is no role for planners in the political system *except* to become actors and enter the game. This is what Brazilian planners have been virtually forced to do. Both Furtado and Campos have entered the

political arena. Both created the one central plan—from the
same stream of ideas, but in differing political circumstances—
and then set out as implementer to make it work. The presidents
served to bring political power to the support of the plan as did
Kubitschek and Branco. Goulart was unable to do this and
planning dissolved. Both Furtado and Campos are, in Robert
Friedman's words, "the Great Man writing the Plan."[1] The
plan, he continues, is foredoomed to failure because it represents nothing but their own private ideas about how things
ought to be. Furtado failed as an implementer. Campos has
been more fortunate in two respects. He has had the full support
of a military-based regime. Secondly, he has moved in a direction away from the Great Man concept. That is, he has increasingly encouraged a broader participation in plan-making
as the incipient procedures of the ten-year plan indicate. This
broader participation, however, may require an increased sophistication about planning both within the bureaucracy and
in regional and local governmental agencies. The natural outcome of such a development would be the development of a
national consensus on both goals and means.

    These considerations raise the question whether it is possi-
ble to institutionalize planning, especially central national
planning, in an unstable political system—one with a high level
of dissensus, and one in which it is the rules of the system
themselves that are in question. What does the Brazilian case
tell us about this?

    We know the manifest function of planning is to produce
change in the direction of "economic development." This is as
true in Brazil as in the rest of the developing world. What is
the Brazilian theory of how planning is expected to produce
more rapid economic development? There are two elements.
First, it is held that the proper allocation of economic resources
will speed economic development. Second, it is held that the
proper allocation of resources can be achieved through the use
of appropriate governmental policies as administered by the

1. Letter to the author, April 26, 1966.

bureaucracy. The great bulk of what has been said in this study is evidence of reliance on these two notions.

The planner, in Brazil, is the economist—the expert. In the early stages of planning engineers were used, but for the past fifteen years the people who have made plans have been economists up to and including the Minister of Planning. With the aid of commissions of experts, economists have increasingly based their plans on the performance of the Brazilian economy. "The plan" has been an economically comprehensive effort to alter economic behavior to improve over-all economic structure. The role of the planner has been to advise the political authorities what remedies to apply at any given time.

The second assumption—that planning decisions will be implemented by the bureaucracy—is intimately related to the first. The Brazilian experience clearly shows the growth of the idea of a permanent central planning staff at the summit of the bureaucracy. During the Goulart regime this staff became a ministry and plans were made to convert it into a control organ. During the Branco regime such plans were revived in somewhat different form and the first steps were taken to make the planning ministry an actual organ of coordination and control. This approach to planning organizations stems from the Weberian ideal type of rational, professional bureaucracy, and from the scientific management ideas of Frederick W. Taylor with his "one best way." The planning experience of the post-Vargas era mirrors the movement toward administrative centralization of the Vargas regime through the mechanism of the DASP. The relation between the two is emphasized in that the DASP was the home of the early Brazilian plans.

The reality is that the Brazilian bureaucracy resembles the Weberian ideal type only on paper. In this respect Brazil seems to conform to the situation in many transitional countries. Fred Riggs accounts for this type of bureaucracy in his theory of prismatic society. In short, Brazil suffered from the same experience with central planning that has become common elsewhere. An ideal type more or less suitable for the developed Western nations was used as the theoretical basis for planning organization and administration. This is not the place to argue the point, but the Western nations themselves are hardly examples of central planning according to the Weberian ideal. The most exhaustive study of development planning to date underlines the irrelevance of planning (in our formal sense of the term) to development. Waterston says, ". . . when a country's leaders in a *stable* government are strongly devoted to development, inadequacies of the particular form of planning used—or even the lack of any formal planning—will not seriously impede the country's development. Conversely, in the absence of political commitment or stability, the most advanced form of planning will not make a significant contribution toward a country's development."[2]

We are forced, then, to consider the role of planning in the total political system.

PLANNING AND THE ELITES: THE FUNCTIONS OF PLANNING

The style of Brazilian planning has varied as between recent Brazilian regimes, but one factor is strikingly constant: the *amount* of governmental participation in the economy, in the name of planning for development, has increased with every recent administration. Both governmental controls of private enterprise and direct participation through public or mixed corporations have increased. To what may we attribute this increased governmental activity, whether by the regimes of right or left? Certainly the answer is not to be found in the strong institutionalization of the planning process in a centralized bureaucracy. Rather we may look to the centers of political power. Economic development in Brazil has meant industrialization. The goals of the traditional landed elite, the new industrial elite, and the omnipresent military elite were not in

2. Albert Waterston, *Development Planning: Lessons of Experience* (Baltimore: Johns Hopkins Press, 1965), p. 6. Emphasis added.

conflict over industrialization and over the planning which sought to control it. In many countries the industrial and agrarian elites came into conflict over development. In Brazil, on the other hand, the very policies which were created for the purpose of favoring the traditional export economy had as a by-product the stimulation of industrialization.[3] The military elite recognized industrialization as an element of military strength and self-sufficiency and remained supportive of the process of industrialization as such.

Moreover, the fortunes of the traditional landed elite, especially based on coffee, have gradually been merging with urban banking, real estate, and industrial enterprises. The dominant stratum of the growing urban population has become a mixture of these traditional and modern centers of power so that no simple delineation of power structure by class can be made. The elites of Brazil have not remained polarized around distinct interests. The political battle is pre-eminently a struggle for access to power rather than for ideology, policy, or protection of a particular interest. This fact has often escaped foreign observers who were puzzled by the leftist tendencies of the wealthy, land owning presidents, Kubitschek and Goulart, in contrast to the parsimonious personal lives of Vargas and the almost propertyless Castelo Branco.

This broad backdrop explains why development *policies* found general acceptance among Brazil's ruling elites. We must be careful to distinguish between the functions of development policies and the functions of a central planning *institution*. The latter, represented by the central planning organ and its embodiment of "the plan," has not always been received with enthusiasm by some elements of the elite. Before considering the sources of conflict over planning, however, let us review the functions of the planning institution for the regime.

The central and presumably comprehensive plan has a num-

3. These import-substitution policies are described in detail by Celso Furtado in "Political Obstacles to Economic Growth in Brazil," 41 *International Affairs* (April, 1965), 253-55.

ber of values not related directly to the attainment of the goals stated in the plan itself. The first of these is the public relations benefits of the plan. The plan asserts that the regime knows where it is going and that it is working for the common good. These sentiments are contained in the plan itself, but they are strongly repeated in the vast number of speeches and other contacts with groups of the citizenry incident to presentation and defense of the plan. The Kubitschek, Furtado, and Campos plans in particular served important public relations purposes. It has been repeatedly pointed out that the Castelo Branco government in particular justified its political existence on the crucial need for planning of the "right" kind.

A second and more subtle function of Brazilian plans has been to provide a specific technique for focusing the effort to arrive at consensus on policy. The technique worked for Kubitschek. It did not work for Goulart, for consensus was never achieved among his own supporters. With the use of CONSPLAN, the Campos plan now appears to have achieved this purpose to a considerable degree. The controversial aspects of the Castelo Branco regime reflect differences over political institutions rather than planning goals. When, as in the Goulart case, the planning institution did *not* achieve its consensus-building purpose, it served an alternative function as a sacrificial goat, leaving the regime itself intact.

Third, the exigencies of the struggle for foreign aid, especially under the Alliance for Progress, required the existence both of a plan and of planners commanding the respect of experts in the organs of international financing.

A fourth, and most important function of the planning institution, is related to all the others. The Brazilian plans have represented a deliberate and calculated effort on the part of the regimes in power to increase the powers both of the incumbent president and of the presidency as an institution. Assembling sufficient power to govern has been the crucial problem of Brazilian governments. The plan, like the creation of the DASP under Vargas, is intended to establish a new centralized control over the administrative hierarchy. The first plans were located within the DASP itself. Later they were attached directly to the president's office. The Plano Trienal was timed to boost the vote for a return to presidentialism under Goulart. Later proposals for organizing the ministry of planning were based on central implementation of plans with varying degrees of compulsion. Even with the firm support of the victorious military forces at his back, President Castelo Branco saw the need to initiate a plan, and justified the Revolution as necessary to carry it out. Much of the rationale for the Institutional Acts was to provide the powers necessary to implement the plan. These powers were notably of a political character, establishing a more centralized government. Among other things, political parties were abolished in favor of two political groupings to replace the fourteen parties; presidents and governors were to be chosen by the legislative bodies rather than by election; and even the mayors of state capitals were no longer to be elected. The commitment to central power for planning was unequivocal.

In all of these ways, then, having a plan has proved functional for the regime ever since the end of World War II. This effect seems to have obtained regardless of the political style of the regime of the day, or of its demand-support system. Regimes of both left and right sought to plan. The labor-based regime of Goulart and the military-based regime of Castelo Branco sought to plan. So, too, did the coalition of Kubitschek.

In speaking of the functions served by planning institutions, we have not commented on the *effectiveness* of planning, but only on the growth of the planning institution. When we turn to the implementation of plans the picture changes.

PLANNING AND THE BUREAUCRACY: THE DYSFUNCTIONS OF PLANNING

The last two Brazilian plans have been characterized by the methods of economic science and rationality. Goals are stated and the means to achieve them are specified. In the hands of Max Weber's bureaucracy, the plans would presumably be implemented. Brazil's bureaucracy is of a different nature.

The functions of the Brazilian bureaucracy are: (1) to provide a channel for upward mobility for the educated middle class, (2) to provide permanent incomes for that portion of the middle class which provides support for the regime, (3) to provide a low level of certain services, and (4) to provide opportunities for private entrepreneurship based on the powers attaching to certain offices. These functions are essentially political in nature. Broadly stated, the purpose of the bureaucracy is to provide patronage, while maintaining a certain minimum level of services. It would be a mistake, however, to regard the bureaucracy as dependent on the political elite in power at a particular time. The bureaucracy has succeeded in insulating itself from all but the most drastic changes of political direction. Tenure provisions favor the incumbent. Actual performance on the job is not required, but may occur if the incumbent wishes to use his post for purposes of advancement or acquisition of power. That the bureaucracy has a will of its own and a more or less independent base of power is underlined if we include, as we must, the military forces. The bureaucracy comprises a set of vested interests established and protected by law.[4]

4. These generalizations about Brazilian bureaucracy require much more study. They are firmly based, however, on a mounting body of empirical material. See, especially, Kleber Tatinge do Nascimento, "Change Strategy and Client Systems: Administrative Reform in Brazil" (Ph.D. dissertation, University of Southern California, 1966); Lawrence Graham, "The Clash Between Formalism and Reality in the Brazilian Civil Service" (Ph.D. dissertation, University of Florida, 1966); Gilbert B. Siegel, "The Vicissitudes of Governmental Reform in Brazil: A Study of the DASP" (Ph.D. dissertation, University of Pittsburgh, 1964); Gilbert B. Siegel, "The Strategy of Public Administration Reform: The Case of Brazil," 26 *Public Administration Review* (March, 1966), 45-55; Gilbert B. Siegel and Kleber Tatinge do Nascimento, "Formalism in Brazilian Administrative Reform: The Example of Position Classification," *International Review of Administrative Sciences*, No. 2 (1966), pp. 175-84; and Robert T. Daland (ed.), *Perspectives of Brazilian Public Administration* (Rio de Janeiro: Brazilian School of Public Administration,

The essence of "rational" planning in a developing country involves sacrifices in the short run in order to achieve long-run gains, the reallocation of existing resources, and the modification of the processes by which allocation decisions for the society are made. All three of these effects of planning run counter to the self-perceived interests of a bureaucracy of the kind described above. They also run counter to interests outside the government to some degree, but let us concentrate on the bureaucracy itself.

In the Brazilian case civil and military personnel have been most reluctant to accept the restrictions on salary increases envisioned in the last two plans. Restriction on the addition of new positions and budget containment generally have been opposed. The imposition of controls over old agencies by new planning and coordinating agencies has been stoutly fought in the political arena. A foretaste of things to come was the controversy between the old Department for Construction of Works against Drought in the Northeast (DNOCS) within the Ministry of Public Works and the new Superintendency for Development of the Northeast (SUDENE) during the Kubitschek and Goulart regimes.

The fate of the "super-ministry" proposals under Furtado and the failure to date of the Campos ministry to establish implementational machinery represent the opposition of powerful elements of the bureaucracy through its highly politicized elements. For example, Amaral Peixoto was Minister of Administrative Reform under the Goulart regime. He is the son-in-law of Getúlio Vargas, a leading member of the former PSD party, a former Minister of Public Works (and partisan of DNOCS). It was completely "safe" to entrust administrative reform to his hands, and basic reforms did not occur.

To orient administrative programs toward achievement and performance, rather than patronage, would strike at the roots of the political balance of power which exists. Even with con-

Getúlio Vargas Foundation, and School of Public Administration, University of Southern California, 1963), pp. 1-61.

trol of the country firmly in the hands of the military, efforts to centrally coordinate and coerce the bureaucracy have proven difficult, though intensive efforts to do so have been made by Castelo Branco. The natural reaction to this situation is to create new entities to carry the programs needed by the plan. This course has been taken through the establishment of additional government corporations. However, this is also a dangerous road. The proliferation of new agencies merely creates more jobs, a larger payroll and an increase in the governmental budget. These trends run counter to the purposes of the plans. Moreover, the new agencies, born into a highly politicized bureaucratic environment, may take on the characteristics of the old agencies. The notorious histories of SUDENE and PETROBRAS (the national gasoline monopoly) are indications of this phenomenon. The Brazilian experience thus seems to show that *implementation* of central plans is dysfunctional from the point of view of the bureaucracy. This fact is perfectly well understood by such Brazilian politicians as Almino Afonso whose view of planning is quite the reverse of that in the United States. We feel that plan making (policy) is a political function and that implementation is a technical-administrative matter. Afonso correctly perceives the Brazilian situation to be the reverse. In practice plan-making has been technical, while implementation is patently political.

A THEORETICAL NOTE

We have now arrived at the frustrating point of noting that planning in Brazil is politically useful, but not for the purpose of achieving development goals. This brings us to the dilemma faced by those impatient to get on with the business of reform and economic development. An advanced industrial society seems to depend on the use of modern governmental techniques among which planning is perhaps the most outstanding. But modern techniques seem to rely equally on the existence of an advanced industrial society, with all its accompanying values.

Since history shows that societies do develop economically from an earlier more primitive stage, we reject the dilemma as inadequate, and search for the factors or conditions which produce the desired changes. Two prominent positions have been advanced which are directly relevant to this search. One holds that there are preconditions which must be met in order to produce movement in the direction of reform. The other rejects the very notion of a precondition. Two students of Brazilian planning have stated these positions. Professor Nelson Mello e Souza of the School of Public Administration of the Getúlio Vargas Foundation argues the case against the indispensability of administrative reform as the antecedent of economic development.[5] After reviewing the failures of Brazilian efforts to rationalize planning and other reforms, he concludes that the situation is just the reverse. Governmental reform is "a consequence of the creation of an industrial base capable of generating tax wealth. Industry then provides the tremendous impetus necessary for improved patterns of administration."[6] Specifically, he says, the problem of planning and administration generally is "less a technical difficulty than a political one, and that this difficulty is linked to the need for a new composition of power centers."[7] The power centers are presently dominated by big landowners who traditionally have controlled the mechanism of government. Thus the political system is a reflection of the traditional social and cultural pattern, he continues.

This deterministic, even Marxian, theory of development is not satisfactory to those who are too impatient to wait for the inevitable, yet slow, industrial and social evolution of society. Brazil is in a hurry to seek economic development. Albert O.

5. Nelson Mello e Souza, "Public Administration and Economic Development," in Robert T. Daland (ed.), *Perspectives of Brazilian Public Administration*, Chapter 12.
6. *Ibid.*, p. 163.
7. *Ibid.*, p. 160.

Hirschman has expressed the other position.[8] He says: "I attempt to answer these questions by avoiding the tempting device—or sleight of hand—which consists in discovering some prerequisite, be it a resource base, a rate of capital formation, an elite, an ideology or a personality structure, that must allegedly be introduced before change can possibly assert itself. Rather, I am trying to show how a society can begin to move forward *as it is, in spite of what it is and because of what it is.* Such an enterprise will involve a systematic search along two closely related lines: *first,* how acknowledged, well-entrenched obstacles to change can be neutralized, out-flanked, and left to be dealt with decisively at some later stage; *secondly,* and perhaps more fundamentally, how many among the conditions and attitudes that are widely considered as inimical to change have a hidden positive dimension and can therefore unexpectedly come to serve and nurture progress."[9]

We suggest that these two positions are by no means antithetical. If this study has shown nothing else, it must now be clear that the failures of planning in Brazil have been political in nature. Yet we observe that the Brazilian economy is in fact expanding at a rapid pace. There are clearly areas of movement and leverages that are constantly being exploited. Short of the monolithic, integrated, coordinated, comprehensive national plan of development there may be as yet unrealized possibilities to introduce planning with less than cosmic scope. If so, the problem is to identify the rigidities which must be taken as relatively permanent in the short-time scale, as well as to identify the areas of flexibility. Professor Mello e Souza identifies seven of the limiting factors: (1) the private enterprise tradition of Brazil, (2) state autonomy, (3) regional disparities, (4) sectorial planning agencies for coal, electricity, alkalies, petroleum, ship-building, auto manufacturing, and others, (5) the defective nature of the tax system, (6) the

8. Albert O. Hirschman, *Journeys Toward Progress: Studies of Economic Policy-Making in Latin America* (New York: Twentieth Century Fund, 1963). 9. *Ibid.,* p. 6.

defective nature of the administrative system, and (7) the composition and structure of Congress. One might add others such as the pressures employed by labor, the military, the civil servants, and other organized groups. However, the list is sufficiently encompassing to pose the problem as a formidable one.

Another way to express these rigidities is to consider their effect. They are associated with political instability and lack of a national consensus on development goals. In a politically stable country, a central plan can have a consensus-building effect. The recent history of French planning during the De-Gaulle period is an example. In the case of Brazil, however, the central plan has had a divisive effect. This was clearly the case under Goulart. During the Castelo Branco regime the divisive effect of central planning has been less apparent, but it nonetheless exists. The increasing tendency to justify added powers on the grounds of the need to implement plans is one indicator. The failure of the planning ministry to establish its projected system of plan implementation is another. Planning remains the very personal product of the influence of its immediate sponsors—in the present case the talented ministers of planning and finance and the President himself.

What hypotheses can we derive from the Brazilian experience with planning?

First, in an unstable political system, the demand for central planning derives from political maintenance needs of the regime. As a corollary, whatever effectiveness planning has derives from the influence lent by the person of the national leader rather than from institutional sources.

Secondly, in a regime with low consensus on goals and high political instability, a central planning institution will be dysfunctional for most actors in the bureaucratic arena if it seeks or threatens to intervene in the existing processes of bureaucratic decision and operation.

SOME INFERENCES

If the argument to this point is valid, certain inferences as to the potential role of planning in a country like Brazil seem appropriate. The first concerns centralization v. decentralization of planning processes. Hirschman and others have suggested that planning be decentralized to whatever "islands" of rationality for planning may be found.[10] In Brazil examples of islands of rationality would certainly include the National Development Bank, the state of São Paulo planning program during Carvalho Pinto's governorship, SUDENE, and the as yet unheralded planning and program budgeting arrangements developed in the state of Guanabara under Carlos Lacerda— who did not like to call it planning.

Certainly such islands should be exploited. Yet the pressure to have a national plan and a central planning institution will continue. This plan can be turned to positive advantage if it is expressed in terms of long-range goals to serve chiefly educational purposes. This, in effect, is what has happened to Brazilian planning. Despite the language of immediacy in the plans of Furtado and Campos, they both express the same general thrust. Neither can be implemented immediately in any complete sense. Yet they represent a goal-oriented framework within which specific plans would achieve governmental support wherever "islands of development" exist or could be created through incentive systems.

10. The notion of "islands" and "nuclei" of planning around which innovation can be created is becoming increasingly prominent in the development planning literature. It runs through Albert Hirschman's stimulating Chapter 4 of *Journeys Toward Progress*; other discussions are in Albert Waterston, "Administrative Obstacles to Planning," 1 *Economia Latinoamericana* (July, 1964), 308-50; Roderick Groves, "Planning and Administrative Reform in Venezuela," Paper, Comparative Administration Group, Latin American Development Administration Committee (Bloomington: International Development Research Center, 1965); and especially Clarence E. Thurber, "Islands of Development: A Political and Social Approach to Development Administration in Latin America," Paper presented to the National Conference of the Comparative Administration Group, University of Maryland, April 17, 1966. Also see John Friedman, "Planning as Innovation, the Chilean Case," 32 *Journal of the American Institute of Planners* (July, 1966), 194-203.

Secondly, Brazil's experience does not suggest that the central planning agency is an appropriate place for implementational responsibilities; but there remains a highly sophisticated role for a central agency as a planning communications center. As such it could develop reliable systems for the collection of needed series of planning data for national, regional, or local use; serve as a central clearinghouse of planning information of all kinds; sponsor research in the governmental areas of policy-making; assist the universities in the creation of programs for the training of planners for various governmental levels and functions; and provide a technical assistance service for departments, states, and municipalities. These functions would not be threatening, but would rather promote consensus-building.

Thirdly, the central planning institution could recommend plans and comment on plans in the general fashion of the United States Council of Economic Advisers. As a part of this function, it could exploit the approach which has already seen its beginnings in the Campos ministry. That is, it could begin to design and recommend noncompulsory incentive systems which, without controls of a compulsory nature, could produce and strengthen "islands of planning." These systems would presumably involve grants in aid and joint federal-state or federal-local programs resembling the United States 701 or urban renewal programs. Any such systems would operate within the accepted political norms of the society, but technical inputs would be encouraged.

Fourthly, if nationally implemented, centrally constructed plans were to be attempted, the process would presumably require early participation and commitment on the part of political leaders in the key decisions. This would involve even earlier consultation procedures than those employed by CONSPLAN. In addition, a less academic and more political style of consultation could be more fruitful.

To summarize, we have said that goal consensus and political stability are the two key independent variables which appear to affect the development planning style of Brazil. We have said that in the presence of dissensus and instability an appropriate planning style would consist of: (1) central establishment of long-range goals for their consensus-building and guidance purposes, (2) provision of central technical, research, and communications services for planners at all levels, and (3) the establishment of incentive systems to encourage goal-oriented decisions within decentralized entities.

We have not said where or how the incentive systems should be established, except that it would *not* be a function of a central planning institution. The rationale here is that the incentive policies would inevitably be so intimately tied to the political regime that they could initially be institutionalized only in terms of the political needs of the administration in power at a certain time. Since the chief rewards would be distributed through the tax, budget, and personnel systems, those who controlled these functions would control the incentive system. Little can be achieved on a centralized basis unless the president has effective control over these central functions and the will to use them within the context of development goals. The point is that the president survives on the basis of rewards which he may dispense. These must not be removed by establishing a central, technocratic planning-decision system. They must be retained. The president must be able to employ these rewards within the limits of the incentive policies while at the same time assuring him continuance of a viable political support system. The object would be to attain both patronage and development objectives by encouraging self-selection of interests into the president's support system. That is, patronage (i.e., rewards through incentives) would be awarded to entities willing to commit themselves to developmentalist goals. Since the elites of Brazil are intermixed, this approach would not set class against class or interest against interest.

The remarks just made presume that the historic character of Brazilian politics and bureaucracy will continue for a considerable period of years. If the military regime remains in power and continues on its course of re-forming the political and administrative norms of the country—and can avoid the creation of civil strife in the process—the centralized planning system could become a reality. Which course will be taken cannot now be predicted. Much depends on the goals and skills of General Costa e Silva. At the very least, he can be described as a man with an opportunity.

A FINAL NOTE

It should be made quite clear what we have left *undone* in this exploratory analysis. Our argument rests on three assumptions which have not been firmly established. First, we have assumed that Brazil is politically unstable. Secondly, we have assumed a relatively low level of consensus in Brazil. Thirdly, we have assumed an increasing intermixture between the traditional and modern elements of the Brazilian elite.

None of these assumptions can now be based on operational criteria or empirical data of a systematic sort. It is suggested that these are the three important frontiers for the study of the political ecology of planning and development.

Finally, one might well infer that we have said that national development will occur once the proper political, administrative, and planning arrangements have been established. In making this implication we have disregarded the theories of geographic, climatic, or racial determinism which have sometimes been used to explain the "backwardness" of Brazil. We are very content to leave these theories in the capable hands of Vianna Moog who has destroyed them sufficiently.[11] One other theory, however, is less easily dismissed. Any total explanation would have to consider it very seriously. This is the notion that "achievement attitudes" must exist in order to obtain a high rate of development. This is relevant to the Brazil-

11. Vianna Moog, *Bandeirantes and Pioneers*, trans. by L. L. Barrett (New York: George Braziller, 1965).

ian case since a study has shown that the "achievement syndrome" is clearly less prevalent in Brazil than in the United States.[12]

12. The theory is developed by David C. McClelland in *The Achieving Society* (Princeton: Van Nostrand, 1961). The Brazilian study is Bernard C. Rosen, "The Achievement Syndrome and Economic Growth in Brazil," 42 *Social Forces* (March, 1964), 341-53.

SELECTED BIBLIOGRAPHY

The following bibliography contains only references to materials relevant to planning in Brazil. Of the Brazilian materials, it contains only items directly related to the contents of this volume. A considerable additional literature on economics of planning is excluded, as well as a body of writings of a hortatory and polemical nature.

Almeida, Cândido Antônio Mendes de. *Nacionalismo e Desenvolvimento*. Rio: Instituto Brasileiro do Estudos Afro-Asiaticos, 1963.

Almeida, Romulo Barreto de. *Clientelismo Contra Desenvolvimento: Dilema dos Nossos Dias*. Salvador: Livraria Progresso, 1958.

——. *Experiência Brasileira de Planejamento, Orientação e Contrôle da Economia*. Rio: Departamento Econômico da Confederação Nacional da Industria, 1950.

Alvim, João Carlos. *A Revolução Sem Rumo*. Rio: Edições do Val, 1964.

Azevedo, Fernando de. *Brazilian Culture*. New York: Macmillan, 1950.

Baer, Werner. "Inflation and Economic Growth: An Interpretation of the Brazilian Case," 11 *Economic Development and Cultural Change* (October, 1962), 85-97.

——. "Regional Inequality and Economic Growth in Brazil," 12 *Economic Development and Cultural Change* (April, 1964), 268-85.

—— and Isaac Kerstenetzky. "Import Substitution and Industrialization in Brazil," 54 *American Economic Review* (May, 1964), 411-25.

Baklanoff, Eric N. (ed.). *New Perspectives of Brazil*. Nashville: Vanderbilt University Press, 1966.

Bemis, George (ed.). *From Crisis to Revolution*. International Public Administration Series No. 1. Los Angeles: University of Southern California, 1964.

Bonilla, Frank. "A National Ideology for Development: Brazil," in K. H. Silvert (ed.), *Expectant Peoples*. New York: Random House, 1963.

Cabral, Castilho. *Tempos de Jânio e Outros Tempos*. Rio: Editôra Civilização Brasileira, 1962.

Campos, Roberto de Oliveira. *Economia, Planejamento e Nacionalismo*. Rio: Análise e Perspectiva Econômica Editôra, 1963.

Cardoso, Fernando Henrique. *Empresário Industrial e Desenvolvimento Econômico*. San Paulo: Difusão Européia do Livro, 1964.

Daland, Robert T. (ed.). *Perspectives of Brazilian Public Administration*. Rio: Brazilian School of Public Administration, Getúlio Vargas Foundation, and University of Southern California, 1963.

Daugherty, Charles, James Rowe, and Ronald Schneider. *Brazil Election Factbook*, No. 2. Washington: Institute for the Comparative Study of Political Systems, 1965.

Dell, E. "Brazil's Partly United States," 33 *Political Quarterly* (July-September, 1962), 282-93.

Dines, Alberto, and Antonio Callado. *Os Idos de Marco e a Queda em Abril*. Rio: José Alvaro Editor, 1964.

Faust, J. J. *A Revolução Devora Seus Presidentes*. Rio: Editôra Saga, 1965.

Freyre, Gilberto. *The Mansions and the Shanties*. New York: Alfred A. Knopf, 1962.

———. *The Masters and the Slaves*. New York: Alfred A. Knopf, 1946.

———. *New World in the Tropics: The Culture of Modern Brazil*. New York: Alfred A. Knopf, 1959.

———. "Patriarchal Basis of Brazilian Society," in Joseph Maier and Richard W. Weatherhead (eds.), *Politics of Change in Latin America*. New York: Praeger, 1946.

Friedman, John. *Introdução ao Planejamento Democrático*. Rio: Fundação Getúlio Vargas, 1959.

Fundação Getúlio Vargas. 16 *Revista Brasileira de Economia* (December, 1962). The entire issue is devoted to an analysis of the Plano Trienal.

Furtado, Celso. "Brazil, What Kind of Revolution?" 41 *Foreign Affairs* (April, 1963), 526-35.

———. "Development and Stagnation in Latin America: A Structuralist Approach," *Studies in Comparative International Development*, Vol. I, No. 11. St. Louis: Washington University, 1965.

———. *Development and Underdevelopment*. Trans. by Ricardo W. de Aguiar and Eric Charles Drysdale. Berkeley: University of California Press, 1964.

———. "The Development of Brazil," 209 *Scientific American* (September, 1963), 208-20.

———. *Dialética do Desenvolvimento*. Rio: Editôra Fundo de Cultura, 1964.

——. *The Economic Growth of Brazil: A Survey from Colonial to Modern Times.* Berkeley: University of California Press, 1963.

——. *A Pre-Revolução Brasileira.* Rio: Editôra Fundo de Cultura, 1962.

Hirschman, Albert. *Journeys Toward Progress: Studies of Economic Policy-Making in Latin America.* New York: Twentieth Century Fund, 1963.

Horowitz, Irving L. *Revolution in Brazil: Politics and Society in a Developing Nation.* New York: E. P. Dutton, 1964.

Ianni, Octávio. *Industrialização e Desenvolvimento Social no Brasil.* Rio: Editôra Civilização Brasileira, 1963.

——, Paulo Singer, Gabriel Cohn, and Francisco C. Weffort. *Política e Revolução Social no Brasil.* Rio: Editôra Civilização Brasileira, 1965.

Jaguaribe, Helio. *Desenvolvimento Econômico e Desenvolvimento Político.* Rio: Editôra Fundo de Cultura, 1962.

——. "Foreign Technical Assistance and National Development." Paper delivered to the Conference on the Role of the Younger Professional Person in Overseas Development Programs, Princeton, September 24-26, 1965.

Jameson, Samuel H. (ed.). *Planejamento.* Vol. 8 of Selected Texts in Public Administration. Rio: Fundação Getúlio Vargas, 1963.

Johnson, John J. "Brazil in Quandary," 48 *Current History* (January, 1965), 9-15.

——. *The Military and Society in Latin America.* Stanford: Stanford University Press, 1964.

——. *Political Change in Latin America: The Emergence of the Middle Sectors.* Stanford: Stanford University Press, 1958.

Joint Brazil-United States Economic Development Commission. *The Development of Brazil.* Washington: Institute of Inter-American Affairs, 1954.

Jurema, Abelardo. *Sexta Feira, 13: Os Últimos Dias do Govêrno João Goulart.* Rio: Ediçoes o Cruzeiro, 1964.

Leeds, Anthony. "Brazil and the Myth of Francisco Julião," in Joseph Maier and Richard W. Weatherhead (eds.), *Politics of Change in Latin America.* New York: Praeger, 1946.

Lieuwen, Edwin. *Arms and Politics in Latin America.* New York: Praeger, 1961.

Lima, Alceu Amoroso. *Revolução, Reação ou Reforma?* 2nd Ed. Rio: Edições Tempo Brasileiro, 1964.

Lipson, Leslie. "Challenges to Constitutional Government: Brazil."

Paper delivered before the American Political Science Association, New York, September 4-7, 1963.

———. "Government in Contemporary Brazil," 22 *Canadian Journal of Economics and Political Science* (May, 1956), 183-98.

Lowenstein, Karl. *Brazil under Vargas*. New York: Macmillan Co., 1942.

Luz, Nícia Vilela. *A Luta Pela Industrialização do Brasil*. São Paulo: Difusão Européia do Livro, 1964.

Marchant, Anyda. "Politics, Government and Law," in T. Lynn Smith and Alexander Marchant (eds.), *Brazil: Portrait of Half a Continent*. New York: Dryden Press, 1951.

Marshall, Andrew. *Brazil*. New York: Walker and Co., 1966.

Moog, Vianna. *Bandeirantes and Pioneers*. New York: George Braziller, 1964.

Nascimento, Kleber Tatinge do. "Change Strategy and Client Systems: Administrative Reform in Brazil." Ph.D. dissertation, University of Southern California, 1966.

———. "Personnel Administration in Brazil and France: An Attempt to Use the Prismatic Model," in Richard W. Gable (ed.), *Papers in Comparative Administration*. Los Angeles: International Public Administration Center, 1965.

Oliveira, Franklin de. *Que é a Revolução Brasileira?* Rio: Editôra Civilização Brasileira, 1963.

Paulson, Belden. "Difficulties and Prospects for Community Development in Northeast Brazil," 17 *Inter-American Economic Affairs*, No. 4 (April, 1964), 37-58.

———. *Local Political Patterns in Northeast Brazil: A Community Case Study*. Madison: Land Tenure Center, 1964.

Pedreira, Fernando. *Março 31: Civis e Militares no Processo da Crise Brasileira*. Rio: José Alvaro Editor, 1964.

Pinto, L. A. Costa. *Sociologia e Desenvolvimento*. Rio: Editôra Civilização Brasileira, 1963.

Poppino, Rollie. "Brazil since 1954," in José Maria Bello (ed.), *A History of Modern Brazil*. Stanford: Stanford University Press, 1966.

———. "Communism in Brazil." Paper delivered before the American Historical Association, Chicago, December 29, 1962.

Ramos, Guerreiro. *A Crise do Poder no Brasil*. Rio: Zahar Editôres, 1961.

———. *Mito e Verdade da Revolução Brasileira*. Rio: Zahar Editôres, 1963.

Richardson, Ivan L. (ed.). *Bibliografia Brasileira de Administração Pública.* Rio: Fundação Getúlio Vargas, 1964.

———. *Political Science in Brazil: A Selected Bibliography.* Bloomington: Comparative Administration Group, 1965.

——— (ed.). *Perspectives of Brazilian State and Local Government.* Los Angeles: International Public Administration Center, 1965.

Robock, Stefan H. *Brazil's Developing Northeast: A Study of Regional Planning and Foreign Aid.* Washington: The Brookings Institution, 1963.

Rodrigues, José Honório. *Aspiracões Nacionais: Interpretação Histórico-Política.* São Paulo: Editôra Fulgor, 1963.

———. *Conciliação e Reforma no Brasil: Um Desafio Histórico-Político.* Rio: Editôra Civilização Brasileira, 1965.

Schurz, William L. *Brazil: The Infinite Country.* New York: E. P. Dutton, 1961.

Siegel, Gilbert B. "The Strategy of Public Administration Reform: The Case of Brazil," 26 *Public Administration Review* (March, 1966), 45-55.

———. "The Vicissitudes of Governmental Reform in Brazil: A Study of the DASP." Ph.D. dissertation, University of Pittsburgh, 1964.

——— and Kleber Tatinge do Nascimento. "Formalism in Brazilian Administrative Reform: The Example of Position Classification," 3 *International Review of Administrative Sciences*, No. 2 (1966), 175-84.

Smith, T. Lynn. *Brazil: People and Institutions.* 3rd ed. Baton Rouge: Louisiana State University Press, 1963.

———. "The Giant Awakes: Brazil," 334 *Latin America's Nationalistic Revolutions: The Annals* (March, 1961), 95-102.

Sodré, Nelson Werneck. *Formação Histórico do Brasil.* Rio: Editôra Brasilense, 1962.

———. *História da Burguesia Brasileira.* Rio: Editôra Civilização Brasileira, 1964.

———. *Introdução a Revolução Brasileira.* 2nd ed. Rio: Editôra Civilização Brasileira, 1963.

Sternberg, Hilgard O'Reilly. "Brazil, Complex Giant," 43 *Foreign Affairs* (January, 1965), 297-311.

Szulc, Tad. *Twilight of the Tyrants.* New York: Henry Holt and Co., 1959.

Theorides, A. *Brazilian Government Finances: Basic Facts, 1956-1966.* Washington: Agency for International Development, 1965.

Victor, Mário. *Cinco Anos que Abalaram o Brasil.* Rio: Editôra Civilização Brasileira, 1965.

Wagley, Charles. *An Introduction to Brazil.* New York: Columbia University Press, 1963.
———. "Luso-Brazilian Kinship Patterns," in Joseph Maier and Richard W. Weatherhead (eds.), *Politics of Change in Latin America.* New York: Praeger, 1946.
Whitaker, Arthur P., and David C. Jordan. *Nationalism in Contemporary Latin America.* New York: Free Press, 1966.

INDEX

A

Abbink, John, 31
Administrative Department of the Public Service, 40, 49, 50, 87, 129, 205, 209; creation of, 16; functions of, 16-17; preparation of five-year plans, 27, 28; during Dutra regime, 29; image of, 49; problems of, 120
Advisory Planning Council, 124, 191, 217; creation of, 45, 72; functions of, 45, 129; purpose of, 108, 110; composition of, 108-9; criticisms of, 110
Afonso, Almino, 155, 160, 166, 212
Alliance for Progress, 28, 37, 91, 208; control over programs of, 94, 95; effects on planning, 102; assistance of, 148; creation of, 171; functioning of, 171-72
Almeida, Paes de, 193
American Technical Mission to Brazil, 27-28
Antunes, Leocádio de Almeida, 89, 93
Assessoria Técnica da Presidência da República, 90
Ato Institucional, 107, 113, 184; definition of, 67-68

B

Barros, Adhemar de, 19, 192, 200; removal from political arena, 22
BNDE. See National Bank for Economic Development
Brazilian Planning Association, 98
Brizzola, Leonel, 160, 166, 176, 179; role in Goulart's succession, 20
Bulhões, Otávio Gouveia de, 31, 108, 175
Bureaucracy, and the middle class, 14; recruitment for, 15; reformed by Vargas, 16; personnel of, 125; corruption in, 126; organization of, 134; political use of, 134; theories on, 143-44; lack of power of, 198, 199; ideal type of, 205; functions of, 210; insulation of, 210

C

Ceara, planning in state of, 113
Calmon Plan, 174
Campos, Roberto de Oliveira, 33, 44, 107, 108, 175, 188, 208; birth of, 33; education of, 33; role in government planning, 68; report on Program of Action, 73; planning of, 80, 110, 111, 114, 119-23, 129, 133, 203-4; controls of, 191
Capanema Amendment, 99
Cartographic Plan, 58
Castelo Branco, Humberto, 31, 92, 119, 175, 192, 207; appointed president, 21; planning of, 44, 68, 74, 80, 81, 107-8, 190-91, 204, 212; extension of term, 45; sources for, 73; political strength of, 128, 209; administrative controls of, 131; reforms of, 194, 201; justification of regime of, 208
COCAP. See Commission for the Alliance for Progress
CODENO. See Council for the Development of the Northeast
Commission for Administrative Studies, 99, 104, 107
Commission for the Alliance for Progress, 94, 95
Commission of General Coordination, 92, 93, 96
Congressional Mixed Commission on Administrative Reform, 98, 99
Consensus, 202
CONSPLAN. See Advisory Planning Council
Consultative Council, 91, 92
COPLAN. See National Planning Commission
Corporations, types of, 130
Correa e Castro, Pedro Luís, 49
Correio da Manhã, 196
Costa e Silva, Arthur da, 21, 191, 194, 219; planning ideas of, 45; views on government policy, 187; atti-

228

INDEX

tudes on Revolution, 192, 193; election of, 200

Council for Development, 42, 91, 92, 93, 104, 114, 126, 136; creation of, 39, 53; function of, 39, 40; composition of, 39, 40, 88; activities of, 41, 94, 112, 113; purpose of, 88, 111; powers of, 88; direction of, 89; role of, 89

Council for the Development of the Northeast, 42

Council of Ministers, 40

Council of Planning and Coordination, 97-98

D

Dantas, Jair, 163

Dantas, San Tiago, 43, 155, 157, 160-68 *passim*, 175, 178, 179; positions of, 156; policy of, 162; negotiations with United States, 174, 177; competence of, 176

DASP. *See* Administrative Department of the Public Service

Department of Construction against Drought in the Northeast, 211

Deliberative Council of the Commission, 91, 92, 96

Denys, Odilio, 20

Development, indicators of, 5; definition of, 7; and industrialists, 17; goals of, 74

Dutra, Eurico Gaspar, 18, 87; presentation of SALTE Plan, 49

E

Economic Commission for Latin America, 38

Economics, Department of, 37

Economy, government intervention in, 22, 23, 181, 182, 206; structure of, 23, 24, 48; growth rate of, 24, 196; inflation in, 24-26, 172-74 *passim*, 190; reforms in, 65; rates of exchange, 163

Elections, 13-21 *passim*

Eletrobrás, creation of, 23

Elites, 206-7

Estado Novo, 16; policies of, 22

F

FINAGRI, 73

FINAME, 73n

Finance, Ministry of, 31, 35, 43, 90, 131, 135, 178, 196; functions of, 28, 29, 30; role in planning, 179

FINEP, 73n, 188

FIPEME, 73n

France, planning system in, 10, 80, 83

FUDECE, 73n

FUNDEPRO, 73n

Furtado, Celso, 52, 97, 102, 106, 107, 129, 148, 152-58 *passim*, 165, 167, 168, 177, 187, 208, 211; birth of, 41; education of, 41; economic ideas of, 41, 132; programs of, 42, 96, 103, 110, 111; removal of, 43; image of, 62; planning of, 87, 116-17, 151-52, 203-4

G

Galvão, Nei, 180

Gaspar, Diogo, 180

General Administrator, 87

General Labor Command, 159, 161

Germany, 12

Getúlio Vargas Foundation, 190; Economic Research Institute of, 25; *Centro de Estudos de Problemas Brasileiros* of, 27

Global Planning Department, 114-15

Gomes, Eduardo, 18

Goulart, João, 19, 31, 33, 41, 42, 64, 92, 106, 153-69 *passim*, 176, 182, 183, 208; as vice-president, 20; succession to presidency, 20; relations with military, 21, 44; image of, 62; economic growth during, 69; planning under, 44, 60, 68, 97, 140-50, 196, 201, 204, 209; corruption during regime of, 126; political support of, 128, 209; constitutional reforms of, 147; developmental ideas, 174, 185; length of term, 198; leftist tendencies of, 207

Gresham's Law, 84

I

India, central planning in, 3

Institutional Act Number Two, 195

Instruction 70, 23

Instruction 239, 163-64

International Monetary Fund, 31, 32, 159; as source of funds, 62; criticisms of, 172, 175; influence of,